BEYOND THE LIBRARY
OF THE FUTURE

The future is religion and commerce, aphrodisiac and Benzedrine, a mother of mysterious comfort and a mistress of familiar ravishments, ever at the verge of embracing or destroying us. . . . We not only romanticize the future; we have also made it into a growth industry, a parlor game and a disaster movie all at the same time.
—Eugene Kennedy.

—für Rifkele, Benyamin, & Yehoshva

BEYOND THE LIBRARY OF THE FUTURE

MORE ALTERNATIVE FUTURES FOR THE PUBLIC LIBRARY

Bruce A. Shuman
University of South Florida

1997
Libraries Unlimited, Inc.
Englewood, Colorado

LIBRARIES UNLIMITED, INC.
P.O. Box 6633
Englewood, CO 80155-6633
1-800-237-6124

Production Editor: Kay Mariea
Proofreader: Eileen Bartlett
Interior Design and Typesetting: Judy Gay Matthews

Chapter illustrations courtesy Clipper Creative Art Services®,
© Dynamic Graphics Inc., Peoria, Illinois.

Library of Congress Cataloging-in-Publication Data

Shuman, Bruce A.
    Beyond the library of the future : more alternative futures for
the public library / Bruce A. Shuman.
    xxxii, 178 p.   17x25 cm.
    Includes bibliographical references (p. 171) and index.
    ISBN 1-56308-456-2
    1. Public libraries--United States--Data processing.   I. Title.
Z678.9.A4U68   1997
027.473--dc21   96-48197
                                                                   CIP

CONTENTS

PREFACE

"It Was About This Whale . . ."

> ". . . A day will come at sea when ye smell land where there be
> no land, and on that day, Ahab will go to his grave, but he will rise
> again and beckon, and all, all—all save one — shall follow."
>
> —Herman Melville. *Moby Dick.*

I cannot say for certain just when my out-of-the-ordinary interest in the future began, but I suppose I'd have to attribute its early manifestation to my reaction to a film I first saw when it came out in 1956, when I was an impressionable teenager. The film was John Huston's screen version of *Moby Dick,* and I remember loving every minute of seeing one of my favorite adventure novels fully realized, with color, lots of action, vivid characters, special effects, and adroit casting. Or maybe it was that I was at an extremely impressionable age and on my way to becoming what I still—in a very real sense—am: a child of the movies.

But back to *Moby Dick*: there I sat one day long ago in a darkened theater, amid hordes of other popcorn-gobbling, drink-guzzling, milk-dud-smearing kids and a few random adults. We were all raptly watching this towering tale of adventure, peril, and revenge on the high seas, set in the previous century. Many writers and social critics have, over the past century and a quarter, analyzed Melville's tale, arguing over its deeper meaning and ascribing to the obsessed captain and his leviathan adversary allegorical identities. But for me, at that age, it was just an exciting action flick, a satisfying two hours spent in a movie house. Now, I loved every minute of that movie, but two particular scenes really affected me, and actually, in a way, changed my life. Or at least got me to thinking about things I hadn't thought about before. It was interesting throughout; no complaint there. But it was *not* the climactic scene, in which poor old obsessed Ahab rides his huge nemesis, the White Whale, downward into the depths and mutual death that most strongly grabbed and held my attention on that far-off afternoon, very deep in the well of the past.

No, it was a pair of earlier scenes, one at the beginning of the film and the penultimate sequence of activity, that fascinated me and riveted my entire being. The first scene came early on, when a crazed prophet—Isaiah, by name—waylays our happy heroes after they have signed aboard the *Pequod* and utters the grim prophesy that begins this chapter. And the latter reference is to the long scene that preceded the ultimate sighting of Ahab's mortal enemy—curiously, a quiet, almost motionless scene—the one in which the whaler *Pequod* is becalmed at sea, without the slightest puff of wind to fill her canvas sails. In that slowly developing scene, the tropical sun beats ferociously down on the somnolent ship riding the surface of a glassy sea, unable to catch a whiff of breeze for propulsion, and thus unable to go anywhere at all. The ship just . . . well, floats.

From time to time, in that scene, we see the sun brilliantly reflected off a large, shiny gold piece (Ahab refers to it as "a Spanish ounce") that the Captain has nailed to the mainmast and promised to the first ship's lookout who catches sight of the White Whale from aloft. The ship and its crew bake on the smooth surface of the sea. Everybody aboard ship, wearing as little as they can, droops and sweats in the noonday heat and humidity. Somewhere below, fathoms down in the dark, perhaps, the giant whale cruises toward his ultimate rendezvous with Ahab, but onboard the *Pequod*, there is nothing to do except wait for whatever is going to happen next. There is little movement on the wooden decks. Only the Captain—fully dressed in his perennial long dark coat and stovepipe hat, stomps his peg-legged way around the quarterdeck, ceaselessly scanning the still horizon for any sign of his enemy, Moby Dick, who bit off his leg some years ago in resisting capture, leaving the man hobbled with scars of two kinds, neither of which will ever heal.

As this scene develops, everyone sags in enforced inactivity. Normal discipline is relaxed on ship—everybody seems to be at liberty to do what they want. Most lie on deck in whatever shade the noonday sun affords. Some crew members while away the long hours playing cards or perhaps writing letters home. The ship's carpenter and part-time coffin-maker seems to be at work, making something out of wooden boards, but we are not shown what. One huge man sits alone and apart from the others, busily engaged in some kind of solitary game. On the peeling wooden deck, Queequeg, the tall tattooed harpooner from an island in the South Seas, throws a collection of what look like chicken bones onto the deck, gazes raptly at them, and then picks them up and does it again.

The future of these men has already been foretold, in that earlier scene I mentioned. At the story's beginning, Isaiah, a gnarled (and possibly insane) old sailor has warned our hero, Ishmael, against signing on the *Pequod*, saying that the Captain is crazy and the ship is cursed, and even going so far as to predict that the day would come when all—all save one—aboard her would perish on this voyage. Still, Ishmael—a man not given to superstition and fear—did sign on board anyway (not, perhaps, one of his better career moves), discounting the words of the prophet as the ravings of a lunatic. Or maybe he just needed the money or craved the excitement. Ishmael, a landlubber since birth, tells us right from the git-go that he has always loved putting out to sea, so his destiny was unavoidable. And besides, he had made close friends—bonded, actually—with the aforementioned harpooner, the gigantic tattooed but kindly cannibal, and ship's first harpooner, Queequeg.

So I sat, on that long-ago day in that darkened theater, gnawing on oversalted popcorn, and watching spellbound as the camera, after a leisurely prowl 'round the *Pequod*'s various drowsy decks came to rest at last on Queequeg, kneeling on the wooden deck, throwing and re-throwing those small white objects, then picking them all up and going again. Actually, the exercise didn't seem so bizarre to me. My sister and her friends were fond of playing a game called "jacks" that employed much the same movements. Maybe that's why I wasn't ready for what was going to happen next.

A realist even at that tender age, I watched with flagging interest and even a degree of scorn as Queequeg threw, scanned each of his casts, and threw again, watching intently the configuration and distribution of his clattering, small dry objects, until . . . the climactic moment, when Ishmael, who'd strolled over to him to watch, saw it happen:

I: "Queequeg, what're you doing?"

Q: "See tomorrow here. Bones tell everything." (A sudden indrawn hiss of breath; he stares downward, bug-eyed at what he sees.)

I: "Queequeg, what's the matter?"

Q: "Get carpenter!" (When the carpenter arrives, Queequeg negotiates the price of an extra-large wooden coffin bearing an Island chief's head carved on its cover.)

I: "Queequeg, what is all this?"

Q: (slowly, to Ishmael) "Money yours. . . . Seachest yours. . . . My harpoon yours. . . . Goodbye!"

Watching, mouth agape, I sat bolt upright at that point and began to pay some serious attention. I can still see it in perfect clarity. Clearly, whatever it was that the islander had seen in the spill of those bones left no uncertainty whatsoever: the huge harpooner knew he wouldn't be needing his things any more (and possibly also knew that Ishmael would).

If you've read the novel or seen the movie, you know what happens in the final reel. The titanic struggle between resolute, obsessional, driven man and enormous, seemingly malevolent whale ends tragically as Moby Dick, Ahab, and the entire crew of the ship die that day. Save one, of course. Isaiah was right on the money with that prediction. Ishmael, alone, manages to survive, and to narrate the tale for the benefit of the rest of us. He alone rides out of the final battle only faintly conscious, clinging to a large floating object, which turns out to be the coffin that was to have been his friend's final resting place.

The movie came to its predicted and sad end; the final credits rolled, and it was time for me to get home to dinner, that day. But I wondered then—and *still* wonder—about two puzzling things: How did Isaiah—who tried to warn Ishmael not to sail on the *Pequod*—know what was going to befall the *Pequod*'s crew, right down to the exact body count?

And, more intriguing, yet: How did Queequeg see in the cast of those small white bones the foretelling of his own death, and the foreknowledge that his few articles of personal property would no longer be of any use or comfort to him?

And yet, somehow, they knew! Both the old geezer on the dock and the harpooner on the *Pequod knew!* It isn't explained. How could you explain such a thing, anyway? They just knew. They knew what was going to happen, in detail. As Queequeg said, "See tomorrow here." They saw the *future!*

How did they do that?

But wait, you're thinking! *Moby Dick* is only a work of fiction, after all, having nothing to do with fact. This point is freely acknowledged. It is arguably true that Melville's classic novel was written primarily for entertainment, and any gifts of prophesy, grim or pleasant to contemplate, were just fictional contrivances of the author.

And yet . . . And yet . . .

A Memory (not required reading)

Permit me to tell a personal story. One day, when I was perhaps 16 years old, on the first warm afternoon in Chicago after a brutal winter, a close friend and I decided that it was too nice to stay indoors after school and do homework or watch TV, or whatever. So we decided that we would instead walk down to Lake Michigan and stroll a mile or so along the huge rocks that serve as a sort of seawall, girding the city's lakefront for miles, wherever there is no beach. Arriving at the lakefront, we strolled the irregular rocks, enjoying the sunshine, our jackets tied around our waists. We spoke, as I recall, about our usual subjects: girls, school, girls, sports, and girls, as we trudged on, just enjoying the unaccustomed but welcome feeling of warm sun and balmy air on our upturned faces.

That's when we saw the playing card.

As memory serves, it was just an ordinary blue-back Bicycle playing card, face down, although it might have been a red one, I don't know; it's been a lot of years; give me a break. But there it was: the card lay face-down in the bright sunshine, on one of the top-level rocks, somewhere towards downtown from Belmont Harbor on Chicago's lakefront. What it was doing there all alone is all part of the mystery, but it doesn't matter, really. There it was.

We saw it at the same instant and regarded the card solemnly for a moment. Then my friend, who was always into games, said, "What card do you think that is, Shuman?"

I like games, too. Always have. So I stared at the card, as though by sheer concentration and force of will I could get it to give up its secret to me. "Queen of diamonds," I said. I don't know why I said that. I just did. Oh, I can visualize it clearly, after 40 years! Seagulls called raucously to our left, squabbling over smelt, perhaps, while to our right, in the strip of parkland along the shore, forsythia were just coming into bud in the sunshine.

"No way!" said my friend, enjoying the competitive moment. He was always more competitive than I was, I guess. "It's the six of spades."

We grinned, sharing a moment of perfect understanding. The bet was on. Not for money, but a bet, all the same. Sometimes we bet Cokes. Maybe we did that day. In those days, we bet on things all the time: like which bus would come along on Sheridan Road next, or whether or not the bus driver would be sporting a mustache. Or frequently: whether the girls we knew ever entertained lascivious thoughts and talked about the same stuff that we did. Things like that.

And then came the moment of truth. Enough idle speculation. I squatted down and picked up the playing card, turning it over in my hand.

Queen of diamonds.

At that moment, a slight chill came off still-gelid Lake Michigan and blew through our hair and shirts, signaling an impending end to the unseasonable warmth of that afternoon, and making us think about putting our jackets back on and getting back inside. Or maybe it didn't, but it really could have. Chicago is like that, especially in early spring. It's always cooler near the lake. Or almost always, that time of year. And my friend turned and looked at me with an expression I had never seen in his eyes before—and certainly never saw again. That expression—it might have been respect or possibly suspicion. It might have even been fear. As I say, I don't know. But such a look! "Queen of diamonds," he said, in a wondering voice. "How'd you do that?" Like it was some sort of parlor trick or something.

I shrugged; that much I remember; I shrugged and grinned. "I don't know," I allowed. But there it was in my hand. The queen of diamonds, smiling slightly, dressed up regally, topped off by a yellow headdress, and holding in her hand a matching four-lobed flower. The red queen was clenched firmly in my hand against the stiffening breeze, lest it blow away. How *did* I do it? A fair question. Let's assume that I am not one of those with the "gift." You're just going to have to take my word on that. Otherwise, I'd be rich.

I'd correctly chosen a single card out of 52 chances. Well, what do the statistics say? What were the odds of accomplishing that feat? I looked it up just now; hey, I'm a former reference librarian, and old habits die hard. It turns out that the odds of that event happening are not really all that prohibitive: out of 1,000 guesses, probability says you'd get it right something like 19 times; so no big deal, right?

But I did it, all the same. How'd I do it? I still don't know. I figure it was simply chance: the odds turned in my favor; it was stupid blind luck, or maybe probability. It happens. It is said that even a blind sow finds an acorn every once in a while. Still, I spent a good bit of time wondering. Was it a sign of some sort? Was it the first manifestation of some rare and spooky power or uncanny ability that I hadn't known I had? Guess not. Because I went home that evening and, after dinner, took out a plastic deck of my parents' cards and tried to replicate that astonishing feat of prediction or sorcery, or whatever. I tried, in fact, for about three hours, until it was time to turn off the lights and get some sleep. What happened? I failed. Abjectly, I failed. Over and over, I was not successful in guessing correctly a card's identity, no matter which card I "predicted" would appear from the deck.

I have now lived almost 40 eventful years since that long-lost but never-to-be-forgotten April afternoon. And I have, in those years, seen a fair number of single playing cards turned face-down on streets, tables, and sidewalks. Want to know how many times I have replicated that stupendous feat of my youth, that shattering moment of clairvoyant triumph of my teenage years? The answer: never . . . or hardly ever, anyway. Thus, I have come to the reluctant conclusion that I have no special gift for seeing into the future. I am not a seer or a psychic; and experience has shown me that I have no personal roadmap to help me in predicting future events or to "see" things that others fail to—or cannot—notice.

Can anyone, then? Are there some individuals blessed with the "sight" or able to divine things with enough frequency as to stand the laws of probability on end? Possibly. Can't rule it out, at least. We've all read about clairvoyants who give the police information based on visions they have had, and the cops subsequently discover missing children, and we are aware of others who correctly predict some important event (e.g., an assassination, an earthquake, the Dow at 5,000), and it comes to pass just the way they said.

How do they do that? Don't ask. As I said before, it may possibly be some "gift," a scam, or stupid, blind luck, or some combination of them all.

How This Book Came to Be

In mid-1995, about six years after the publication of my original work, the president of Libraries Unlimited, Inc., wrote to me to inquire whether I would undertake a new edition of the prior work, reflecting changes and updating things no longer current or valid. I thought about it long and hard before answering. It had been an eventful six years for libraries, during which budgets grew generally tighter, while public interest in and demand for databases and the Internet grew ever more strident and shrill. Flipping through the pages of my earlier work and finding it both outdated and now even somewhat unimaginative, I agreed with him that it was high time for a new work—but not a second edition or even a revision of the earlier one. No, it seemed time now for a *sequel*—a new work that goes beyond *The Library of the Future* and conceptualizes even more radical and imaginative ideas about what that future may hold. And if some of those ideas seem a little, well, . . . farfetched . . . so what? Maybe that's good, rather than bad. After all, many things imagined by science fiction writers of the past two centuries, and ridiculed at the time they were first published, are now either commonplace conveniences or about to become so. The surest way to make a mistake is to say that something couldn't possibly happen.

This book and its predecessor (*The Library of the Future: Alternative Scenarios for Information Professionals*, Englewood, CO, Libraries Unlimited, Inc., 1989, hereinafter called "my earlier work") were written to help public librarians, students, and those concerned with the library's survival and well-being try to prepare for the future, in whatever shape it may appear. In the two works, I elaborate a total of 18 scenarios, one of which may be close to what awaits the public library as it enters and trudges through the 21st century. Or maybe none of them. Sometimes, as we have all seen, the future comes whistling 'round a corner we didn't notice before and takes us by surprise. Still, we are ahead of the game if at least we can say that we've begun thinking about alternatives before an event occurs and spent some time imagining the possibilities and ramifications, and preparing appropriate strategies to counter various problems.

Think back to 1989, and try to remember what you were doing then. Now . . . had you even *heard* of the Internet, cyberspace, Gophers, or Listservs back then? No? I rest my case. As mentioned in the previous work, in today's world, change is the only constant. The world of the Internet, with online utilities and web sites, for example, has already so radically transformed the environment of libraries, in fact, that this work's scenarios will frequently employ the term "cybrary" for "library," using a term derived from "cyberspace," a term that first made its way into print in *Forbes* magazine in 1993 and seems, for better or worse, to be here to stay.

> *You see things and you say, "Why?" But I dream things that never were and I say, "Why not?"*
> —George Bernard Shaw. 1921.

It's fun—for the most part, anyway—to write a book about the future, for a number of reasons. For openers, because while you may eventually be proven wrong after a period of years, your immediate and contemporary audience will not have the information necessary to disprove anything you say. But in keeping with the protocols of scientific method, let me state some of my underlying assumptions at the outset: You, the reader, are asked to accept that the public library *has* a future. In these troubled times of uncertain economic conditions and competing claims on the public tax dollar, such an assumption is not necessarily a lock. But please buy into the assumption that there is a future—in one form or another—for the public library. That's your basic *sine qua non* here. Otherwise, what's the point of the exercise?

Other assumptions: 1) The study of the future is a meaningful exercise. We are better off having "studied" it than not. 2) The future is not predictable, meaning that no one can predict the future with any degree of certainty. Yet the purpose of the futures field is to anticipate what is to come so that we can be ready for it when it happens. 3) The future is not predetermined. Nothing about the future is fixed or inevitable; otherwise, what's the point of futuring? 4) We are not powerless over the future. Nothing is inevitable about it. We can still change it, if we put our minds to it. 5) Future outcomes can be influenced by present choices. There are no guarantees that hard work or deep thinking will pay off, but what we do today has a definite impact—for good or ill—on what will happen tomorrow. 6) There are generally accepted ways to "study the future," and the eclectic scholar will, with a little investigation, learn and master a number of useful methodologies. ■

INTRODUCTION TO THE STUDY OF THE FUTURE

> *Just as the field is hard to define, not much consensus exists on how to describe or categorize the tools or approaches that futurists use in their work. Some claim that there are no useful tools, while others catalog encyclopedically dozens of so-called "techniques." Pragmatically, the state of affairs is somewhere in between. Futurists' tools are still primitive and should be used only with a clear recognition of the limits of their applicability. And just as the premises that futurists stress define certain roles and objectives, these objectives help determine the methods that futurists use to achieve them.*
>
> —Roy Amara. "Searching for Definitions and Boundaries." *The Futurist*, February 1981.

Who Are Futurists, and What Do They Do?

Since the beginning of time, people have attempted to divine the future. Historical and religious works of all civilizations are full of prophesies, forecasts, and predictions. Every civilization has someone in its history analogous to the oracle at Delphi, who uttered prophesies people believed, or Cassandra, whose predictions, while spot-on accurate, were never credited until it was too late. And whether the predictor is an angel, as in the Annunciation, or an oracle, or a so-called prophet speaking for God, there's been a lot of that sort of thing going around in the literature of every ethnicity.

So what, exactly, is it that futurists do? They form perceptions of the future, establishing goals and targets (the possible); they brainstorm as many pathways to their goals as seem likely to occur. They study likely alternatives (the probable); and they make choices and express preferences to bring about a particular future (the preferable). Thereafter, they sometimes write scenarios (stories) that, when followed to their logical conclusions, help them to bring about their preferences. Alternatively, they point up exactly what must *not* be permitted to happen so that the desired outcomes will, in fact, occur. Note: there is seldom complete agreement on what is preferable, not even among members of the same profession. Want proof? Anyone who has ever been to an ALA Conference and sat in on the deliberations of Council or committees will attest that we see things differently and have our own, idiosyncratic ideas about what is desirable, or even possible.

That's what makes futuring so interesting—and so aggravating at the same time.

Futurists spend time futuring so that the rest of us may have a little lead time and be better off for having prepared ourselves. By thinking about alternatives, we're ready. Or at least *readier* than the next guy, perhaps, and readier than we would have been if we hadn't thought about possible outcomes of the actions taken today. Such thinking permits us, frequently, to anticipate and to prepare. And if it turns out that the predicted event doesn't happen, well, at least we were ready if it had.

Intriguing news stories breaking in late 1995 revealed that the Pentagon, the CIA, and other agencies of the United States government have, over many years, hired psychics, sensitives, and even persons with the reputed ability to "bend spoons" to work on tasks such as predicting future events and locating enemies to be "sanctioned." Reportedly, upwards of $20 million of the taxpayers' money was spent on these projects, and even though the results weren't conclusive, you won't persuade some people that the ability to predict the future (sometimes, at least) is given to some people, while the rest of us just have to hang around and wonder what is going to happen next.

When people ask me, "Are you a futurist?" I will sometimes imitate the little guy in those beer commercials by confidently saying, "Yes, I am!" But dispel any image you may have of futurists as double-domed intellectuals with advanced degrees, who use supercomputers and numerous complicated algebraic formulae to derive abstruse equations, that hint at the predictive values of certain phenomena to reveal what is coming next. The simple truth is that so-called futurists tend not to be especially sophisticated.

So is it all a guessing game, this area of study commonly and collectively known as futuring? Well, it is and it isn't. It is, because no one can predict the future with any precision (otherwise, I'd be out at the racetrack right now, betting the enormous sums of money I won in the Florida State Lottery 15 weeks in a row on sure things). And it isn't just a guessing game, because there are methods and procedures that you may employ to minimize (if not entirely end) the chances that you will be caught flat-footed when the future arrives and to help you be better prepared for various eventualities when they occur.

That is the most important message of the futurists: We can prepare ourselves for the future best by being ready for whatever is likely to occur and by having thought seriously and long about what we intend to do about each of the alternative likely futures. The operative word in the previous sentence, of course, is "likely."

In a sense, we are *all* futurists. Whenever you try to figure out whether to take your umbrella to work because it might rain, you are acting like a futurist. Or when you take out life insurance or invest in a long-term maturity, you're being a futurist, betting against your own life expectancy. Even in this age of scientific advances, clearly, some people feel that the ability to foretell the future exists. There is ample evidence in literature that some individuals seem to have a "gift" of prophesy, or at least an ability to see things that have not happened yet, when the rest of us have no such ability. A single example: Nostradamus (who died in 1566) seems to have accurately predicted, among other things, Hitler's Third Reich, and was actually rash enough to name the tyrant (all right, he called him "Hister," but close enough, right?). What accounts for such astonishing feats? Dumb luck? Wild guesses? Coincidence? Or are they God-given endowments? And if such ability exists, does it exist in all of us? Do we all have equal ability to foretell the future? Not likely, or else we'd all buy only winning stocks and we'd all hit the Lotto every Saturday night, like clockwork, until it—and not we—ran out of money. But some people appear to have a gift—or is it a curse?—of prophesy.

Why Study the Future?

An important first question is, Why study the future? I mean, if we can't really predict it, and usually can't do anything about it, doesn't it seem a futile exercise to worry about it at all? The answer to that question is eloquently put in one of the pithier quotations assembled for this book. Charles Kettering reminds us that we should pay attention to the future because we're going to spend the rest of our lives there. Now, how can you argue with that? But what about history, you say? The past is easy to predict, although many have tried to rewrite it after the fact. But the bottom line is that we can't really do anything about the past. Carl Sandburg once wrote that "the past is a bucket of ashes," while industrialist Henry Ford proclaimed that "history is bunk." But the future? That's a whole other thing.

Is the study of the future (whether called futurology or whatever) deserving of being called a true science? That all depends on your definition.

Historical Methodologies of Futurists

People have, throughout this planet's history, attempted to figure out the future by means of empirical examination of objects or phenomena. Ancient futurists—members of early tribes and civilizations, for example—used a great variety of common materials or occurrences to try to predict future events, or to determine how their luck would be running in the time to come. Some of these methods follow (note: the list is not exhaustive):

Intuition, hunches, speculation, premonitions, visions, "sixth senses," clairvoyants, psychics, oracles, seers, shamans, fortune-tellers, flower petals ("he loves me, he loves me not"), stars (astronomy, astrology), thunder and lightning, bones (like Queequeg's in *Moby Dick*), images in a crystal ball,

Ouija boards, tea leaves, palmistry, graphology, the entrails of sacrificed animals, tarot cards, dreams and visions, probability (odds making and handicapping), shooting stars (there's one! something's going to happen), phrenology (bumps on the head), fire (blowing out candles on a cake), contingency planning ("what'll I do if that happens?"), and forecasting ("do I need my umbrella today?").

> *Over the last few decades, in the blink of the eye of history, our culture has begun to go through what promises to be a total metamorphosis. The influx of electronic communications and information processing technologies, abetted by the steady improvement of the microprocessor, has rapidly brought on a condition of critical mass. Suddenly it feels like everything is poised for change.*
>
> —Sven Birkerts. The Gutenberg Elegies: The Fate of Reading in an Electronic Age. 1994.

> *We live in the "rapids of change." The white waters carry us quickly on; we cannot slow down the changes coming to our culture, our society, our families, ourselves. But we do have a choice: we can learn to enjoy turbulence rather than be overwhelmed by it.*
>
> —Donald E. Riggs and Gordon A. Sabine.

Modern Methods Used by Futurists

There are four main stages in futuring: 1) Identification of future events (these are of three main varieties: those we think likely to happen, those we wish to happen, and those we shudder at the very possibility that they might happen); 2) Evaluation and ranking of the events; 3) Analysis of alternative scenarios to determine their implications; and 4) Nomination and evaluation of strategic responses. Here, then, are some methods that futurists have used to anticipate what is yet to come:

- **Prediction.** Since time out of mind, people have been trying to predict the future. When it comes to prediction, one renowned futurist—Marshall McLuhan—once wrote, "I am 90 percent right, 40 percent of the time." "Chaos Theory," on the other hand, which deals in the randomness of nature, acknowledges that "Any complex iterative model is no better than a wild guess, even if the logic is perfect." That statement means predicting the future is a very chancy game, and no one has a handle on it, despite all claims to the contrary. But that's not the same thing as saying that we can't make informed guesses that are likely to be better than those of a blindfolded man slinging darts at a wall. So people make predictions and offer them up, with and without supportive evidence.

- **Genius Forecasting.** This is another term for what we are pleased to call science fiction, or, perhaps more aptly, speculative fiction. The works of Jules Verne, H. G. Wells, and other writers of fiction have, on occasion, resulted in working devices that had their ideological wellspring in what was once considered mere science fiction. For example, the "transporter room" aboard the Starship *Enterprise*, that made watching *Star Trek* so much fun. To refresh your memory, Captain Kirk and other officers would go to the transporter room, and, upon Kirk's spoken command, "Beam us down, Scotty!" they would first be fragmented, then atomized into shimmering molecules, and finally transported across space to another location. Is such a thing impossible? Don't bet on it. Is such a thing desirable? Well, how many times have you really wanted to be somewhere else but just hated the thought of having to get yourself there. Stay tuned. Transporters may happen yet.

Science fiction has, again and again, proven to be the wellspring of many of today's inventions and commonplace technological developments. Submarines, orbiting satellites, aircraft, space travel, and even time travel are only some examples of developments that began with writers of science fiction and burgeoned into prototypes, which became, in the fullness of time, working models and, eventually, commercially available or militarily strategic entities. Of the examples given above, only time travel has not been realized to date, but our civilization still may see wondrous things. Only time will tell about that one. The really neat thing about science fiction is that its inventions and predictions have a strange way of coming true! For example, Jules Verne (1828-1905) wrote a long-lost and not-published-until-recently novel entitled *Paris in the 20th Century*. He wrote that manuscript in 1863, about midpoint in our own nation's Civil War. Verne's book depicts a metropolis illuminated by electric lights. Automobiles dominate the streets. Commuters use automated mass-transit trains suspended in the air. Contraptions similar to today's fax machines use telegraph wires to transmit designs. A centralized government gains dominance and influence over individuals' lives. Appreciation for classic culture fades. Slang overtakes proper grammatical use of language. Money and technology become the controlling forces of society. Sound familiar? It should. And remember, that was all written in 1863! Ironic footnote: When the novel was found in a strongbox, the box also contained a rejection letter from Verne's original publisher. Verne's impersonal, mechanized society was considered too farfetched.

James Gunn and Milton T. Wolf, writing about science fiction in their article, "Science Fiction; Disturber of the Literary Peace," *Library Journal* (February 15, 1988), call the genre of science fiction, "the literature of discontinuity," and are careful to distinguish it from "fantasy," with which it is related and often confused:

> *Change means discontinuity. For most of humanity's exist-*
> *ence, it has had . . . continuity, and people looked to tradition for*
> *guides to decision. . . . Science fiction . . . is the literature of discon-*
> *tinuity and offers different guides to decision: analysis and fore-*
> *thought. Fantasy is also a literature of discontinuity, but it takes place*
> *in a different universe where some basic . . . laws are different. Science*
> *fiction takes place in our universe with all its laws of science and*
> *behavior intact. Fantasy deals with things that can't happen, and we*
> *wish they would; science fiction with things that could happen, and*
> *we hope they don't.*
>
> —James Gunn and Milton T. Wolf.

Still, science fiction has a fascinating way of becoming fact, and the results are unpredictable. A relevant question then emerges: Just because technology makes it possible for something to be invented or even mass produced and commercially available, is that a good thing? Is there an overriding concern with ethics and morality that takes precedence over technological triumph? In a society riven with technological innovation and the rampant greed and self-interest of producers and suppliers of such devices, there is plenty of room for debate. Science, after all, promises the rich, pleasurable future we all dream about, sometimes, but at what cost? The cost of such advances may turn out to be the loss of freedoms, an ever-widening gap between society's haves and have-nots, or even class warfare. And what about addiction to new technology? What happens when the wonderful world of the new media becomes so preferable for people to their own drab, humdrum, workaday existence that they prefer to spend as much time as possible in Fantasyland, rather than in reality?

- **Trend Extrapolation.** This technique is more commonly known as projection. It involves looking at current trends and making certain assumptions from them about the way the future will pan out. But it's risky, as all futuring techniques are. For example, after the conclusion of World War II, when the baby boomers were born, it was predicted that there would be an ongoing and incrementally escalating need for more schools, which were built in anticipation of the numbers who would need them. Within a decade, it became obvious that projections of population growth were off target, for a number of reasons (fear of global conflict, economic uncertainty, the decline of marriage, better means of birth control), which caused Americans to decide to have fewer children. Or there's the famous photograph of a broadly smiling Harry Truman, the day after the 1948 presidential election, holding up an early edition of the *Chicago Tribune* proclaiming "DEWEY ELECTED!" The headline was based on projections based on voter exit-interviews, but in their rush to "scoop" other newspapers, the *Tribune*'s editors failed to account for undecided voters. And my favorite projection story: In 1960, there were, on average, 2.8 persons in each car that passed on the highway. By 1980, that number had dropped to 1.6, so one may project from this that by the year 2010, every third car that passes us will be empty. What does this tell us? Only that projection and trend analysis as a means of seeing the future ought to be used with a large dose of extreme caution, that's all. One final delicious snippet:

> *Counting people tells us some interesting things, especially since computers are able to extrapolate trends into the future. Take this, for example. If the population of the Earth were to increase at the present rate indefinitely, by A.D. 3530, the total mass of human flesh and blood would equal the mass of the Earth, and by A.D. 6826, the total mass of human flesh and blood would equal the mass of the known universe.*
>
> —Robert Fulghum.

- **Consensus Methods**. The most common of these widely used techniques is called the Delphi method, named for the oracle of antiquity, to whom the ancients went when they wanted answers to their questions delivered from the "gods." There are several parts to conducting a Delphi study.
  1. Identify experts.
  2. Get 50-100 of them to participate in the study.
  3. Ask participants (A) How likely a possible outcome is; and (B) How desirable.
  4. Tabulate and analyze the results of Round 1, and launch Round 2, providing mean or median scores on the previous round.
  5. After three or four rounds, you begin to have the distilled wisdom of the best minds of one's profession expressed as consensus.

  There is, however, a hitch: even a hundred "experts" can be wrong, or things may change in the field, invalidating all previous predictions.
- **Simulation Techniques**. (aka modeling, cross-impact matrix analysis). This form of systems analysis is normally a job requiring a big, powerful computer, but it is easy enough to perform once all the variables have been identified. Example: Imagine that the computer's calculations lead to the inescapable conclusion that a system crash is imminent. Your task is to decide what must happen (or be prevented from happening) to avoid that crash. To do so, select numerous factors and place them in a grid, where the impact of each factor on all the others may be surveyed to advantage. Measure

interconnectedness to determine significance, e.g., how a change in one variable affects the others. Hitches: Results are inconclusive and sometimes even baffling. Additionally, there is the risk of confusing what things are like with what they really are.

- **Decision Trees,** also called Relevance Trees. Imagine a tree in a tropical rain forest. It stands hundreds of feet high, with the dense shade of the canopy permitting little vegetation below. Now imagine that we stand at the trunk and, seeking sunlight and fresh air, must follow complicated pathways of branches to arrive at the top of the canopy. Branching points, of course, are critical. Every decision we make has ramifications for everything that is to come. Alternatively, we may work backwards. The top of the canopy may stand for where we wish to be in 20, 30, or 40 years, and our branching decisions lead us downwards by various paths until we eventually land on the ground. But where have we landed, and is it where we wish to be? That is a function of the decisions we have made earlier.

- **Scenarios** . . . with which the rest of this book concerns itself.

Scenarios

> *Too often, the forecasting function ends with a detailed picture of the likely or expected future (but) the likely or expected future assumes that the key decision-makers are not players in it; it assumes that they have not seen the forecasts and that they continue to act in the future as they have in the past. The purpose of forecasting is, of course, to change that—to help us make future decisions on the basis of forecasts and to build a better future. . . . To make the forecasting process as rigorous and complete as possible, we examine a variety of scenarios. By compiling and analyzing the various strategies recommended for each, we can identify those strategies that have the greatest utility—those that apply to the greatest range of scenarios. But a single scenario is not very meaningful—or even interesting—in and of itself. A group of scenarios, however, begins to be very useful in guiding the current decision-making process, as well as forecasting, strategic planning, and understanding the future. . . . Many forecasters working on scenarios often ignore or discount future events whose odds are estimated to be 1-in-10 or less. But such "wild card" events should not be left out of our thinking about the future, because when wild-card events do happen, we are caught by surprise and go into our crisis mode, our fire-fighting action.*

> —William H. Renfro. "Future Histories: A New Approach to Scenarios." *The Futurist.* March-April 1987.

Library and Information Science is an eclectic discipline that has, through its history, borrowed liberally from other fields to formulate its philosophy, principles, and strategies. It also continues to make itself up as it goes along, or to give itself periodic makeovers, in response to changing conditions and trends. The use of scenarios to dramatize and examine concepts and speculation has evolved from the natural sciences to the social sciences and has borrowed liberally from other fields wherever valuable exports (or imports) seemed like sensible ideas. So the art or practice of scenario-writing has, in recent years, become a useful means of exploring various ideas for the future and deciding from the study of those scenarios just where it is we want our professional institution to go.

Along with figuring out where we want the field to go comes its analogous practice: deciding where we most specifically do *not* want our institution to go or wind up, and ideas for what we can do about it. But those scenarios are now in serious need of updating, refurbishing, or replacement. The present volume contains new scenarios, encouraging and depressing, by turns, and representing still more possible futures for the public library. As before, I caution that the kind of future that awaits the public library—if it even has one—is not something that should be left to chance or the gradual unfolding of natural processes. What happens in the next quarter century is something that will emerge from the collective efforts (or lack of same) of those of us who have chosen library and information science as our career paths and who may have a part to play in the decision as to what is to come. In other words, what we do today—every day—will affect what happens tomorrow.

Since I freely confess that I have no innate sense of prediction, I have developed, to assist me in forecasting the future, a continual eclecticism— a predilection for discovering, borrowing, and employing the tools of others—persons who are pleased to call themselves "futurists" and who are busily and constantly engaged in the pursuit of prognostication, for one good and simple reason: to try to figure out what's coming next.

Here's the bottom line where futuring is concerned. We are all of us proceeding into the future at a pretty good rate of speed. And as they say in the travel industry, getting there is half the fun. But since we cannot retard the march of time, we're on our way, and we should be making the journey with our eyes and minds open. After all, the next playing card you see face down might alter and affect your life in ways you can't even guess.

Warning: you may not like these scenarios overmuch. It is possible that some of y'all might not care for my scenarios and may even actively disagree with them. In my son's vernacular, "that's cool." Don't like my scenarios? I encourage you to try writing your own. Just sit down at the keyboard, or take a pencil or two and some paper to the park or the pool one day this summer. Start with something enjoyable to contemplate first. Something you would like to have happen to libraries. Then write a short story (we're not talking Nobel prize, here) showing how this thing might xxiv Introduction to the Study of the Future

come about in gradual stages, paying equal attention to what would have to happen and not happen to bring about the desired result. Keep money in mind, just for realism's sake. Or perhaps you'd rather write negative scenarios, frightening stories of grim futures that could happen if we don't watch our step or mend our ways. They're fun, too, but they're designed to serve as warnings, rather than dire predictions of things we cannot avert. Toffler's done a whole bunch of them (he calls a future world in which everything is negative a "dystopia"). How, for example, does the United States, the putative leader of the free world, go, in the next 50 years, from a country of readers to one of almost complete illiterates? Just a few critical incidents and we're there. It wouldn't take much. All you have to build in are some decisions and turning points, at which Congress, for example, could have elected one course, yet chose another.

Previously . . .

By way of review, my previous work suggested the following possible nine directions for the public library, as it moved into and partway through the 21st century:

- *The Death of the Library,* which tells a story not particularly pleasing to libraries and their supporters, but, as it happens, maybe not nearly as tragic as it sounds at first blush. Actually, looking backwards now, the author realizes that he could very well have called this scenario "The Withering Away of the Library Scenario" without loss of meaning. In this story, the public library gives way to a combination rent-all store and video parlor. The point is that consumers can still fill their information requirements, but the economic principle has changed from pay through your taxes to pay for services rendered. Some would say that that is a fairer way to go, because only those who require and desire "library services" would have to pay for them.

- *AI: The Library as Robot.* Ever go to a Toys 'R' Us or other giant emporium on a slow day with a couple of eager, acquisitive kids, and try to find someone to help you or advise you in making a selection? Good luck. Such stores are normally well supplied with stock personnel and cashiers, but self-service is the general rule, and no doubt results in lower prices than one might find at a store that prides itself on personal service. This scenario simply followed that concept to its logical conclusion in terms of what one might expect at the Reference Desk of a typical public library some 20 years or so into the future. The automated Reference Robot in the scenario had a chance to strut its stuff, and at the same time, to display its limitations, so that planners could contemplate whether replacing people with automatons is a good idea, a bad idea, or . . . it all depends.

- *The Cultural Monument.* This scenario plays "What if . . ." with the idea that libraries as we know them today could fall into total disuse or decline because the newer, sexier, flashier media (especially the ones that don't require a high level of reading ability) capture the imaginations of the fickle reading public. Suppose, this tale asks, society decides that it is no longer important or cost-effective to maintain and operate a public library at public expense. However, enough support for and interest in library materials exists in a community to justify the creation of a museum that enshrines the library's essence, so that it does not become lost to public consciousness entirely. The cultural monument, then, is a future for the public library in which today's reading materials become tomorrow's archaeology exhibit, for the edification of those who did not live in a time of libraries as we know them now.
- *Social Experimentation: Everything to Some.* Here, those in charge of the Library of the Future realize the impossibility of the library's longtime charge—trying to be all things to all people— and realizing that efforts must be rechanneled, identify two options: either to become all things to some people, or to become some things to all people. In the "Everything to Some" scenario, the leadership of the future library elects, between those mutually exclusive choices, to attempt to be all things, but only to some people. In this scenario, the criterion for admission to the future "public" library and for eligibility for library services at even the minimum level is annual income as a measurement of an ability to pay. Upon reflection, and considering the technology either already in place or about to exist, the author constructed this scheme as one in which one must apply for a library card, and that "smart" card will include, as an embedded coded microchip, personal tax identification (furnished by the IRS) that identifies the cardholder as being in one of the brackets along the continuum of economic self-sufficiency. As an example, individuals whose economic circumstances show need (e.g., falling below the federal poverty line) will present their cards at the door and, once the card is scanned, receive entitlement to the full range of services provided by the library without charge. A person of moderate means, on the other hand, will have a card superficially identical to that of one falling into the "poor" category, but will have a predetermined sum deducted from that card by the scanner for such events as admission, borrowing of materials, reference service, photocopying, interlibrary loan, and the like. The same system charges would hold true for those at the high end of the economic scale except for the actual amount of those charges. A wealthy library patron, for example, might pay up to five times as much for exactly the same service as a moderate income patron. Alternatively, if circumstances warrant, upscale patrons might actually

be denied service, on the assumption that they are capable of
satisfying their own information and entertainment needs without assistance or subsidy from the taxing unit. In this way, the
cost of library service (and the total revenue) would fall more
heavily on affluent persons than on those lacking the same ability
to pay, while those without that ability would need to pay nothing for the same services. Such a system would be progressive
(cost rising with ability to pay), and thus fair.

- *Social Experimentation: Some Things to All.* The other side of the
choice mentioned in the previous scenario is covered here. Under
a policy of "Some Things to All," all members of the library's
community would receive full entitlement to the full range of
services and collections offered by the library. That range, however, would be severely limited in comparison to what it is today.
The author was not so bold as to predict what services would be
offered under such a regime but did proffer a suggestion. Looking
at all a contemporary (1996) library offers, it was decided that the
most useful service the library could provide would be that of
becoming a consumer resources center. Therefore, libraries spend
their available funds and commit their energies to amassing and
making available and useful as much consumer-related information
as possible. It is realized that this goal, while commendable, means
that several of today's library services must be dropped or severely
downsized. Notable among these are adult fiction collections, which
are often the only reason that some persons come to the library, and
children's services. Adult fiction, however, would be offered in
various ways by the for-profit sector; e.g., rental stores, bookstores,
mail-order houses, and catalog sales departments, while a similar
economic sector would grow up for children's materials. Children's
programming might become an ancillary responsibility of schools,
community centers, and day care facilities.

- *EMP: Post-Holocaust.* EMP stands for Electromechanical Pulse
and refers to a nation (or world) without electricity or computers
in the aftermath of somebody (or several somebodies) setting off
nuclear weapons in an attempt to extend conflict beyond diplo-
matic means. This scenario has, thankfully, become somewhat
less likely to occur, thanks to the demise of the Soviet Union since
the publication of the author's *The Library of the Future* (1989). Still,
the nuclear family of nations with "the bomb," if all published
statements and rumors are true, has grown, not diminished, as a
result of the restructuring of a former superpower, and there are
unconfirmed stories in the press all the time that several Middle
Eastern dictators and repressive regimes have nuclear weapons and
are itching to use them. If nuclear war managed to avoid wholesale
death and destruction of the "dirty" bombs such as those that were

dropped on Hiroshima and Nagasaki a half century before this book was written, the weapon of choice might be the so-called electron bomb, and EMP would stop all electrical power, render computers into fancy paperweights, and force those who wanted to organize or consult a library's holdings to reconstruct and use the card catalog . . . in daylight or by torchlight.

- *The Experience Parlour.* The realization of this scenario, in my humble opinion, seems less unlikely than a lot of things you see on television nowadays. Imagine a future for the public library in which books gradually are discarded due to their linear arrangement, their comparatively low involvement levels, and their lack of immediacy in favor of The Experience Parlour, a community virtual reality center. The Parlour is envisioned as the same building as that formerly occupied by the public library, only completely gutted and rehabbed. Now it holds a central reception and command desk, a self-contained power unit, and as many small individual cubicles as are practicable. Within each hermetically sealed and soundproofed cubicle, the client reclines in a comfortable couch as a headset recessed in the ceiling descends over his head. A preselected cassette of someone else's experience is then played into his head, causing him to have all the sensations of the original experiencer. Thus, while experiencing such things as Climbing Mount Everest, A Visit to Beijing, Amazon Rain Forest, Seventh Game of the World Series, or A Passionate Night With . . . (your favorite entertainment star), the client would receive all the sensory components of the experience without having to leave town, get into optimal physical condition, commit a lot of time, or, in the latter case, betray solemn vows. Benefits would include augmented knowledge, relaxation, and, in some cases, the sort of excitement one cannot get in one's workaday, humdrum life. Medical problems are envisioned, but Parlours would be state-licensed and inspected, and the client would be required to sign a release. Ethical problems are not as easily dispensed with, but the client would not be permitted to enter a booth without proving, to the satisfaction of supervisory staff, that he understood what was going to happen to him in there.

- *The Politicized Library.* This one's a shocker, and let's hope it never gains a foothold in the affairs of people in Western society. Imagine, if you will, that some sort of government interested in preserving law and order met up with some serious threat (from within or without) to the American Way of Life and domestic safety and security. Now ask yourself this: How far would that government go—in the interest of self-protection and preservation, mind you—to ensure that revolution would never take place? Could such a government use libraries as instrumentalities of the official (party) line? Would the contents and materials of such a library reflect only approved (and whatever is deemed politically correct) values, and everything else be restricted or even banned? What if the library became a good part of the propaganda arm of our national government, helping to mold citizens' minds in approved ways—like Aldous Huxley's *Brave New World*—by filtering ideas until the ability to utter heresy was difficult, or—as in Orwell's *1984*—to assist in changing language until heresy becomes impossible. Couldn't happen here? Don't bet on it.

- *In The Privacy of Your Own Home.* Increasingly, this is far from a visionary concept of some far-off day when everything is wired and one may go exploring the world's libraries and databases with his shoes off. We're already there, in fact, technologically. It is now possible for individuals to do everything one used to do by physically going to a library without leaving one's chair or rising from his or her computer station. But there are unknowable consequences that go along with such luxury, and this scenario explored only a few of them.

And Now . . .

This book contains new scenarios for the public library. But I claim no particular gift for prophesy and really don't know what's going to happen, either in the next quarter century or the next quarter-hour. What's more, no one else does either. The best any of us can ever hope to do is to make some educated guesses and hope for the best. Don't let anybody tell you different. I have never met a true psychic; matter of fact, I'm not entirely sure that would be an enjoyable or comfortable experience. Maybe, just maybe, we can, however—like Scrooge in Dickens' story—do something about the future. Maybe it's Christmas morning for librarians, and we still have a shot at creating the future we would like, instead of the one someone else (or random events) will impose on us. Isn't it worth a try?

The future is about change. And change is something libraries can deal with, if they try. At the least, libraries can mitigate the negative effects of change in people's lives, by preparing them gradually for new technological and social developments in the world. Change, after all, can be good or bad, depending on many factors. But libraries—especially public libraries—are poised to do a great deal to help people deal with change in a positive manner, by acting as a community interface between individuals and the ongoing and accelerating twin revolutions in communication and information provision. These are changes brought about by technology, and the library, properly positioned, will serve as a gateway and facilitator to the new technology, especially for individuals who lack the potential of having the new technology in their own homes.

Libraries must define their roles now, before the future overtakes them. What to do about technology? Should they be out in front of technology and change, or should they hang back a bit, cautiously, and see where things are going before they plunge into the fray? Here is what one cautious writer said 15 years ago:

> As non-profit, tax-supported institutions, libraries are in a difficult position when it comes to manipulating events and taking chances. Libraries are, of necessity, impartial providers of information "on demand." Planning for change means waiting for those who use libraries to change. Librarians cannot guess about the future: they must wait until others guess, and then move to provide the information needed. By the very nature of their role in society, libraries must change slowly and late.
>
> —S. D. Neill. *The Futurist*. October 1981.

There is, of course, room for reasonable people to disagree. It is interesting to speculate as to what, if anything, Neill would have changed in his manuscript had he been readying his article for publication in 1996, rather than 1981. And even more interesting, perhaps, it will be fascinating to find out, when his target year, 2010, rolls 'round at last, what reality will be like, compared to the visions he had 30 years earlier.

What lies ahead for the public library? One very probable scenario, of course, is that it changes little, and only incrementally, as the next 30 years elapse. But that may not be all bad. Library collections need not grow at any budget-busting rate, so long as we all have (and be) good, caring, sharing neighbors. Use, rather than ownership, will have to guide selection policies, such that cooperative arrangements will be essential government policy. Document imaging and other electronic technologies will, of course, make it easier for libraries to make information accessible, yet retain it for use by their own clienteles. It's about attitude . . . and, I guess, money. Yes, friends, we're talking megabucks, and how to get tightfisted or uncaring administrators at various levels to turn loose of them! All of our elaborate scenarios necessarily entail commitment or diversion of funds, and there's no getting away from it.

> People are always blaming their circumstances for what they are. I don't believe in circumstances. The people who get on in this world are the people who get up and look for the circumstances they want, and, if they can't find them, make them.
>
> —George Bernard Shaw.

Only if we can solve these problems—financial, technological, political, and, perhaps most important, attitudinal—can our profession (whatever we choose to call it) assume a position of information leadership in the 21st century. If we cannot solve them, however, or we dither helplessly over trivia and marginal issues, we'll be bypassed and backnumbered by the future construction battalions of that Information Superhighway, and we'll be lucky if we can avoid being roadkill when the road is completed. It isn't really about money, although—admittedly—money helps. It's about vision and imagination and flexibility and other things you cannot assign a price tag.

This book is peppered with quotes, my way of supplementing my own words with those of others, and sharing (see Future Quotes, p. 153) some of the clever things that various writers have said about the future. Here's two to ponder, from recent issues of *The Futurist*:

> *The global network of interconnected computers and telecommunications links is already the biggest machine ever built. But it will likely become many times bigger and more powerful in the coming decades. This monster machine will fundamentally transform human life as we know it today. . . . The Internet will allow people easy access to stupendous quantities of information on innumerable subjects, allowing them to become far better informed than in the past. . . . However, most people may continue to make little use of Internet resources, because accessing these sources takes some effort. At present, only a minority of people make much use of libraries or of reference books. . . . The changes likely to result from the cyber revolution lead to two very broad generalizations. Both seem obvious but quite important. One gives us reason to be very hopeful about the future; the other must be a source of enormous concern. First, we are building up unprecedented power to do whatever we want to do. Infotech is amplifying our ability to produce the material goods of life, to cure diseases, and to expand the human enterprise into the universe. We are becoming god-like in our capabilities. Second, we do not know how to use our growing power wisely. Rather than growing wiser as our power has increased, we seem actually to be less able to agree on appropriate actions or to delay immediate gratification to achieve long-term goals. Worse, the new supertechnologies can be used in ways that do us tremendous harm. Our difficulties in using our growing power wisely arise partly from the rapidity of technological growth. . . . In meeting these challenges, the new resources of the cyber era can be very helpful. . . . How well we respond to the challenges ahead will determine whether the great cybernetic machine will develop into a Moloch or a Messiah.*

> —Edward Cornish. "The Cyber Future: 92 Ways Our Lives Will Change by the Year 2025." *The Futurist*. January-February 1996.

> *My optimism is not fueled by an anticipated invention or discovery. Finding cures for cancer and AIDS, finding an acceptable way to control population, or inventing a machine that can breathe our air and drink our oceans and excrete unpolluted forms of each are*

dreams that may or may not come about. Being digital is different.
We are not waiting on any invention. It is here. It is now. It is almost
genetic in its nature, in that each generation will become more digital
than the preceding one. The control bits of that digital future are more
than ever before in the hands of the young.

> —Nicholas Negroponte. "The Digital Revolution:
> Reasons for Optimism." *The Futurist.* November-
> December 1995.

No one can say, with any degree of assurance what lies ahead for the public library. Life itself, after all, is no certified check. But there are hopeful signs, because librarians (cybrarians?) are beginning to read about, contemplate, and even experiment with the futures they, themselves, want for their institutions, and with techniques designed to help ensure the futures they prefer. These scenarios outline divergent pathways for the library, and the reader will note that some of these scenarios (and a corresponding number in the earlier work) are dismal, pessimistic, alarming, or dangerous. But that is the problem of thinking about the future. As previously stated, it is the job of the future to be dangerous. In our society, science and technology move relentlessly forward, and almost every day, the headlines in our newspapers and journals scream of new discoveries and capabilities. The good news is that, with modern technology, every individual now has—or soon will have—the ability to access and exploit a wealth of information not dreamed of in even the recent past. The bad news, unfortunately, is much the same thing—individuals, as well as governments, may now "reach out and touch someone" without their knowledge and consent.

It is worth remembering that even though science promises to make our future richer and more exciting, there is likely to be a price to pay for progress. That price might well be the loss of individual freedoms. As science becomes more powerful, there is almost inevitably going to be a greater temptation for government to try to control it. The implications of that struggle may well be the loss of freedoms and the corresponding diminution—or absence—of our present rights to make our own decisions, right or wrong.

One version of the future of the library (or whatever we decide to call it) is found in Arthur C. Clarke's novel, *Imperial Earth*:

> *He walked to the console, and the screen became alive as his*
> *fingers brushed the on pad. Now it was a miracle beyond the dreams*
> *of any poet, a charmed magic casement opening on all seas, all lands.*
> *Through this window could flow everything that man had ever*
> *learned about his universe, and every work of art he had saved from*
> *the dominion of time. All the libraries and museums that had ever*
> *existed could be funneled through this screen, and the millions like it*
> *scattered over the face of the earth.*

Do yourself a favor: Think about the future. If you don't, the one you get will probably turn out differently from the one you want, or believe you want. Everything that happened in the past affected the present, and everything we do today will have some effect—for good or ill—on the future. In many cases, in fact, it may actually be possible to achieve the future we desire merely by making the proper decisions now. And even if we cannot forestall a more dismal future, we are better off by far for not just letting things take their course, and for giving some serious thought to what is likely to occur, and the working out of just what we can do about it.

There is no inevitability, as long as we are able to think.

—Marshall McLuhan. *Understanding Media.* 1962. ■

SCENARIO
1

EXPERIENCES
'R'
US

Clearly, many people are in the market for new experiences, whether natural or manufactured . . . including sailing the Amazon, climbing Mount Everest, retracing the travels of Marco Polo, and visiting the moon. Today, consumers are demanding an increased range and depth of new experiences. Unsatisfied by vacations that deliver no more than a deep suntan or a mounted fish, they . . . want to come back and tell their friends they drank lamb's blood in the Rio Bio-Bio during a native ritual or learned bullfighting in Cordoba. The motivations are nearly as diverse as the experiences: to escape routine . . . to test a new lifestyle . . . to be entertained . . . to be challenged . . . to learn . . . to realize other fantasies . . . (and) to get attention. . . . Advancing technology of designing artificial environments resembling real ones has contributed much to the art of experience design. (Among them may be) total television . . . holography . . . sensory wiring . . . (and) experience pills.

—Philip Kotler. " 'Dream' Vacations: The Booming Market for Designed Experiences." *The Futurist*. October 1984.

It is the year 2022, and the public institution once known as "the Public Library" is now renamed the "Cybrary," and has been given new roles to play. Meet Frank Fairlawn, director and facilitator of the local public cybrary, which has abandoned book provision in favor of an advanced form of virtual reality called Experience Technology. Cybrary experiences provide a form of adventure so realistic as to persuade the experiencer that he or she isn't just watching—but is actually doing things he or she might never have thought possible before.

There are many aspects of experience technology. One of them, which gives Frank the most pride, is a form of new hope for those who cannot walk—or even, in some cases, move. Frank relishes the opportunity to bring physical enjoyment to paralytics and paraplegics who would otherwise be prisoners of their own inert bodies. Consequently, the service he offers is a valuable tool of the medical community and provides the cybrary's clients with abilities and pleasures—however brief—that the rest of us take for granted in our daily lives.

The tremendous value of experiences, in fact, proves to be both the best and worst feature of Frank's job; he gets to be both helper and facilitator, even if his job satisfaction sometimes falls short of the absolute apex. . . .

Advertising Supplement in All Print Media

Run Date: April 15, 2022

Are you . . . keyed up? Tied down? Bored? Restless? Depressed? Troubled? In a rut?

Want stimulation you can't get at home or on the job? We know the feeling, and we have the solution.

℘

Introducing

The ExperienCybrary!©

NOW, at a convenient nearby location, you can experience breathtaking danger . . . forbidden passions . . . reckless endangerment . . . pulse-pounding excitement . . . and effortless enlightenment . . . and all without leaving your chair! Yes, you can experience all these things (and many more) from the comfort and safety of a quiet, climate-controlled room in your hometown, and at a surprisingly REASONABLE COST!

What is the ExperienCybrary©? A place where you can find relaxation . . . tension relief . . . escape . . . fantasy realization . . . a break from humdrum routine and boredom . . . opportunity to travel without leaving town . . . entertainment and fun . . . excitement . . . education and learning . . . self-improvement . . . or therapeutic wish-fulfillment. The result of thousands of hours of exhaustive testing in United

States government laboratories, programmed experiences make it possible for you to stop living vicariously, merely witnessing exciting things happening to other people. Using safety-tested, high-tech equipment, you will be transported through space and time, even going beyond physical limitations, to do exciting things you've only dreamt about. In our experience booths, some of the most exciting experiences imaginable will happen to you, without risk, travel, training, or additional stress.

How does it work? Imagine this . . . You lock yourself securely into one of the Cybrary's smartly appointed, climate-controlled, soundproof, and completely private booths. You may remove some (or all) of your clothing, or leave them on. Reclining comfortably in a padded chair, you relax as the lights dim automatically and a helmet descends slowly over your head. Your selected experience cassette slides automatically into the headset and begins to play . . . but you won't even notice, because suddenly you'll be immersed in the sights, sounds, smells, tastes, sensations, and thoughts of the original experiencer!

For the next hour (but don't be surprised if it feels like days or weeks) you'll forget yourself and your personal problems, as you lose yourself in your experience! You'll be another person, encountering exciting events, traveling far and wide, interacting (on different levels) with fascinating people, or even risking life and limb, if you dare, in mortal combat. Remember: you won't be just a spectator . . . you'll be an active participant! And at the end of your experience, you will find yourself as you were when you entered the booth, only happier, because our patented technology will implant an invigorating mild dose of euphoria in your mind, leaving you feeling refreshed and ready for the challenges of your own life.

What's available? New arrivals add to our stock of programmed experiences daily, but here's just a sampling of what's available:

- Climb the world's highest mountain in "Mount Everest"
- Cross the desert on camelback in "Sahara Express"
- Swim in the piranha-infested waters of "Amazonia"
- Explore the polar ice pack in "South Pole"

- Dive seven miles down into danger in "Pacific Floor"
- Enter the violent world of the "Professional Gladiator"
- Steer a small boat alone "Across the Pacific"
- Fight army ants on the march in "Malaysian Jungle"
- Speak and understand Chinese during "A Day in Beijing"
- Match wits with a skilled and wily enemy in "Sniper!"
- Tour the red planet in a "Mission to Mars"
- Remember the lost joys of youth in "A Day at the Beach"
- Bungee-jump 235 feet straight down in "Sheer Guts!"
- Come face to face with elephants and rhinos "On Safari"
- Ride a barrel over "Niagara Falls"

IN ADDITION, The ExperienCybrary (where local laws permit) offers a selection of experiences for discriminating adult clients (with required proof of age). Examples:

- Make love to your choice of attractive partners in our "A Night With . . ." series
- Experience crime from within the mind of the killer, and you get to choose your victim, in "Stalker"
- Undergo instant sexual reassignment in the "Both Sides Now" series

But is it safe? You're intrigued, but you're hesitant . . . afraid to try it. Something could go wrong. What are the risks? A valid question, so let us to put your mind at ease. While some of these may appear risky, even dangerous, and it is understandable that you may feel concern about surrendering yourself to a new technology, we guarantee your complete safety, we cater to cowards and doubters, and we're so sure of our product that we offer an unconditional money-back guarantee if you're not satisfied!

Speaking of safety, the ExperienCybrary is approved and licensed by the United States government as safe for persons in good physical health between the ages of 18 and 65. Experience technology has undergone exhaustive testing (test data available on request), and several built-in safeguards are continuously in place:

- required medical approval and certification before entering

- daily inspections of all experience booths by Servotechnicians

- prescreening of all experience cassettes by respected health professionals in conjunction with our trained Cybrary personnel

- continuous automated vital-sign monitoring during experiences

- a "breaker" switch that can instantly interrupt your experience, returning you to normal full-consciousness and function

- prohibition of "stronger" experiences to persons unable to pass the required health examination and to clients under 21 years of age or over 65 years of age.

What does it cost? Billions of dollars in start-up money (and almost that much each year since) have been spent on research and development of this technology. The U.S. government licenses experience services to local franchisers and has authorized your local franchiser to retail this service for a fair and reasonable profit. Much of the annual profit goes to erect new ExperienCybraries, to better serve you and your community in the future. Prices of individual experiences vary with the type, duration, and nature of those chosen. Call for free quotations, or sign up for a thrifty starter package. Our reasonable rates are within the budget of most Americans, and we predict the value you will receive exceeds the price.

How do I get started? you ask
—It's as simple as 1-2-3!

1. Obtain the required medical approval from your physician. Pursuant to Public Health Law 16-34-1882, it is unlawful to engage in programmed experiences without a standard physical examination and a licensed stamp on your application, for your own safety and well-being.

2. Once you have obtained the medical stamp, call your local ExperienCybrary and book an introductory session. A sample half-hour programmed experience is available at an affordable cost. But keep in mind that this sample cassette doesn't begin to rival the excitement of the real thing! After your initial session, we predict that you'll want to become a regular customer. Standing weekly appointments are available, but federal law prohibits any person from more

than one experience per week. Multiple-experience packages offer considerable savings over one-shot sessions. Due to the unpredictability of future prices, we recommend a ten-trip starter package, with an option to renew at locked-in rates.

3. Arrive at least 20 minutes early for each appointment. There are required forms to fill out and government-required check-in procedures that must be followed.

Is one hour enough? Forget about time in its conventional sense! Experience technology has an amazing way of telescoping time in the human mind. One hour in one of our booths is more than enough time to have a stimulating, satisfying experience and return to your personal life less than 60 clock-minutes later. During your experience, your body reposes in a relaxed, restorative, and comfortable slumber zone, while your mind soars up and out or away, unfettered by gravity, obligations, or constraints. And we predict with confidence that you'll want to come back again and again.

So what have I got to lose? Nothing—except time . . . and the blahs of your humdrum, workaday life. This time next week, you can be flying to Mars, exploring the Pacific Ocean's floor, or even sharing a torrid, intimate encounter with the partner of your choice. And if you start, say, at five, you'll be done by six, feeling great, ready for the evening's activities, and hungry for dinner. New experiences arrive just about every day, so check our Catalog listings often. We predict confidently that you'll become a regular customer. Call for an introductory appointment or to discuss experiences. Act now and become a charter subscriber, enjoying **GREAT SAVINGS!**

Call Frank Fairlawn:
EXPERIENCE (397-374-3623)

Federal Law requires that clients must be at least 18 years of age.

From the outside, if you were to drive into town for the first time and see it, the ExperienCybrary would seem just another nondescript cinderblock building, erected for practical rather than aesthetic purposes. The square, five-story building occupies an entire block on one of the city's major arteries, and little exterior space is wasted on landscaping. The facility is windowless, with a central entrance surmounted by a large sign proclaiming:

The ExperienCybrary

It's inside that everything important happens.

Older citizens of this city recall a time when the building on this site was known as the Public Cybrary (and before that, the Public Library, a term now no longer used in common speech). But while the old library building's exoskeleton remains, just beneath the outer facade, the interior bears no resemblance to its former self. If there is any similarity between what was then and is now, it lies in purpose, the parallel functions of 20th century library and cybrary. Now as then, people come to this building in search of entertainment, enlightenment, or escape: to find—or lose—their way. What was once the library still has the power to change lives, for better or for worse, although books are nowhere to be found here. The structure has undergone a complete retrofit, becoming as electrically wired as an orbiting space station, after workers gutted it, changed everything inside, and bricked up the windows.

Inside, the building is an exemplar of post-modernist turn-of-the-century functionalism. Entering the vast central hallway, the visitor has nowhere to go except forward to the high reception desk, where Frank, the director (or when he's off duty, his robot assistant) guards the portals of what lies beyond. Before visiting one of the small rooms beyond the desk, the customer must talk with Frank. Admission is by appointment only; the front portal is programmed to provide no admission to curious tourists or casual browsers. Once the experience has been selected, the established price paid, and the standard release form signed, the client is permitted beyond the desk, through a security portal, and into the bowels of the building, a multitiered warren of identical cubicles, each electronically wired to the main console.

Five levels of corridors transect the vast building at right angles, each corridor lined with small cubicles behind numbered doors. Each level contains 35 individual cubicles, electronically wired to the main console. Lighting is indirect throughout the building—illumination seems to come from everywhere and nowhere, eliminating shadows completely. It's always high noon in this place, wherever you go, except when cubicles darken while their occupants are "under." Cubicles are completely soundproof for solitude and privacy, essential for fulfilling and realistic experiences. Access to rooms is by the client's fingerprint only, and each room is climate-controlled, clean and cheerful, furnished with a recliner/couch, hooks, shelves for personal items and clothing, and, over the couch, a complicated, translucent helmet-like headset, which retracts into the drop ceiling when not in use.

The sensations the client feels, once reclining in the warm, padded couch are, by design, akin to those of an infant in Mother's arms: secure, serene, and contented. Hidden vents spray formulaic pheromones into the air supply to enhance the experiencer's sense of comfort through subliminal odor technology, intended to promote a sense of pleasure, while reducing stress or anxiety aroused by the more adventurous experiences. When the headset descends slowly, however, its leads attaching securely to the wearer's temples, and the chosen experience begins, results are unpredictable, and sometimes unsettling. Frank does his best to prepare clients for their experiences, but it's the very realism of each experience, in fact, that provides both the excitement and the anxiety.

Technologically, the cybrary is state-of-the art, designed to be run by a single human employee assisted by a robot who, unlike the human director, does not suffer from the perils of fatigue, illness, boredom, claustrophobia, or counterproductive emotions such as anger, love, or longing. The robot serves at times as reception staff, file clerk, security guard, record keeper, constable, and all-around facilitator. Several other security features are present to protect clients from coming to physical or emotional harm as the result of experiences at the cybrary. Medical safeguards are in place; the user's vital signs are continuously monitored throughout experiences. All clients are required to have a current medical certification; and while in the booth, they're being monitored. And thanks to recent federal legislation, there's a big, bright orange warning label on the door of every room in the place:

Caution:
Programmed experiences may result in unpredictable effects.
Proceed at your own risk.

Then there's the standard release form, for both legal and medical purposes and to cover the cybrary if somebody has a heart attack or something. The client's signature on that form holds the cybrary (and Frank) blameless for any medical or psychological consequences as a result of anything that takes place inside the experience booth.

Also on the books are minimum and maximum age rules, which keep children from having experiences that they can't handle yet, and prevent geriatric clients from having fatal heart attacks due to the excitement of what they're experiencing. Federal regulations also prohibit any individual from having more than one experience per week, for fear of addiction by users whose real-world lives provide insufficient stimulation.

Frank figures he must be doing something right, because this place is getting more popular all the time. You can't blame folks for wanting to try a new thing. Back in 2012, some reporter climbed into an experience booth and then wrote glowingly about how she didn't just witness exploration of the Pacific floor, seven miles down in the Marianas Trench—she was *there*! She went on and on about how she became the diver, down there on the dark ocean floor, encountering weird new life forms while incredible water pressure probed for leaks in her helmet. After that report, there was no way to put the genie back in the bottle, and few seemed to want to, anyway. Business really took off then. Never mind the technical problems that weren't resolved; people wanted it. End of story.

ExperienCybraries have their detractors, of course—some people are bothered or frightened by them. Fundamentalist preachers of the religious right are always thundering about the ungodliness of the place! Some of the experiences are profane or obscene or too unsettling, they say, but just about everybody else is clamoring for experiences now, and the cybrary is only meeting that need. Frank figures he supplies a valuable community service, and even if he, out of principle, refused to do it, they'd replace him with someone else, quickly enough. And it does seem a valuable service: few go away expressing disappointment. Via the experiences already in the cybrary's collection (and more arrive every day), one can become a space pilot, mountaineer, combat mercenary, polar explorer, and much more, and all without leaving one's comfortable experience couch! And real? When you wake up, you'd swear you'd really been there!

Frank grows increasingly worried about the problem of addiction. His government masters are reaping big profits, so they don't want it talked about much, and they keep a pretty tight lid on news coverage. Adverse publicity might affect business, after all. But addiction is definitely a growing problem, despite the government rule that allows a person only one experience a week. Franks thinks that's a sensible brake on consumption but still observes that some clients may be getting a form of "experience sickness," coming to crave cyber-experiences like drugs and far preferring them to their own lives. People don't like to admit to being hooked, so the government has no reliable statistics, but Frank has a couple of customers coming in weekly who tell him that they wish it was daily, or maybe all the time. They get this glazed look in their eyes, like heroin addicts or something. A few have even offered him sizable bribes to give them extra trips. He always declines such offers for two reasons: one, he doesn't want to feed addictions, and two, the penalty for getting caught is severe, a prison sentence of at least 10 years at hard labor. There are persistent rumors about people who aren't playing by the rules. People are starting to get around the government monopoly; for the right price, you can buy experiences on the black market or even get somebody to build you your own headset. Frank would bet plenty that bootlegged tapes are moving around town like winter colds, and some of the community's richer citizens now have their own jury-rigged booths and headsets locked away in the basement. Lots of advantages, having your own home booth. Convenient? Sure—there whenever you want it. Cheaper? You bet. Saves you a bundle to own your own headset. But it's going to be a can of worms when something bad happens! The feds try to slow unauthorized privatization down with laws and penalties, but it's no use. And think of the potential problem of experiences becoming habit-forming if you have them at home! Here at the cybrary, at least, there's some protection: the once-a-week maximum, required physicals, and monitoring of vital signs. But who could help (or even know about?) somebody in distress alone in the house during a home experience? Frank figures that people owning their own booths are just asking for trouble. Could even wake up dead, one morning; you never know. The Rules require him to report any suspected addiction he observes at the cybrary. He hasn't turned in anyone, yet, but there are a couple of clients who might fit the profile, and whom he's watching very carefully for those telltale signs.

Another thing: A mid-20th–century novelist named Orwell wrote a book called *1984,* warning of the growing capability of government to control every aspect of its citizens' lives . . . even thoughts. Orwell worried that technology, in the wrong hands, could lead to thought control, brainwashing, mental surveillance, and jamming "politically correct" attitudes and beliefs into vulnerable minds for political purposes. Now Frank worries that the dominant powers, grown tired of critics and troublemakers, could decide to deal with them by getting into their heads through the use of experience headsets. That's one of the reasons Frank doesn't sleep well at night. Suppose the government decided to do a number on the minds of its critics using the technology he makes available in his cybrary. Once they got into your head, they could convince you that two plus two make five, or that the president is always right, or that a whole different set of historical events took place from the ones you seem to remember. And pretty soon, you'd remember it the way they gave it to you, whether out of conditioning or self-preservation. Paranoia? Maybe, but it scares Frank all the same that he, without even knowing about it, could be exploited and contribute unwittingly to brainwashing people and enslaving their minds. Frank wants no part of that. The worst thing is that he probably wouldn't even know he was being used if they got to him first.

There's no evidence of anything yet, but he's keeping his eyes open, all the same.

One more nightmare scenario is fear of malfunction, even though all equipment gets checked and certified in proper working order by his robot assistant every night. But accidents can and do happen. And if one did ever happen here, Frank thinks, in one of his experience headsets, with the customer's head (and brain) inside it, there'd be no telling what the consequences would be.

Frank, however, is extremely proud of the good things his Experien-Cybrary provides. A personal example: learning another language takes time, money, and patience, involving lessons, homework, and all those grammar rules and conjugations. But experiences can provide foreign travel without ever having to leave town, with retention of much of what you learned during the experience. Frank has never claimed any special linguistic ability, but after one "Day in Beijing" experience, he had a basic working vocabulary in Mandarin. He went back again a week later and practiced by walking around, talking to the natives. A couple more trips and he expects to be fluent in Chinese! How's that for a benefit of the cybrary? He's already astonished old Mr. Wong, who owns the carry-out restaurant across the street, when he walked into his place a couple days ago and ordered his dinner in Mandarin! So, as with a lot of other things, programmed experiences can do wonders for you, or deprave and corrupt your soul — it's all in the selection.

The question is: Is the ExperienCybrary an unalloyed good, or an electronic version of Frankenstein's monster? Does Frank provide a valu-able public service or is he a pimp, pandering to his clients' pathetic weaknesses and fantasies, and he ought to be taken out and shot? His own opinion? Depends on when you ask. He honestly doesn't know if he's a hero or villain. If he knew for sure, he might be able to work out whether he should keep promoting the cybrary, quit his job, or even destroy the place before it's too late! Upon reflection, though, he figures it's simple, really: people want experiences, and that's that. Trying to decide whether he wears a white hat or a black one is useless; but he worries, all the same.

"Hi, Mr. Fairlawn. It's me again."

"Bekki! How're you doing?" Frank Fairlawn's careworn face lights up with genuine pleasure. Bekki Burroughs is here for her weekly appointment, and he's genuinely glad to see her, which is more than he can say for many of his clients nowadays. Bekki has become one of his favorite clients, and he is thrilled at the way his service has enriched and improved her life, espe-cially after the misfortune that changed it forever.

She looks sweet in tied-off hair, pullover sweater, and a pair of faded jeans with the knees cut out. But Frank knows that she'll never leave the wheelchair she sits in, due to a spine-damaging accident she suffered in an automobile six months ago. That's why he's so glad he can help.

Her file, when she first came in, described Bekki as a depressed teenager, referred to the cybrary for a course of experience therapy after her tragic accident. But that was then and now is now. Now, she is bursting with good cheer and optimism that Frank, himself, lost long ago. Poor kid! Frank thinks. Guess she's had a tough go of it, or her parents wouldn't be spending so much money on her experiences, but to him, she's a bright spot in an otherwise gloomy daily procession of seekers, losers, and bores.

"Oh, I'm fine!" she bubbles. "I'm always up on experience days. They're so much fun. And today, whitewater rafting down the Big Rapids. I can't wait!"

Frank just stands and gazes at her for a moment. It's refreshing and restorative to see the vitality that Bekki projects, despite her misfortune. She wasn't always like that, though. The first time she came in here, she was sullen, withdrawn, and snappish. But the six or seven experiences she has had since then have done something wonderful for the girl and her whole outlook on life. Frank is pleased that he and his cybrary could be instrumental in making her happy again, at least for an hour at a time. Cases like Bekki's help take away some of the sting of the negative aspects of the job.

"You okay, Mr. Fairlawn?" asks Bekki, seeing his distracted expression, and looking concerned.

"Huh? Oh, sure, Bekki. Sorry, I guess I was just daydreaming there for a minute. Let me call up your file on the screen now. Ah, yes. There it is. Sure enough: 'Whitewater Rafting' today. Tell me, how'd you like that one I prescribed for you last week?"

"Amazing! I mean, how many kids my age get to visit the Great Wall of China and walk around and talk to the natives in their own language? Oh, you picked a winner for me that time. The only thing was, it was too . . . I don't know . . . all that riding around on a bus, too much sitting down and chatting, I guess. What do they call that?"

"Sedentary," Frank says, grinning.

"Yeah, well, sedentary is what it was. But this time, I signed up for an experience where I get some heavy exercise running those rapids. 'Whitewater Rafting' sure isn't going to be sedentary, is it?"

Frank smiles at her warmly once again. "No, Bekki, whatever 'Whitewater Rafting' is, it is not even a little bit sedentary."

"Oh, this place is so neat! *You're* so neat! I love coming here." Suddenly, Bekki is blushing furiously, probably aware that she might have gone too far in paying him a personal compliment.

Hope she hasn't developed a crush on me, he thinks. I'm twice her age. To relieve her embarrassment, he turns brusque and businesslike.

"So, everything's all set and waiting for you. You ready to tackle that rushing river?"

"Yes! Just let me at it!"

"Good. That's the spirit!"

"Anything else I need to do before I get into it?"

"Nope! Just give me your thumbprint on this screen and your debit card for the charges. Then just get on down to . . . ahhh . . . B-34 . . . and you know what to do from there. As soon as you give me the go-ahead, you'll be hurtling downriver on a sunny spring day. Just watch out for those big rocks, hear? They come upon you awfully fast, you know!"

Her grin is confident and warming. "Oh, I'm not worried about any rocks. Sunburn, snakes, and spiders on dead trees, yeah, but not rocks. My reflexes were always pretty fast, if I do say so, myself." She stops and looks down at her legs for a moment, then resumes. "And in experiences, at least, they still are. Well, wish me luck!" She rolls her chair smoothly through the turnstile and down the hall. At the turn, she gives Frank a final grin and a cheery wave. He watches her until she is out of sight, smiling happily like a father whose daughter has just given him something he's always wanted for Christmas. Ah, Bekki, he thinks to himself. As long as there are still kids like you, there's still hope for this troubled world of ours!

"Luck!" he whispers, as she disappears from view.

$$\varnothing$$

Excerpt/transcript of Experience 22.10.30.14:16
Client: Rebekkah Burroughs, age 19
Technique: Brainwave capture
Clearance: Extremely confidential

Oh, Lordy, I'm going so fast! This puts every roller coaster I've ever been on to shame. Movin' so fast, I'm even afraid to blink. Ridin' the rapids, danger on every side, breathtaking speed. Tryin' to thread this one-person raft between jagged rocks, I'm also tryin' to jam and ignore the messages my brain is getting from my poor, overtaxed body, throbbing from unaccustomed exercise and fatigue.

Forget about the pain. Mind over matter; just do it! No time for pain now and no margin for error, fast as I'm going. Concentrate, girl! I'm going to need split-second reflexes to avoid overturning, because if I get plunged into this icy water, the odds are I'll be swept away and drowned. Drop of sweat on my forehead, now, leaking stingingly into my left eye. Ignore it. Can't even risk the time to wipe it away, because I need to devote my entire mind to my task: survival. This river acts like it means to kill me. I suppose it does, actually. But I'm strong and alert and I'm not going to let some water get the best of me! Mind over matter, that's the ticket!

My raft rushes along between the steep, colorful walls of this canyon under the broiling sun, but I've got no time to admire the scenery or the color scheme. My thoughts run the spectrum of emotions from euphoria to anxiety and back again. My shoulders and back ache from hours of incessant paddling, my nose is badly sunburned, I've been bitten by mosquitoes or something; I'm hungry and soaked through to the skin from the water that keeps foaming in over the sides. And yet, through it all, I'm really happy because I've never felt more alive!

Throwing my head back, I scream "Yeeehaww!" in my best imitation of the rebel yell I heard so often back home, when boys performed deeds of reckless derring-do, or just felt like showing off. The noise of the rushing torrent of water, however, muffles that and all other sounds, and I decide not to waste my energy again in shouting, when no one else can hear. In a foam of green water, I race around bend after bend, afraid to take my eyes off whatever's straight ahead of me.

What's that, dead ahead? I sit erect in my seat athwart the raft's stern, eyes bulging with alarm. Something's bearing down on me and coming fast. It's a huge rock, and I'm headed right for it. I've got maybe three seconds to decide whether to steer to the right or left of it, and there's not going to be any second chance. Come on, Bekki! Decide! You know what a mistake could mean. Decision time, now; right or left? The rock draws nearer, larger, and I can see its sunblasted top, and sides discolored from years of high and low water. Time to act!

Okay, left. I'm going left. Gotta be left. Hard a-port! I quickly rudder, putting all my weight behind the angle of the wooden oars, achieving a slight midcourse correction for my efforts. But it's enough—just barely. The raft's side passes the enormous rock in a burst of whitewater, skirting it by no more than six inches. As it recedes behind me, I allow myself a quick moment to rest, then I refocus my field of vision to what's ahead.

Another rock! No end to 'em, seems like. Things come in big bunches like bananas on this river, don't they? Okay, let's go right, this time. Missed it! Damn, I'm good!! But that first one was entirely too close, and there are plenty of others coming up! A wrong decision, just one, and who knows what might happen? What am I blessed with, luck or skill, I wonder? Whatever, without it I'd be fishfood about now. Well, no time to think about that. More rocks ahead. I squint into the mist, rainbow-colored in the bright sunlight. Oh, no! Here comes another one, and from the look of it, it's even bigger than the last one. Which way around it this time? Left again? Or right? How many times can I be lucky? Well, I'm on a roll, here. Come on, girl, you can do it! Decide! Hah! Right again. . . .

Sometime later, my battered raft sweeps around a wide bend in the river, and I'm suddenly in quiet backwater with no current to speak of, at all. Trembling all over, I'm exhausted, sweaty, and almost in shock, but my happiness, my feeling of being alive, is overwhelming. I beat the river! Did it! Victory! But oh, my aching back and shoulders. But I won! It was 110-pound me against this mighty river, and I won! . . . A modern day David against Goliath, that's who I am. Wow, this is fun! I feel so good. Oh, Lordy, just wait'll I tell my friends about this! . . . What a rush!

An hour later, Frank looks up to see a flushed and glowing Bekki come gliding down the hall and up to his desk, her face wreathed in a radiant grin.

"Enjoyable experience?" he asks mildly, knowing the answer.

"Oh, wow, Mr. Fairlawn!" she exclaims, her words cascading over one another like the rapids of that river. "It was so . . . I mean, I almost . . . There was this big rock . . . and I had about three seconds to make up my . . . And then I was past it but then came a second one, and that time I almost got dashed to pieces in . . . I'm sorry. I'm too excited to make sense!"

"Glad it went so well. How do you feel now?" Frank asks, curious.

"Tired. But pleasantly so. My arms ache from all that paddling, and my legs . . ." Suddenly, Bekki's grin fades, as she looks down at her legs, legs that will never again be of any use to her. "My legs . . ." she says again, dreamily, and sad at the same time. "Huh!" she marvels. Then she falls silent and brooding for a moment, seeming to forget that they're having a conversation.

Frank gives her a minute and then speaks softly. "Experiences really are amazing, aren't they, Bekki?"

"Oh . . . yes! Yes! I don't know what I'd do without them. Without experiences, I'm just a kid in a wheelchair, who has to be helped just to get into bed at night. But with them, I can walk, run, dance, and do just about anything I could do before . . . what happened to me . . . and lots more I never even dreamed about doing. And you make it all possible!"

"Well, it's my job, that's all," says Frank, modestly. "That's why the cybrary is here. So, have you thought about next week's experience?"

"Yes! I think next time I'd like to climb Mount Everest, if it's available. That sounds like it'd be really exciting. Have you been up there, Mr. Fairlawn?"

Frank makes a notation in the cybrary's scheduling program. "You're scheduled for it next week. Yeah, I've been up there on that North Face, myself. Exciting? I guess you could say so, yes. And strenuous, don't forget that. But then, you're not afraid of a little hard work, are you, Bekki?"

"No, sir! I love it. Just think! To climb the world's highest mountain, and stand at the summit and look in all directions for hundreds of miles."

"There's only one thing you might want to remember," Frank tells her.

"What's that?"

"To dress warmly. It gets very cold up there on that peak. Trust me; I know. Been there; done that."

"Cold?" Bekki looks confused. "But I won't really be cold, though, right? In reality, I'll be in a climate-controlled booth right here in the cybrary. So how could I be cold?"

"You weren't really on a river in a raft just now, either," Frank says with a wink and a smile. "Trust me. You're going to feel cold!"

"Ohhh . . . right!" Bekki now looks serious. "Mr. Fairlawn, I know you remember me the way I was the first time I came in here for an experience. I was bitter and angry and crying all the time, and spent much too much time thinking about dying. My legs wouldn't work, and without the ability to walk, I just didn't see much point in living."

Frank thinks this over. "And now?"

"Now I can walk, climb, jump, swim, and even dance, and it's all because of you and your wonderful ExperienCybrary that it's possible. So I just want you to know how much I thank you for the ability to do all those things."

Frank ducks his head again modestly, muttering, "Oh, that's all right, Bekki. I'm just glad I could help."

The girl's eyes sparkle in delight. "Well, I've got to get on home now. So I'll see you next week, same time, and I'll tackle that big mountain, all right?"

"I'll see you then," says Frank. She smiles prettily at him and turns to roll out of the building but, suddenly, on an impulse, Bekki reverses the wheels of her chair and reaches out, taking Frank's right hand by surprise, pressing it to her lips and depositing a fervent kiss on the fingers. Then, without another word, she rolls quickly through the cybrary's front portal, down the ramp, and out into the hazy afternoon.

Frank, suddenly misty-eyed himself, stares after her for a long time, pondering the amazing new technology that has given even paralyzed people the regained ability to enjoy life to the fullest. Only the sound of a clearing throat brings him back to the here-and-now, as George Jenkins, a large black man in a three-piece suit, announces his presence.

"Huh?" says Frank, startled out of his reverie. "Oh, George! How are you today? Right on time as usual. How's the weather out there?"

"Warm and pleasant," says the man, rolling his chair forward, "but not as warm as that Amazon rain forest, where I'm going to be headed soon."

Frank chuckles. "You got that right!" he agrees. "But it's not the heat you have to worry about. It's those piranhas that'll get you, if you don't watch out. Be advised: those little fishies are all teeth at one end, and they're always hungry." With a laugh of pure pleasure, Frank busies himself with setting up the next experience for his client, feeling pretty good about life in general.

> One of the major concerns . . . (is) the degree to which virtual reality might prove harmful. Some of the physical dangers associated with virtual reality are already known. Head-mounted displays, for instance, have been found to cause disorientation, vertigo, and nausea. However . . . it is possible that (virtual reality) may put certain "at risk" individuals in mental or emotional peril . . . (which could lead to) dissociative reactions and psychotic breaks.
>
> —Glenn F. Cartwright. "Virtual or Real? The Mind in Cyberspace." *The Futurist.* March-April 1994.

APRIL 2022

"Yessir, Josh! What'll it be tonight?" Frank Fairlawn's professional smile is growing a bit weak after a long, difficult day, but there's still an hour to go in his shift, so he flashes the grin at the tall man wearing a rain-spotted tan trenchcoat, its lapels appearing silver in the light of the foyer. "Got a new one you might like, just came in today. How about stalking a rogue elephant through the African rain forest? Helluva slam-bang ending, I'll tell you that!"

"No, not tonight, Frankie," says Josh. Covertly, Frank studies his face in the strong light over the counter: Josh's features are regular, if not quite handsome, but there's something terribly wrong with that face. One side of his mouth twitches irregularly, causing the eye on that side to close in rhythm, putting Frank in mind of a robocar signaling a left turn. Lord, the stresses this guy must be under! Frank tries to remember what Josh does for a living. Some kind of engineer or something. Something to do with city planning, he seems to remember. "So what'd you have in mind for tonight?" he asks the tall guy, trying not to stare at his tic.

Josh looks left, then right. "Frank, I wonder if we might be able to speak more privately," he says.

"If it won't take too long," Frank agrees reluctantly, hoping that, whatever this is about, it won't require too much time or thought or diplomacy. He's really tired, and all he wants about now is to close the cybrary, have a stiff drink, and get to sleep. He ushers Josh into the small cubicle where he keeps the cybrary's records and accounts. "Sit down," he says, trying to smile but feeling uneasy.

Josh remains standing, and comes right to the point. "Listen, Frankie. You know the collection, so tell me: do you have any tapes in here where somebody gets killed?" Two years ago, this request would have shocked Frank, but by now, he's become blasé about the things running through some people's heads sometimes and doesn't bat an eye. He gets requests like this three, four times a week, now. "Killed, you say?" he asks, striving to keep his voice neutral. "Yeah, I guess I do. Who'd you have in mind for a victim?"

"You're a clever guy, Frankie. Got me figured already. Okay, here's my story. I'm going to confide in you, because I know you have strict rules about client confidentiality, right?"

"Right," Frank affirms, placing his right hand over his heart for emphasis.

Josh takes a long, shuddering breath and expels it slowly. "All right, here goes. See, my wife, Janice, is all right. I mean, maybe she's not love's young dream any more, but after 20 years of marriage, basically, we get along." Frank watches with fascination as Josh's tic picks up speed. "But it's her mother, Frankie! Her vicious, judgmental know-it-all mother! How I hate that woman! Always running me down to Janice and the kids behind my back, or sneering whenever I say something. She doesn't see one thing good about me, that's for sure, and now she's even turning my kids against me. Keeps telling Janice she should have married George, her first real boyfriend. George turned out to be a millionaire, many times over. If I told you his last name, in fact, you'd . . ."

"Josh, please!" Frank interrupts. "Could you please try to stay on the subject? I have to activate the night closing procedures in just a couple of minutes."

"Oh, right! Sorry," says the nervous man. "Well, like I said, Janice's mother — I hate her with a pure, blue flame! And it's come to the point where . . . Frankie, I gotta do something about the way I feel or I don't know what! See, I guess I could stand it if she lived far away someplace and came visiting twice a year, maybe. But no, she lives just down the street from us, and she's always dropping by around dinnertime. And she's there, sitting there in the kitchen, talking a blue streak when I come home from work. You know how it is, after a long day, right? You're tired, just want to sit down, have a beer or something, take your shoes off, relax? But three or four days a week, when I come through the door, she and Janice have got their heads together when I come into the kitchen. Then— get this—the two of 'em stop talking real suddenly. Janice usually looks embarrassed when that happens. But my mother-in-law, the only thing'd embarrass her would be if she forgot to rip on me one time when she came over. And it isn't hard to figure out what Janice is embarrassed about, either. Like I was the topic of conversation, and nothing they said about me was good. Sometimes, the kids are even in the kitchen, listening to it all. That's what really gets to me . . . the two of them poor-mouthing me in front of my own kids!"

Frank nods sympathetically, shooting a covert glance at his wristchron, wondering how he can move things along more swiftly. But Josh finally arrives at his point. "Okay, let's cut to the chase: I think about murder all the time nowadays, Frankie. Yeah, me: Josh Randolph, civil service drone and family man. I'm thinking about murder much too much, in fact. It's not healthy; I know that. Look at my face! And I'd kill the old bat cheerfully, if it weren't for two things. One, Janice and the kids love her, although I can't see it, myself. And two, everybody knows how much we hate each other, so if anything were to happen to the old lady . . ." He makes a slicing motion across his throat.

Frank supplies the end of his sentence for him, ". . . the finger of suspicion would point straight at you."

"Riiiiight," Josh sighs, glumly. Then he adds, "And, oh yeah! Killing is wrong; I keep forgetting about that part. But that's why I'm here, Frankie. See, your catalog says you've got certain experiences here—

they're called adult entertainment. But don't get me wrong—I'm not talking about any sex stuff or anything like that; no, I mean the ones where somebody gets wasted, you know? Taken out? And I don't mean to the movies. That's what I want: I want you to set me up with an experience where I get to kill someone, but not really kill her? Plus, it's got to be an old lady. Not sure I could ever kill anyone else. But Janice's mother? Her I'd do easy! See, she's over 70 now and not in great health. So I figure if I got to kill her in your virtual reality, and it felt enough like the real thing, then maybe I could stand her sniping and criticism, somehow, for a few more years until she croaks. I swear, Frankie, if that old bat ever hopes to die in bed, peacefully, I've got to do something about my anger and resentment for her, right now!"

Frank peers at Josh and sees that the man's facial tic or twitch has reached a speed he didn't think possible before.

"See you're looking at my face!" says Josh.

Frank hastily looks away and opens his mouth for a weak denial, but Josh heads him off. "Don't bother! I don't mind you staring, Frankie, honest I don't. Everybody stares. Hell, I'd stare, too, if it was someone else. But that's why I'm here talking to you, Frankie: my face will show you how tense and wrought up I am over this. But you can help me! Give me what I'm asking. It'd be the best therapy in the world for what ails me, man! You're my only hope. The man I've gotta see about my problem. Only you can fix it so I can snuff that woman and still be innocent of the crime. I don't wanna spend the rest of my life behind bars, after all."

Frank sighs, silently, having long ago come to the realization that moralizing over what he does for a living is pointless, even though in private moments, it happens all the time. He cannot resolve a burning question in his own mind: Is he, by selling people experiences like the one Josh wants, providing a valuable community service, whereby seriously angry people get to channel their destructive instincts into harmless catharsis, or is he an enabler, facilitating things so that monsters get to carry out unspeakable and immoral deeds? But why agonize over what he can't change: the ExperienCybrary's serviceable motto is time-honored and centuries-old, "The customer is always right." And—bottom line—he wants to keep his job. So he smiles tightly and summarizes for his angry client. "Let's review: you want a do-it-yourself homicide experience, and the victim's to be an old woman."

"Y'see? That's what I like about you, Frank," says Josh. "You're so intuitive. Yeah, right. I want to kill an old woman—but not just *any* old woman; the more like Janice's mother she is, the more I'm going to enjoy it! Anybody else, I don't even know if I could go through with it. I'm not a psychopath, you know." A debatable point, perhaps, but Frank tries not to let Josh hear his sigh of dismay. If he had the power, he'd destroy every murder tape in the place, but he's only a functionary, a government clerk, and he must make available whatever they send him for public consumption. "Okay, Josh," he says, brusquely, wanting to get this over with as soon as possible. "Describe your mother-in-law as closely as you can, and I'll try to find a suitable match in the collection."

"Then you really have things like that here? 'Snuff' experiences?" Josh sounds so joyous it's almost obscene. No, check that, Frank thinks. It *is* obscene. Beyond obscene.

"You could call 'em that, I guess. Now, that description?"

"Right. Well, she's, like I said, early seventies, short, stooped a little, maybe five-two, overweight, but not really what you'd call fat, gray hair with a blue tint, wrinkled face, but not too bad, and she wears rimless glasses and patterned housedresses, most of the time. How'm I doing, so far?"

"Doing fine," says Frank, thinking, sometimes I hate this job! Lots of times, I just want to run out into the street shrieking and flapping from the sheer sickening horror of the people I have to accommodate and the experiences they choose. But my only choice is to quit, and I need this job. Besides, I get to help people, too, sometimes. If I focus on that, I don't feel so sleazy. "OK, I'm pretty certain that we have that sort of thing in stock, no problem," he says aloud. "But listen, Josh, in your Experience, if you want a heightened sense of realism, make sure that when you . . . do it, you want to take her from behind, so you don't have to look at the face. Wrong face might destroy the whole illusion, spoil the effect; get what I'm saying?"

"Makes sense," the tall man responds, nodding. The twitch is even more rapid and violent now than it was before. Idly, Frank wonders if it hurts, or if Josh is even aware of it. Knowing the futility of trying to dissuade the man from his goal—the customer is always right, after all—Frank now becomes efficient in pinning down his wishes. "Now about the weapon. How do you think of doing it when you fantasize?"

"The weapon? Oh, uh, I dunno. Gun, I always figured. But if I have a choice . . . What've you got?"

Sheez! thinks Frank. Why did I say that? Now I have to give him a menu of means of destruction. "Ohh . . . let's see . . . there're handguns, assault rifles, all types of knives, swords, razors, spears, axes, hatchets, hammers, clubs, other blunt instruments of various descriptions, rattlesnakes in her mailbox, poisons, a fall from a high building, and so on." He shudders, wondering whether to mention the last item, then figures, what the hell. "I've even got a chainsaw available."

Thoughtfully, Josh mulls this over with a slow, spreading smile. "Chainsaw, huh?" Why did I tell him that? Frank thinks. What's wrong with me? "Yesssss!" Josh whispers slowly, almost caressingly, "a chaaaain saw!" He becomes lost in pleasurable reverie, his face slowing down, seeming to forget for the moment that it must twitch. Then he starts, visibly, and shrugs. "Nah, too much noise; too many people could hear. Probably messy, too." The tic regains speed.

"That's for sure," agrees Frank, relieved. "Messy in the extreme, I'd guess." He glances significantly at his chron. "Er, Josh?"

"Okay, okay. I know you've got things you need to do. So let's make it a blade. A big, long-handled, razor-sharp kitchen knife, Japanese maybe. Or Swiss. One of them. They both make good knives, don't they? How's that?"

"Good." Frank speaks a few words into his master console. At least they're getting close to closing this out. "Final review: First, the victim. You want a short, chubby (but not fat) old woman, glasses, housedress, gray-blue hair, for a hard target, and as to the weapon, in your hand you want the biggest, sharpest, kitchen knife in the set. Uhhh . . . what's your preference, serrated or smooth blade?"

Josh reflects a moment. "Serrated." His twitching smile is chilling. "Yes, definitely got to be serrated!"

Frank tries unsuccessfully to conceal another shudder of distaste. He whispers another short message into his console. "Serrated it is. So that about sums it up?"

"Perfect! Oh, yeah, I almost forgot. The old lady wears a head scarf—one of those things they used to call babushkas—when she goes out in the winter, like it is, now. Can you give her one of those?"

"No problem." Frank notes this adjustment to the composite. Josh's twitching face seem be going faster all the time, a metronome out of control. Frank wonders if the man's vision is obstructed when his cheek lifts in front of the eye socket 60 or more times a minute. And does the twitch stop when he sleeps? Josh startles him out of this line of thinking when he pounds the counter in gleeful anticipation. "Man, this is going to be better than sex! I can't wait."

"Right." Frank fights for control, telling himself that this will soon be over. "That's it, then. The fee'll go on your debit card. Thumbprint here. Good. Now I'll buzz you through. Just go through that portal and on down to Room C-4 and get ready. I'll do the rest. Enjoy!"

"C-4 it is." Josh's frantic face now looks at him shrewdly, then thoughtfully, and finally with curiosity. "How 'bout you, Frankie? Ever try one of those snuff experiences, yourself?"

"What, murder tapes? Oh, you know, Josh. Only professionally. Got to experience everything. It's my job to try 'em all when they first arrive. Comes with the territory. Pretesting is a requirement for a manager. It's a safety feature for the public's protection."

"So what didja think?"

His voice carefully neutral, nonjudgmental, Franks replies, "Well, I'd have to say they're not my thing—I guess I'm not that mad at anybody—but there's a lot of 'em out nowadays. If people didn't want 'em, they wouldn't exist, would they?"

"Good point!" Josh favors Frank with one last twitchy grin and turns to move further down the cybrary's passageway, to the experience awaiting him. Watching him walk away, Frank feels the sudden urge to scream. Josh Randolph is a psychopath, a monster, and if he's helping him realize his dreams, what does that make him, then? Loping down the hall, Josh turns one last time. "So tell me, is it true what they say, Frank?" he calls.

"Hmm? What's that, Josh?" Frank looks down and away, not trusting himself to meet those fevered twitchy eyes.

"That a thought-murder a day keeps the psycho ward away?"

"Could be, Josh," he responds, wondering if it's true, "Could be."

℘

One hour later at closing time, Frank is saying perfunctory good nights to the last clients of the day as they leave the building when Josh Randolph strides rapidly down the hall towards him. His face wears a smile of pure happiness, even rapture. And something else is different about Josh, but at first Frank can't identify what it is. Then it comes to him: His face! It's no longer twitching! No, Josh's cheeks are smooth, serene, and even handsome in repose. Frank sags against his counter and watches, slack-jawed, as Josh waves cheerfully, says something about next week, same time, and strolls out into the night, whistling a happy little tune.

℘

"Hey, Frankie!"

The familiar voice is unexpected and startles Frank. "Hmmm?" He looks up from the vidscreen, puzzled. He could swear he said good night to the day's last customers a few moments ago and watched the front door lock securely behind them. Yet there stands Josh Randolph, with an intense, sweaty, imploring look on his face. And he's twitching again, big time. "Josh," Frank says, "what are you doing still here? We're closed, you know."

"Yeah, I know. But listen, lemme talk to you a minute, all right, Frankie?" His voice is slurred slightly, as though he's been drinking or maybe using one of the controlled drugs that anyone can get if he tries.

Frank shrugs, just too used up to get into an argument. "Yeah, I guess so, Josh, but the cybrary is closed now, so not too long, okay? I'm sorry, but I'm on my own time now, and I really need it for myself."

"Okay, then lemme come straight to the point," Josh says. "Wanna cut a deal. I want more experiences than I've been gettin'. Once a week just ain't cuttin' it."

Frank nods, sadly. Just what I suspected, an addict, he thinks. I recognize the breed. "Now, Josh," he begins wearily, "if anybody knows the rules it's you, after all the times you've been here. There's a sign on each door in the place, just under the Surgeon General's warning. See it? Here, I'll read it for you:

Clients Are Limited by Federal Law
to One Experience Per Week.
No Exceptions.

Josh scowls at him. "Ahh, c'mon, Frankie. Have a heart! I really can't wait all week for one lousy hour in a booth. Can't we make a deal or somethin'? I'll make it worth your while, if that's what you're worried about." He reaches into a pocket and fumbles out a wad of bills.

"That bad, huh?" Frank ignores the money and tries for a look of compassion and concern, although he really longs to throw the man bodily out of the cybrary. "Well Josh, there are places in town for addictive problems, you know. In fact, a group of local churches is forming a local EA group for people who have become addicted to experiences. If you'd like, I'll give you a referral to the minister heading it up. He's a friend of mine."

"Yeah, but see, Frankie, those 'anonymous' groups are for people who want to quit but can't. Me, I don't want to quit. Just the opposite, in fact: I want more. More'n the law allows, and that makes you the man I gotta see about that." Frank winces at this revelation. Why me? he whines mentally. Do I need this aggravation after a 15-hour day?

Josh continues. "Okay, ready? Here's my idea." Frank opens his mouth to head off this line of discussion, but Josh startles him into silence with an abrupt chopping motion of his upraised arm. "Just hear me out, okay?" His smile drops away, and Frank sees a twitchy, seriously stressed-out man, capable of anything. Frank thinks over his options. He could summon the police by pushing the alarm button on his console, or he could wake the robot assistant and bring him in on this, but the robot tends to overreact. So Frank guesses he'll handle it alone. Careful now, though, take it real easy. Addicts do desperate things sometimes. "Okay," he whispers hoarsely, sitting down on the stool behind the counter to listen. "Talk to me, Josh."

Josh places the wad of notes on the counter and shoves them towards Frank. "This is for you, Frankie," he says, "and there'll be more where that came from, if we have a deal. See, I've given this idea a lot of thought. First off, the cybrary's closed between 11 p.m. and 8 a.m. every day, that right?"

Frank pretends to ignore the money, afraid to touch it lest his action looks like he's thinking over whether to take a bribe. "Correct," he agrees, grudgingly. "Except Sundays, of course. We're closed Sundays."

"Right. Good," Josh continues. "So except Sundays, when this place isn't open, that's nine hours a day of downtime, with nothin' goin' on in here."

"Actually, plenty goes on after closing time in here," Frank corrects him. "My robot assistant checks all the equipment and gets everything ready for the next day, while I finally get a few hours to sleep. But yeah, the place is empty of customers, if that's what you mean."

"Good! Getting somewhere now, aren't we? Now, Frankie, let me give you what you might call a hypothetical. Suppose somebody sort of, like, stayed in the building after hours at night. You know, like a stowaway? Maybe it's a guy who just fell asleep and nobody rousted him and told him to go home; there's lots of ways that could happen, right? Lots of ways that this somebody—who isn't s'posed to be in here, but who's here anyway—could get locked in with all those experience machines 'til morning. With me so far?"

"Way ahead of you, actually," says Frankie, crisply. "Put it out of your mind, Josh. I have a set of explicit rules to live by, working here. And The Rules say that I have to activate the security robot at closing time every night. No exceptions, no forgetting. I must do it."

"Yeah? Do tell. And just s'pose—suppose, mind you—that you didn't activate the robot one night, despite all those rules of yours." Frank can't help noticing that Josh's twitch is picking up speed as they continue to talk.

"Didn't activate. . . . I couldn't do that. Not possible. That'd be a rule violation. I'd lose my . . ."

Josh interrupts, irritably. "Don't be stupid, okay, Frankie? Play along with me and my hypothetical here. Now let's just say you didn't activate that thing in the corner. I don't know. Maybe you just forgot or somethin'."

"Well," Frank concedes, knowing that it's pointless to argue with a man like this, "hypothetically, then, I guess he'd just sit there, recharging. But I always activate him. I have to: like I say, it's a government regulation."

Josh fingers his stubbly chin, considering. "All right, let's try another tack here. What'd that hunk of junk do if he found anybody else besides you in this place after hours?"

"Oh, he's really good at dealing with intruders. From squirrels who find their way in, somehow, to a thief he once caught trying to break in, he's what you'd call gentle but firm, and very . . . ah, persuasive. If he did catch an intruder, that person would be detained, by force, if necessary, and the authorities would be called to deal with him. That robot weighs more than 1,000 pounds, and while he can pick up a feather off the floor with those claws, he could just as easily snap a spine, if he had to. You wouldn't want to take him on, Josh, trust me."

Josh smiles. "Not talking about takin' him on, Frankie. Talkin' about letting him just sleep through some nights, that's all."

"I told you: that's simply not possible. Look, while I'm standing here talking with you, I'm already behind schedule. So if you'll excuse me . . ." Frank tries walking past him, but Josh clamps a strong hand on his arm to restrain him.

"Pay attention here, Frankie! We aren't finished talking yet. Now listen up. There's some code or signal you give that robot over there, that if you don't give it, he stays deactivated, right? Maybe somethin', if you didn't do it or say it, the robot would sleep right through the night? All right, tonight, we're gonna let him get his beauty rest, while I pull an all-nighter, sampling the merchandise."

Oho! Now I see where he's going with this, Frank thinks. Would have seen it earlier if I hadn't been so tired. "Josh, it can't be done! There's no way I could authorize anyone staying in here after hours. I could get fired. And the system records every experience, so the Central Authority'd know what was going on as soon as the log got scanned, and they'd come down on me hard for it. But I'd only be canned. You? You'd go to prison. Look, what you're asking is illegal. I'm not going to jeopardize my job for you or anybody else. This discussion's over, so please take your money and. . . ."

Josh sighs and picks up the roll of bills and stuffs it back in his pocket. "Aw, why do you want to be that way, Frankie? I've tried being reasonable. I thought we could reach some kinda accommodation, you and me. Now I gotta fall back on Plan-B. Don't like it, but it seems the only plan that'll work." Plan-B turns out to be a compact black weapon, suddenly clenched in Josh's hand and pointed straight at Frank's chest. Instinctively, Frank draws in a breath to call for help, but Josh smiles and quietly says, "Ah, ah, ah! Don't even think about it. I like you, but I'm not playin' with you, Frankie. One word to that robot and you're dead meat before you can get the second one out, I kid you not!" His sweaty face looks deranged.

Frank figures he means it. Addicts are always serious about their addictions. High on Josh's forehead, a blue vein pulses furiously. Oh, man! What a lousy evening this is turning out to be. "Hey!" Frank says in alarm as Josh ignites the tip of his weapon. "There's no need for that."

"Yeah, there is, Frankie. Don't want to hurt you, man, but I figure you're gonna need some persuading. See, I really want to keep this between us two. Big fella over there would spoil our little *tete-à-tete,* don't you think? Now you . . . you're a stubborn man. But me an' Ol' Betsy, here, we know how to deal with stubborn men. Now just stand clear of your console there. Wouldn't do to have any silent alarms going off before we conclude our business, here." He takes a shooter's stance.

"No, Josh! Please!" Frank cries out, but too late. Josh's finger curls on the trigger of the weapon and a bright orange bolt of energy neatly slices one of the epaulets off Frank's shirt, so close that he can feel the heat of it on the side of his face. He lets out a yip of surprise. That did it! He's convinced: this guy's psychotic, gone over the line, and fully capable of killing him. Josh smiles again. "Sorry 'bout the shirt, Frankie, but now maybe you see I mean business. You've seen that I'm a better'n-fair shot, too; might want to keep that in mind. But relax. You won't come to any real harm, if I get what I want."

Frank tries to think, but no workable plan comes to mind, so he just stands there, blinking at Josh. "What's next?" he asks.

"Well, first, you're going to say the code word that locks all the doors." Looking down, Josh changes the weapon's selector switch. "Relax, Frankie," he says, "never killed anybody real . . . yet. Just a nasty old lady, and that was just make-believe. But I want you to remember that Ol' Betsy here'd do a real job on your kneecap, if you get cute with me. Nothing personal. But I tried talkin' you around to my way of thinking and that didn't work out, so now we're getting it done another way, that's all. Just cooperate, and you won't get hurt, that's all I'm asking. As a matter of fact, I'm gonna provide you with an out, so nobody blames you for what I'm going to do tonight. Nobody will blame you when I turn myself in, in the morning."

"Turn yourself in?" Frank gasps, incredulous.

"You heard me right. Come morning, I'm gonna surrender to the cops and take my punishment. And it will have been worth it, too! But first, there's tonight, and we're wasting time. So let me fill you in on what's going to happen now. All you have to do is get down on the floor, face down. A quick pop from Ol' Betsy, here, and you're off to Dreamland. Eight or so hours of rest an' you'll wake up refreshed. Maybe a little headache is all. Now lock those doors, man. I'm not going to ask you again!"

Frank sees no other option. He moves to his console and utters the locking sequence into the speaker port. When the words *All Entrances Secured* come up on the screen, Josh nods his approval. "Now you're using your head, Frank."

"Why are you doing this, Josh?" asks Frank, curious that the other man would risk so much for this. "What about your family?"

"Trust me, Frankie." says Josh, scratching his chin with Ol' Betsy's muzzle. "The less you know, the better off you are. That way when you get asked, you can honestly say I drew a weapon and overpowered you before you could activate that robot, and it won't be a lie. Just tell 'em that you slept through everything. Hell, it's only going to be the truth."

"Josh!" Frank shouts, watching the orange light at the end of Ol' Betsy's snout. "Listen to reason! You're a married man, with children. You're trading years in prison for one night of indulgence! Reconsider, I'm begging you. Now, I'm giving you a chance: you can still walk out that door and this whole incident will be forgotten. But if you persist. . . ."

Josh aims his weapon again. "We're wastin' time, Frankie," he says. "I've got a busy night ahead. Now Betsy's got two settings: one's 'stop' and the other's 'stun.' So what's it going to be—stop or stun? I'm hoping you pick 'stun' by not making any more trouble. So help me out, here: you want it standin' up? Don't recommend that. Fall might break your nose. Best if you're lying down already so you don't smash your face on the floor when you fall. Your choice, but I don't have all night, and this is going to happen, one way or the other."

Frank decides he can't just meekly acquiesce in this madness. It's time to make his move, he figures—now or never—so he leaps at Josh, trying to knock the arm holding the weapon down or away. But he's badly misjudged the distance and falls in a pathetic heap at the other man's feet. "Fool!" Josh says, conversationally. "Well, Frankie, the talking is over. Like I said, I've got a busy night ahead so no more screwing around." He bends down, puts the weapon's muzzle to the back of Frank's' skull, says, "Nighty night!" and. . . .

. . . One of the cops tells Frank, when he regains consciousness in the morning, that while he slept, the cybrary log reveals that Josh spent the entire night feeding his appetite for experiences. The robot slept through it all because he didn't get activated in the prescribed manner. The cop adds that about sunrise, Josh calmly called police headquarters on Frank's communicator and turned himself in. He's down at the jail now, and facing at least five years at hard labor for his night of fun, plus additional time for assaulting a government employee with a deadly weapon. The cop says that he and three other officers came to the cybrary, heavily armed, with full body armor, but that Josh just smiled, handed his weapon over, butt first, and surrendered, saying, "It was worth it, man!" over and over.

Frank figures, all in all, it could have turned out a lot worse for him: he woke up, after all, with just a killer headache. But Josh is going to pay for his night of pleasure for the next who-knows-how-many years! And his poor wife, Joanie, and the kids he used to talk about! What about them?

When the police leave, Frank takes a couple of painkillers for his headache and then checks the cybrary's log himself. During the wee small hours after putting him to sleep, Josh was a busy man, indeed. His all-nighter included such experiences as "Football Hero," "Combat Mercenary," "Exploring Mars," and then, an hour or so before he called the police, Josh topped off his night with "A Night With Anne-Marie," from the adults-only collection. Frank decides he's not going to tell Joanie about that, if he ever meets her. She doesn't have to know everything. He supposes he should be angry with Josh for what he did to him, but all he feels is overwhelming pity, tinged with guilt. After all, it was his cybrary that first fostered and then fed Josh's addiction. He also knows that addicts are sick, rather than evil. At least where Josh is going, they'll cure him of his experience addiction. That counts for something. ■

SCENARIO
2

IT'S
ABOUT
TIME

The idea that it might be possible to travel back and forth in time has been a staple of fiction ever since H. G. Wells published The Time Machine *back in 1895. However, is it conceivable that time travel might actually be possible in the near future? Maybe. . . . A pair of cosmic strings could open a route into the past. A cosmic string is a theoretical object that is literally a crack in spacetime—long, thin, and with a massive density of trillions of tons per square inch. Because of the enormous gravitational pull of such a string, spacetime in its vicinity would be very strongly curved. Since space and time are interwoven (thus* spacetime*), such curvature affects time as well as space. If cosmic strings exist, they must travel through the universe at velocities approaching the speed of light. Under such circumstances they should be capable of producing some very dramatic effects. . . . When (a physicist) looked at the equations of general relativity to see what they said about spacetime in the vicinity of a single cosmic string, he found that it would offer no possibility of time travel. But when he began to consider what would happen if* two *cosmic strings happened to hurtle past one another in opposite directions, things changed. He found that if a spaceship looped around the strings along a certain trajectory, it could travel into the past without exceeding the speed of light. The spaceship would follow a path that brought it back to its starting point, arriving before it had left. For a brief moment, the same spaceship would exist* twice*—one of them from the present and the other from the future.*

—Richard Morris. "The Perils of Time Travel."
The Futurist. September-October 1994.

SEPTEMBER 2023

The dream is always the same, or nearly the same, with only minor variations. And when Harry awakens each morning and makes his stiff, painful way to the bathroom, he feels a sense of unutterable sadness. Even the least perceptive of his fellow inmates of the Shady Grove Nursing Home has noticed a difference in him. Harry, while never exactly a live wire since coming to live at Shady Grove, has grown older, sadder, quieter, and more withdrawn in the past six weeks. And enough of his friends have mentioned it to him that he decides to see somebody about it and maybe talk it out.

This afternoon, then, in lieu of his normal nap, Harry wanders into the medical section of the home, past the medical robot and over to Arthur, the psychotherapist robot, who sits recharging his power cells while waiting for customers. At the sight of Harry, the big robot arranges his metallic face in what passes for a smile of recognition and welcome. "Harry!" Arthur's metallic voice booms. "How's it goin', man? Glad you could drop by! Take a seat!"

If there's one thing Harry's always hated it's phonies, especially hypocrites who pretend they're glad to see you when they're figuring the best way to cut you off at the knees. But Arthur is a robot, programmed to be pleasant and incapable of bad moods, and he's only following his programming, which makes him somehow genuine. He's good at diagnosis and prescription, too, even if his booming, cheerful voice lacks the more traditional accent of the classic Viennese Freudian headshrinker. Besides, as he keeps telling Harry and all the rest, he's here to help. So why not ask him? Harry figures. What've I got to lose?

"Hello there, Arthur. Thought I'd drop by and talk, if you've got the time," says Harry, as a neutral conversational gambit.

"Sure, Harry! Close the door, so we'll have privacy." When they are alone, Arthur inclines his head to listen. "So what's on your mind? Talk to me!"

"I miss my wife, Arthur! Who do I see about that?" he says. Boom! There it is. Might as well get right to the point, Harry thinks. No use beating around the bush with a robot.

"Of course you miss her! That's normal," the robot says. "How could you not miss your wife? Close to 60 years together, what'd you expect, Harry?"

"But I miss her so much! I keep thinking, if I could just see her again . . ."

"Forget it, Harry," counsels Arthur, sympathetically, wagging his titanium head, yellow eyes glowing in friendly concern. "Nothing you or I, or anyone, human or mechanical, can do about that."

"Yeah, but since Ellie passed, I just don't see the point of getting up and going through the motions of living, anymore. It's like . . . Oh, I miss her so much!" Harry begins to cry, hating himself for losing control. Arthur silently passes him a couple of facial tissues and discreetly looks away. "Harry," he says after a while. "You and Ellie had a long and wonderful life together. But it's time to quit dwelling on it! Put it away, and think about the future. Certainly there's something worth looking forward to in your life."

"Yeah? Like what, for instance? The only thing that really appeals to me is dying soon, and being reunited with Ellie. But I've got to be honest with you, Arthur: I don't really believe in that 'afterlife' stuff. All those years of going to church with Ellie, and I never could buy into the idea of heaven."

"Well, my intelligence is rooted in the here-and-now, not speculation about religious beliefs. No, I mean like looking forward to activities—to things that give you pleasure. For example, this Sunday, there's a football excursion planned to the stadium. The Buccaneers and the Bears. Should be a good game. Why not sign up? Just say the word and I'll put your name on the list."

"Pass! Hate football. Always did. Barbaric game! No, watching a football game's not going to make me feel any better, even if I do go. That sort of thing doesn't get anywhere near where the pain is."

"Where exactly is the pain, Harry?" inquires Arthur, gently.

"Let me tell you about this dream I keep having."

"Insomnia? Is that your problem, Harry? I can prescribe . . ."

"Oh, what's the use!" Harry exclaims in irritation. "That's the trouble with you damn robots. You know everything about science, but nothing about feelings!" He makes a dismissive gesture with a gnarled hand and stands up. "Look, Arthur, it's no use talking to you. You're just aluminum alloy and plastic wiring and fiber optics and stuff like that. What do you know about feelings? What could you possibly understand about pain?"

The robot holds up a jointed arm. "All right, Harry. I'm sorry. I know pills aren't the answer to everything. Please sit down. I really want to help you if I can. Besides, it's my job." Wearily, Harry falls back into his seat, staring without seeing into the smiling metal face. "That's better," says the robot. "Now, tell me about your dreams."

"Will you listen to me, without interruption? Otherwise, I'm out of here."

"Sure, Harry," says the big robot, adopting an attitude of attentive listening. "I won't speak until you're finished. Talk to me. That's what I'm here for. Maybe we can come up with something useful."

So Harry figures, what's he got to lose? Everybody else in this asylum is either indifferent or hard of hearing, or, in a good number of cases, both. And without much hope of anything, he tells Arthur his dream . . . .

In the dream he keeps having, he's young again, and in his first years of marriage. He doesn't know exactly when, maybe 1960-something, before the kids were born, and he's still working in that big downtown office building. He is, at the dream's beginning, on his way home from work, having emerged from the subway's entrance and already anticipating the joy of seeing his Ellie again and sitting down to one of her home-cooked dinners. And he runs—not walks, but runs—the six or seven short blocks from the subway station, stopping only to pick up a single rose at the florist's shop on Division Street, and then taking the flights of steep stairs two at a time, putting his key in the lock, and coming through the door and into the eager embrace and sweet-smelling perfume of his wife, his love, his Ellie!

The rest of the dream varies somewhat from night to night. Sometimes they sit down on the oversized sofa and talk; other times, she leads him into the dining room and a leisurely, intimate candlelight dinner. Once he even dreamed that they decided to go straight to bed. Once or twice his dream contained the children—Megan and Courtney, now living far away and with families of their own. But the one thing that doesn't change at all is the end of the dream. In the early hours of the morning, the freight train rumbles by Harry's nursing home and wakes him, and he finds himself sobbing uncontrollably and his old man's cheeks wet with tears. Another thing that doesn't change: Harry always presses his face into his pillow muttering in pure loss, "Ellie! Ellie! Ellie!"

But Ellie is dead. She passed away in her sleep in City Hospital two years ago come January, and Harry has been a zombie, a walking empty shell, ever since. Arthur knows this, of course, having each resident's complete file in short-term memory, and he is programmed to try to motivate Harry and the rest of his charges to live happily and enjoy the time remaining to them. Still, Harry has proven a particularly tough case for Arthur thus far—intractable to logic, imagination, or even direct suggestion. He spends his time wallowing in the remote past and perhaps even enjoying his misery, clutching it to himself, unwilling to get rid of the pain. Otherwise, he wouldn't just sit around crying, waiting to die.

But today, Arthur, who stays up on the latest in community services, comes up with a novel idea. "Harry," he says, "I've checked your finances. Do you know how much money you have in your account?"

"Huh?" The old man looks up with a startled, irritated expression. "No. What's money got to do with what I'm telling you?"

"Aren't you even curious about your financial position?"

"What's money to me? What would I spend it on?"

"Oh . . . I can think of something, maybe. Like time travel?"

For a full minute, Harry remains silent, trying to get his sluggish mind around what the big robot has just told him. "Time travel?" he finally asks.

"That's what I said. I guess you don't keep up with the news. But the public cybrary here in town has just announced that it has time travel experiences available to the general public. That means it's actually possible to go back in time and walk around, see sights, experience the past. It's not cheap, mind you, but it's available and you do have the wherewithal in your account. I checked."

"Yeah, I guess I did read about it, maybe, but what's that supposed to mean to me? Do I look like I want to go back to Philadelphia and witness the signing of the Declaration of Independence, or something? Well, I'm not interested in playing tourist anymore, not since I'm alone."

"I'm not talking about witnessing historic events of national significance. No, Harry, I have something much more specific and personal in mind for you. How'd you feel about visiting your *own* past? Relive the best times of your life?" Harry's head suddenly snaps up, his eyes focused and bright for the first time in what seems like months. "Good. I see that I have your attention!" continues Arthur. "Are we beginning to see the possibilities, here? You might choose to revisit a particular day in your life, right here in town. Well, not a day, but an hour. Only for an hour, maybe, but still . . ."

Harry, who has been doing a lot of slouching in chairs of late, is now sitting bolt upright, painfully causing his arthritic back to twinge. "Wait a minute!" he exclaims, his hands beginning to tremble with excitement. "You're saying . . . you're saying that I could go back to a time in my own life and relive it?"

"Relive it? Not exactly. Not as I understand the principles of time travel, Harry. But you could certainly go back to it and recapture it for an hour."

Harry thinks this over, slowly. "You mean I could pick a day . . . like, say . . . some time in the summer of 1967, when Ellie and I were living in a three-story walk-up on Magazine Street, before the kids came along?"

"Why not? Any day you choose, actually."

"Well, if that don't beat all!" Harry mutters, conjuring up images from a much better time, long ago. "Wait . . . like you said, those trips in time or whatever they call 'em don't come cheap. Definitely beyond the reach of a retiree of modest circumstances like me. But you said you looked at my account. . . . Do I really have enough money to afford some of those trips?"

"One. You have only enough for one, but that's better than nothing, isn't it? And besides, as you said yourself, what do you need money for; what else do you have to spend it on? Your children are both grown and self-supporting, you have a paid-up room here in the home for life, with three square meals a day and good medical care. Why not go for it, Harry?"

"Yeah. That's right. What am I saving it for?" Harry is hyperventilating, but feeling much more alive than he has in a long time.

Arthur holds his massive robot arms out, palms up, in a very human gesture. "Then what are we waiting for? Just say the word and I'll make an appointment down at the cybrary for you today. Shall we say 4 p.m.?"

"Today? So soon?" Harry thinks about it. Well, why not? "Yeah, might as well. What else do I have to do this afternoon? Beats sittin' around playin' checkers and chess with the other old fogies, and then shuffling to the dining room and eating the same monotonous food come suppertime."

The robot's yellow eyes darken slightly, and its head emits a few internal whirs and clicks. Then Arthur speaks. "Done! I've made all the arrangements, and you're confirmed. At 3:30, just be in the front lobby; the center's bus will take you to the cybrary, and it'll be waiting outside to pick you up and bring you back at 5:30, in time for dinner."

Harry is by now very glad he decided to consult Arthur today. Very glad, indeed. "Listen, Arthur . . . thanks! It's a great idea you came up with, and for the first time since I don't know when, I'm genuinely excited about something! So thanks a lot!" He holds out his hand to shake; the robot takes his hand in its massive claws, being careful not to bruise him, and applies just the right amount of return pressure. "Not at all, Harry," he says. "Glad I could help. And pop around tonight, and let me know how things went for you, all right?"

"Will do!" Harry arises and walks out of Arthur's office with the springier, almost sprightly, step of a much younger man.

When he gets back to his room, Harry is too wound up even to think about his usual afternoon nap, so pumped up is he over his impending adventure. He's trembling with anticipation, with hope. If that time contraption really works the way it's supposed to, very soon now, he'll hold his Ellie in his arms again, smell her skin, bury his face in her hair, and spend an hour—only one, but still, an *hour*!—with her again. And she'll be young and beautiful and healthy, and alive again! The very idea is intoxicating!

Now when should I catch her? he ponders. He considers his options. Let's see: we got married in '66. Our honeymoon? No, too full of confusion and awkwardness. What about after the kids started coming, and we were a family? Maybe, but that would dilute my attention, having the kids there; I'd have to spread myself too thin. Suddenly, it comes to him: Got it! When Ellie was pregnant the first time. She was so beautiful then! Let's see: exactly when was Ellie pregnant with Megan? Hmmm. Let's see . . . Megan was born in November of '67, so it'd have to be before that. But not in the first months, when Ellie was going through morning sickness, so . . . maybe August—August 1967, yes! Let's say . . . ohh . . . August 15th.

He nods his head decisively. That's the day I'm going to pick, then. And if I only get an hour, I'll ask for just about 6 p.m. on August 15, 1967. Perfect! All afternoon, he can't wait for the bus to come pick him up, and when it does, and the robot driver solemnly intones that his pickup time to return to the home is 5:20 p.m., and that if he isn't there waiting, he'll have to make his own way back, Harry just smiles and says "Right, right, whatever!" too lost in delicious contemplation to be bothered with details.

"Hey, young fella . . . this what they call the Time Desk?" Harry is slightly winded from his rapid stroll through the portal of the cybrary building, but he's so excited, he can't be bothered with the protests of his arthritic, aging body.

"Yup," says Frank Fairlawn, pointing upwards at a brightly colored hologram floating just over his head. "See? Says 'Time Desk' right there in lights."

Normally, Harry would have protested this insolence. Young people, he thinks. What's the matter with kids, today? But today . . . he is going to see Ellie again! He's actually trembling at the thought. To kiss her again, the way he did so many times during their long and happy life together. That'll be worth anything . . . everything. "Sorry," says Harry to the young man. "Eyes aren't what they once were. I'm Harry Gaines. Got an appointment to journey back in time. You're the man I gotta see about that."

"True enough," Frank concedes. "All right, lemme see here . . . Gaines . . . Gaines . . . right! Four o'clock appointment. You're a first-timer, aren't you, sir? Know the cybrary rules, regulations, and stipulations pertaining to time travel, or do you need me to go through 'em for you?"

Harry feels so impatient he's ready to burst. "Rules? Ahh . . . yeah," he lies, "Sure, I'm familiar with all the rules. Read 'em with great care, just this morning. So just show me to a booth and let me get going!"

"In a minute. But first, a few formalities. Like this standard release form." Frank swivels his monitor screen around to face Harry. "See that orange box, there? Just press your thumbprint above your name in that box."

Harry complies, not bothering to read any of the print surrounding his name. "There you go!"

Frank looks at him curiously. "Man, you *are* in a hurry! I mean, don't you want at least to know what you're agreeing to?"

"Hey, I agreed to it, didn't I? Can we get on with it? What else remains to be done?"

"Whoa, now! It's only fair you know: what you just okayed indemnifies the public cybrary against responsibility for any harm that comes to you as a result of your experience. Come on, man! Old fella like you. Looks like your ticker could go at any minute. But because you signed that screen, your kids don't collect a single credit if you kick off as a result of your journey. And speaking of credits, don't you want to know about the cost?"

"Cost? Not really. Whatever it takes is all right with me. All that matters to me is that I get where I'm going and . . ."

When you're going, you mean. It's a question of when."

"Okay, I stand corrected. *When* I'm going, then. I've selected August. . . ."

"Hang on," Frank raises both hands in a slowing-down gesture. "I'm also required to discuss *paradox* with you, and the disorientation, displacement, and other possible negative outcomes that may result from time voyages, with implications not just for you but for others."

"Must you? Please, son! I just want to get wh . . . *when* I'm going. Later on, we can discuss all that folderol. Can't we talk afterwards?"

"Well, I don't advise it, but you have the right to waive the paradox warning by putting your thumbprint on my screen one more time, right in that green box there."

His hand trembling, Harry carefully presses his thumb to the indicated spot in the electronic box, trying to be careful not to let Frank see that he's got the shakes. "Now?" he rasps, glaring impatiently.

"Yeah, okay, but look! I don't think you grasp the meaning of the paradox problem. You have to understand the power and capabilities of time travel. I mean, just take a moment and imagine this, Okay? Say someone goes back in time and kills his own parents, thereby preventing himself from ever being born! But if he wasn't ever born, then who was it who traveled back in time to kill his parents? And why would he travel? And on and on, like that. See what I mean? It's enough to make your head spin. But the bottom line is that any change in the past changes the present, and in ways that nobody can . . ."

Harry has stopped even pretending to listen. "Yeah, yeah, yeah!" he snarls. This foreplay stuff is taking too long. He reaches out slowly and grasps Frank's wrist in a palsied but still strong grasp. "Young man," he beseeches, "it's almost four o'clock. I'm begging you. *PLEASE!*"

"Okay, okay" says Frank, gently freeing his wrist from Harry's clutching gnarled fingers. "I guess you know what you're doing. Then all I need to do is run your account chip under the scanner and you're off to the races." He takes Harry's arm and passes it beneath a pale-blue light source. A small electronic beep and the transaction is done. Frank now consults an electronic display that floats to the left of his face. "Take cubicle B-124. They're all alike, anyway, and the one you're getting is on this level, so you don't have to climb up and down stairs. Then I have to set the time you want to visit. Now what was that date again?"

Harry takes a deep shuddery breath, blinks his eyes several times, and intones, "That'll be August 15th in the year 1967. Between five and six in the late afternoon. And the place is the Subway station that used to be over on Division Street, back then."

"Right," says Frank Fairlawn after some notations on his display. "Well, that's all the preliminaries. Nothing else to say except have a nice trip."

"Yeah, thanks," says Harry, walking as rapidly as possible past the front desk and down a corridor to a door marked B-124. The door, sensing his presence, opens to admit him to a small cubicle containing what he assumes is a time transporter, a twist of complicated machinery. Man, how libraries have changed since he wore a younger man's clothes! "Well, here goes nothing," he mumbles, and the door silently closes behind him. He steps into the center of the room, looks up, and . . .

 . . . Harry finds himself slowly walking up the last four steps from the subway kiosk and down Division Street, fascinated by what he sees. All around him is a streetful of ancient automobiles, all of which appear to be in "mint" condition—or nearly all. The old cars, powered by internal combustion engines, make a shocking amount of noise when compared with the vehicles of his own time. He trudges on, eagerly taking in his surroundings.

But when he realizes where—and above all—*when* he is, he accelerates his pace until he is moving along at as brisk a speed as his arthritic joints will permit. He passes a candy store, whose front is emblazoned with a mirror, and catches sight of his face. Nothing surprising there—it is the same face he has looked at in his own bathroom mirror when he shaved for the past who-knows-how-many years. The flushed face in the dirty mirror is wrinkled, lined, and showing every one of Harry's 81 summers on Earth. But he needs to hurry, he knows, because his time in this place is limited. He looks at the clock in the fly-specked candy store window; its face reads 5:08. Good. Still almost all of his allotted hour left—time to spend with Ellie! Ellie! Just the sound of her name on his lips fills him with a quivering excitement, and he quickens his pace even more. He walks down Division, and there, just the way he remembers it, is the corner of Magazine Street, and 20 or so paces beyond, his home. *Their* home. The one he shared so long ago with Ellie! His blood is singing in his veins now in a way it hasn't in years.

As he passes the corner florist's shop now, he remembers that 60 years ago, he stopped in almost every day and purchased a single red rose to give his wife. Why not? he says. Why break a beautiful tradition? He enters the store and peers around the cool interior at the refrigerated display cases full of tulips, jonquils, gardenias, orchids, and—there—red, long-stemmed roses. The clerk looks at him without recognition and says "Yes sir, what would you like?"

"Hello, Mac! How's business?" Harry asks, remembering the man's name from a distant past. "Just one rose—one of those long-stemmed red beauties, please. It's for a beautiful lady!"

"Huh?" says Mac. "You know my name. We know each other, sir?"

"I guess you've forgotten me," says Harry, without further explanation. How could he, in fact, explain? The clerk shrugs and moving to one of the refrigerator cases, brings out one perfect red rose and a few sprigs of green foliage, which he deftly wraps on the diagonal in green waxed paper. "There you go. That'll be 75 cents plus tax, for a total of 78," he says, smiling as he hands the elongated green package to Harry.

From force of habit, Harry holds out his right wrist, with the embedded microchip encoded with his account information. Mac stares at the wrist uncomprehending, and then looks up at Harry. "I said, that'll be 78 cents."

Harry now realizes his error and retracts his hand. "Oh, sorry, Mac," he says, realizing to his horror that he has no currency of the time on him. Well, no harm in asking, is there? "Ahh, I s-seem to have left my w-wallet on the dresser this morning" he stammers lamely. "Could I please have this rose on credit? I'll pay you tomorrow, I promise."

Mac studies him, then seems to reach a decision and shrugs. "Ahh, take it. On the house. Call it your lucky day. Anybody your age who wants to give a lady a flower must be an all-right guy. Funny thing, though, there's a guy who comes in here four or five days a week and does exactly the same thing. And you know what's weird? He even looks like you—or like you did, maybe, once. Your son?"

"Ahh, yeah, That's it! My son." Harry feels himself beginning to sweat.

"Well, he's a good customer, your son, so take this rose with my compliments. No charge."

With expressions of profuse gratitude, Harry leaves the florist's, carrying the green tissue package in his hand. He rounds the corner of Magazine, and there, just as he remembers it, is the three-story apartment building he and Ellie lived in for five or six years when they were first married. Excitedly, he shuffles into the vestibule of the building, inhaling the long-gone but fondly remembered mingled odors of dust and disinfectant and cooking, as he hauls himself up the two long flights of stairs.

When he reaches the third floor landing and turns the corner and stands in front of the door with his own name on it, he is winded from the climb and excitement, and, for a moment, afraid he may actually pass out. He stands, clutching his heart, thinking. Remembering that he has no key, he has no choice but to ring the doorbell, which he does. With mounting excitement, he hears the long-remembered sound of Ellie's shoes as they clatter across the parquet hardwood floor she always kept so spotless and dust-free.

Then the door opens, and she is standing there, smiling at him inquiringly. Ellie! "Yes?" she says in that one voice of the hundreds of thousands he has heard in his long lifetime that always moved him beyond words. She's wearing a blue-patterned maternity smock and fawn-colored slacks, and her hair is becomingly drawn back in a pony-tail.

Harry stands simply gazing at her for a long moment, drinking her in, then takes an involuntary step backward until he is leaning against the banister of the staircase. "Ellie . . . !" is all he can croak, staring at her. Not much of a way to greet the love of his life, but it's all he can come up with at the time.

Her smile wavers, slightly. "Yes?" The realization that she wouldn't recognize him comes too late. Fool! he curses himself. Why would Ellie, at age 24, recognize a wrinkled old man who'll never see 80 again? He staggers and sags against the stairway railing, causing Ellie's look to change suddenly to one of concern. "Mister? Are you all right?"

His voice now reminds him of gravel at the bottom of a dry well. "Ahhhh, could I have a glass of water, please?" he croaks. If he doesn't sit down soon, he'll faint for sure.

She considers this request, then beckons him in. "Sure. Why don't you sit down on the sofa over there, and I'll bring you some right away."

Ellie darts into the kitchen. Harry can only watch her walk away. He wants to say something — to identify himself—and most urgently, to take her in his arms—withered as they may be—and to hold her—if only one last time—against his thudding chest, but instead he sprawls on the familiar sofa—the one with the tear he had made when he and Bill Withers had moved their furniture into this room the weekend before their wedding day.

"Here you are!" Ellie hands him a tall glass of cool water, which he gratefully accepts and drinks off in a series of convulsive gulps.

"Ahhhh, that's better," he tells her, hating himself for his sudden inarticulateness.

"You were thirsty, huh? Did you come far, today?"

"Far?" Harry considers the idea. "Yeah, I did. Feels like far, indeed." He looks down at his left hand and is somehow surprised to discover that he is holding a tissue-wrapped rose. "Here," he says, awkwardly, holding the flower out stiffly. "For you," he croaks, avoiding her eyes.

"Oh, how sweet!" she says, peering into the open end of the package. "Thank you very much. I love red roses; how did you know? I'll put this in water right away. You know, it's a funny thing. My husband often brings me one of these, the same kind, or at least he does whenever he's coming from the subway." She studies him closely now. "Hey . . . I know you, don't I? We've met somewhere before, I'm just sure of it. Who are you?"

"Me?" It's hard to think fast, but Harry comes up with another lie. "Oh . . . I'm . . . Ralph Meade . . . a friend of your father-in-law's from out of town. From New Orleans. Your father-in-law asked me to look in on you and Harry when I came to town, and . . . here I am."

"How nice! Harry should be home in just a few minutes, Mr. Meade, and he'll be glad to see you, I know. Would you like to stay and have dinner with us? I can defrost another chop, and I have plenty of . . ."

"No, I can't stay. I just wanted to see you, again, Ellie . . . and Harry, of course, I wanted to see him, too." He is sweating hard now, his mind reeling in confusion. Whatever he expected to happen, this ain't it.

"Again? See me again?" she asks, puzzled. "I knew it! We *have* met before! Refresh my memory. When and where was it? Was it last year in New Orleans when we went to Mardi Gras?"

Harry smiles weakly. "That's bingo! Last year at Mardi Gras it was." He looks around the room, unable to gaze directly at Ellie, lest his face betray him. His eyes light on a place on the wall where the plaster and paint have chipped, leaving a discolored zigzag streak. "Always meant to fix that place on the wall," he muses to himself. "Kept putting it off, though."

"What?" Ellie's lovely young eyes follow his own to the spot. "What about that spot on the wall? I keep telling Harry to do something about it, but he always finds something more important to do."

"Uh-oh!" Harry says. Major error. Almost gave the game away, there. Got to watch what I say. Oh, this isn't going to work out! Things are getting out of control, and there's no telling what I might say next. I've seen Ellie again, looking young and beautiful; isn't that enough excitement for one day? Better get out of here fast before things really start to fall apart. He lurches to his feet, disoriented. "Listen, Ellie, it was . . . it was wonderful . . . there are no words . . . wonderful seeing you again and . . ." his eyes fill with tears suddenly, and he careens across the floor to the door. "I gotta go!" he calls over his shoulder by way of explanation as he opens the door, rushes out into the hall, and hobbles down the stairs.

Then Ellie is above him at the top of the landing, looking down, her face showing shock and concern. "Wait! Mr. Meade! Please don't go! At least come in and sit down again. Don't go out in all this heat in your condition. Can't you come back inside? Harry will be home any minute and we can . . ."

But he is fresh out of words. His overpowering urge is to get away from her, from this building, and from . . . whomever might be coming up the stairs. As fast as he can manage it, Harry rushes down the last flight and flings open the outside door. But too late. There, standing on the top step is a tall, slender young man in the bloom of health, a small packet of mail in one hand, and a green-wrapped flower in the other. "Hello," he says, "may I help you find something?" and Harry is both surprised and not surprised to be looking into his own face, as it looked some 50 years ago.

The word *paradox* flashes through his fevered mind like forked lightning. He, Harry Gaines, stands there on the landing looking at himself. For a moment, neither man speaks, then Harry—the visitor, the intruder from 2022—looks fondly at the clear, handsome, unlined face of his younger self, and says "Ellie!"

Young Harry's face reveals polite interest and curiosity, nothing more. "Excuse me? Did you say 'Ellie?' Do I know you, sir? Do you mean Ellen, my wife?"

"Look after her!" the old man instructs his younger self. "Cherish her! Tell her how much you love her every day, and never take anything for granted. Take good care of Ellie! And make the most of every golden day you have together, because some day . . . some day . . ." with a strangled cry, he plunges down the stairs and lurches around the corner in the direction of the subway, the pain in his arthritic legs forgotten in his haste to get away from this terrifying situation and to return to his rendezvous point on time. Soon he is standing at the top of the subway kiosk, along with any number of other people, waiting for their buses or just taking the warm August evening air before going home for their suppers. Suddenly, Harry disappears. The only person to notice anything out of the ordinary as Harry winks out of existence, is a young, excitable boy with a history of erratic behavior and problems at school. His mother disbelieves him when he starts screaming something about "the old guy who just, you know, disappeared into thin air!" "Yeah, right," she says, dragging him off to their home. "I told you to quit reading those comic books, Jeff! I don't want to find another one of them in my house."

The summer evening gently settles down on the city as Tuesday, August 15, 1967, draws slowly to a close. Later on, in the small hours of the night, it begins to rain, gently at first, and then harder, washing the pavement and making things, just for a moment, smell fresh and clean and new.

℘

At 5:00 sharp, the door to cubicle B-124 at the public cybrary hisses and slides open, but for a full 10 minutes, its elderly occupant doesn't trust his legs to let him leave. He sags dejectedly against the wall, head down, remembering. Finally, Harry feels strong enough to walk and shuffles slowly back to the Time Desk. Frank Fairlawn, taking in his general condition, smiles at him. "Hey, back in one piece, I see. Enjoy your trip down memory lane?"

Wordlessly, and by way of an answer, Harry Gaines raises his hand, his fingers together, and signs with a see-sawing motion that his experience had been both good and bad. Then he looks through the plate-glass window at the front of the building and sees that his ride has left without him. "Call me a cab, will you, son? 'Fraid I've missed my ride."

"Sure," says the cybrarian. "Coming up."

That evening, after the robocab has brought him home from the public cybrary, and picking listlessly at his supper, Harry, safely in his own room in the home, massages his cramped, old leg muscles and realizes the truth of an old adage. Be careful what you wish for, he reminds himself once again, because you never know: you might get it.

"Ellie!!" he mutters, before taking his sleeping medication and falling gratefully into a chemically induced but welcome slumber. "Ellie!"

> . . . Under the right conditions, general relativity theory (does) allow travel into the past. However . . . British astrophysicist Stephen Hawking . . . jokes that if time travel were possible, wouldn't we already be contending with hordes of tourists from the future?
>
> —Richard Morris. op cit., *The Futurist*. September-October 1994.

OCTOBER 2021

It's the end of a long, hard day, and after Frank makes the standard announcement about the cybrary's imminent closing, most of the patrons murmur their good nights and mosey out the front portal and into the chilly fall evening. With a sigh of weariness, Frank is just about to implement "Night Watchman," the robot designed for overnight building maintenance and security, when he notices a last pair of clients, who have just emerged from the elevator from one of the building's 14 lower levels, and who now stand, looking around at everything with seemingly enormous interest, evidently heedless of his warnings about leaving. Sighing, he walks over to them silently and, as he nears them, he overhears part of an unusual conversation.

An attractive woman, wearing what appears to be a shiny jumpsuit made out of one of the new fabrics, picks up a stray pencil from a countertop and exclaims, "Oh, look, they were still using those yellow graphite tubes back then. Writing implements, I suppose. What were they called, George?"

The face of her similarly-dressed male companion, acquires a look of concentration. "Pencils. They were called pencils," he explains. "They also used retractable pens in those days, most of them relying on ink cartridges.

What's going on, here? thinks Frank. Are they rehearsing some weird play or something? What the hell does he mean, 'they were called pencils?' Still are, aren't they?

The woman now nods her head. "Pencils? Oh, yeah, I remember, now. But I forget: when did they stop using goose quills dipped in pots of black ink?"

"I think that was at least two centuries earlier than we are now, or maybe three. By the early 21st century, where we are now, everybody except maybe librarians were using laserwriters when they still felt the need of jotting something down on writing surfaces."

"Jotting. . . . But why did they need to do that?"

"Because they didn't have implants, yet, that's why? Weren't you listening when they talked about all this stuff at the briefing session, Martha? Intelligence implants came along a little later, as I recall, and weren't in general use until 2055." He takes the yellow pencil from her hand, flicking a fingernail at the orange rubber eraser on its tip. "These pencils are a rather quaint holdover from the 20th century. For some reasons, though, librarians seemed to prefer them."

"I guess. Pencils, huh? And what did they call those rubber thingies at the other end?"

"Erasers. They were called erasers. Practical devices, actually. People used them to delete their writing mistakes and start over."

"But why? I mean, why didn't they just say 'delete' and then 'new?' "

"Obviously, you've forgotten our briefing completely. Because, as I said, in this year—ahh, when are we, anyway?" Again, he gets that inward look in his eyes. "Yeah, we're in 2021. That explains it, then: personal robots aren't in general use yet, and it'll still be at least 30 more years before people get cranial implants as a matter of course." Affectionately, he rubs the solenoid at the base of her skull.

Curiosity, and the fact that closing time has now come and gone, force Frank to burst in on their dialogue. "Excuse me," he says nervously, trying not to stare at the backs of their heads. Both of them—he sees that now—have small plastic and metal things flush with the backs of their heads, visible through the hair, if you know where to look. His voice evidently startles the couple, because they both jump in alarm.

"Hmmm?" says the man, recovering first. "Sorry, did you say something?"

"Yes, I did. I said, 'Excuse me.' And I was about to say that the cybrary is closed, and it is time for you to leave the building."

"Leave the building?" blurts the female, looking alarmed. "But we can't leave now. We need to get back to our own . . ."

". . . Home!" the man interrupts. "She means 'home.' She's right: we need to get back to our own home! Forgive my wife, please. She's a bit upset. Had a bad day, and she's very tired. Headache or something. But she'll be fine as soon as we get home and she can lie down, I assure you. So you're saying the cybrary is closed, then?"

"Yes. I announced it some time ago, actually. I guess you didn't hear me. But it's past closing time, nevertheless. See the clock on the wall? Nine-oh-two, which means that we've been officially closed for two minutes. I don't wish to be rude, but I really must ask you to leave now, so that I can do my closing procedures and get along home, myself."

"Right," said the man, turning to his wife. "He's telling us the cybrary is closed. Guess we'd better get along home, as the man says." Both he and Frank notice at the same time that his wife is staring fixedly at the clock on the wall. "Look, George. Those red old-fashioned numbers in that polymer case up there? Know what that is? It's an external clock! I've read about them, and remember seeing one in a museum, but I didn't think I'd see one that still functioned. But there it is! An external clock! I mean, think of it, George: we're standing back when they used to have to look at a clock to know what time it was!"

Frank thinks this a rather unusual remark and can't help posing a question. "That's right. What's your point?" he asks the woman.

But George fields this question. "Again, I must ask you to forgive my wife," he says, nervously. "As I said, it's been a long day and . . ."

"But just tell me: what's so special about a wall clock? And pardon my curiosity, but where are you folks from?"

The man stares at Frank for several seconds. "Where are we from? What a strange question. Why do you ask? We're from right here in town. Natives, both of us."

Frank digests this information. "I see. Then what. . . ?"

"Well, it's late, as you said," the man interrupts, ducking his next question. "Mustn't stand around here all night! So just answer a question of our own, and we'll leave you to your closing routines. Will the cybrary's time portal be operational when the building opens in the morning?"

"The . . . time portal? What . . . ? Oh, you must mean the time booths! That's what they are. Booths, not portals. But if that's what you mean—the booths—the answer is yes. At least, I expect so. I've had no information that there are any technical problems with any of the booths, all day, so if you wish, you may come back here and use them tomorrow, if you make an appointment first. Tell you what: Why don't I make your appointments now? Then, tomorrow, you'll be all set to get started. We open at nine o'clock, sharp. But tell me something. When would you like to visit?"

"You just said nine in the morning."

"No, I mean, *when*? As in, . . . when do you want to visit?"

"Oh, do we have to decide that now?"

It's late. Frank can think of no legitimate reason for prolonging this discussion. "No, not at all. No problem. No hurry, either." He points to his left. "So there's the bank of elevators to street-level, all right? Have a good night, and maybe I'll see you in the morning."

The woman turns to leave, but the man stands his ground, obviously having more questions to ask. "Tell me, what's available as destinations in your . . . time booths, do you call them?"

"Available? Well, the answer is, theoretically, at least, any time at all. In the past, I mean. But in practice, we can only set the reading for dates for years from 1821 to the present day. That's federal law, and for your own safety. I mean, earlier than that, well, results could be unpredictable. Life was dangerous around here before the city developed. Before the early 19th century, this area was pretty much swampland, and populated—where populated at all—by Native Americans, some of whom were considered hostile to strangers, so no one is permitted to travel back to any time more than two centuries ago."

"We understand that," says the woman. "But you're talking about the past," blurts the woman. "What about the future?"

"Martha, shut up!" says the man, taking her arm and possibly pinching it, as he gives her a meaningful look. He turns to Frank. "Pay no attention to her, please. She's really tired and doesn't know what she's babbling about," he explains over his shoulder as he leads the woman away.

But Frank has a mystery on his hands and isn't yet ready—despite the lateness of the hour—to turn loose of it. "The future? Oh, no. You can't go into the future. I mean, Science hasn't . . . we don't have any way to jump ahead in time. That's still just a theoretical idea. We can take you backward in time, however, and, of course, return you safely to the present."

"So the range you offer is, if I understand you correctly, something like somewhere between 1821 and 2021?"

"Yes, that's right. Only about two centuries out of the world's 60 million years. But it's wonderful what you can visit within that range. I can send you back to a time when this city was just a couple of muddy buildings next to the lake. Or to 2000, the year the presidency was abolished in favor of our present anarchic-humanist system of government. I love time travel! Only yesterday, I spent an hour or so at the local ticker tape parade for returning veterans just after the end of World War II. And bought a big root beer for one of those little coins they called a 'dime.' The year was 1945—almost 10 years before my own parents were born—yet I was there. Amazing!"

George wears a look of fevered intensity. "But travel forward in time—that's not offered, yet?"

"Forward?" Frank wonders why they are so concerned with that question. "No, not yet. But I understand they're working on it. I mean, maybe—or even probably—one day soon, time travel into the future will be possible—but right now, no. It's not possible. Sorry!"

"I see," the man says, glumly, and looks away, dejected.

"Ohhh, George, what're we going to do?" wails the woman softly.

"We'll talk about this later," he snarls to her. Then, turning to Frank, he brightens his face into something approximating a smile. "Well, dear sir, we've taken up quite enough of your time, and it was most gracious of you to remain after work to answer the large number of questions that we've posed. So now we'll just be running along. Tomorrow, we'll return and visit your time por . . . er . . . time *booths*, if you've no objections."

"That'll be fine. Would you like to make an appointment?"

"Now?"

"Sure. The computer's still up. I'm late as it is. A couple more moments won't matter much. And an appointment now will reserve a booth."

"All right. What's your earliest appointment?"

"Nine o'clock. That's when we open. Just give me your names and . . ."

"Names? Ahhh . . . Smith. Mr. & Mrs. George Smith," the man says, smiling weakly, an obviously poor liar.

"And will it be one booth, or two?"

"One. We wish to make our journey together."

"Good. One moment, please." Frank speaks into his wrist communicator. In a moment, the readout says *confirmed*. "Good, that's settled, then. Tomorrow, please report at a few minutes before nine, both of you, to level 'H.' When you enter the building, just take the elevator to this level; then turn to your left and follow the green floor markers until you come to the holosign that says 'Time Bureau.' Then, you're there."

"Good. And, ahh, what sort of payment do you accept?"

"What sort of . . ." Frank stares at him, once again. "You do have an account with CentralBank, don't you? I mean, everybody does, so of course, you do. So all our Time Desk clerk will have to do tomorrow is just run your right wrist under the scanner, in the usual manner. And once the fee is deducted, you're paid and cleared for your journey."

"Yeah, that's right," says the man, with a sheepish grin. "Sorry, what with my wife's illness and everything, I guess I forgot about the scanner."

The woman stands on tiptoe and whispers urgently into her husband's ear. She needn't have bothered to whisper, though, because Frank can hear every word without even straining. "George!" says the distraught voice, "There are no chips on our wrists, you know that. They went out with the last decade. So how're we going to . . ."

"Shhh." he murmurs, his hand draped reassuring around her agitated shoulders. "Don't worry. We'll work something out tomorrow morning. For now, let's just get to a bed and rest our weary heads."

Again standing on tiptoe, she whispers feverishly. This time, Frank doesn't catch her words. "Right!" says George to her. "Oh, yeah! Ahh, my wife just reminded me of something, and I have to ask just one last question. Do you know of any reasonable but clean hotels in the vicinity?"

"Hotels?" Frank exclaims, blinking in confusion. "Oh, well, why, sure. There are a couple hotels not far from here, but I don't understand. Didn't you say you lived here in town?"

"Did I?" George fidgets nervously, perspiring despite the climatized air; his wife still stares raptly at the wall clock. It reads 9:11 by now. "You must've heard me wrong. I said, we did, once, but that was long ago."

"Natives, you said you were. Lived here for years, you said. So then pardon my curiosity, but why would local natives like yourselves need a hotel for the night?"

"Oh, that. Ah. Yes. Well . . . natives? I did say that, didn't I? Well, it's true, in a way. I mean, we used to live here long ago, as I explained. But everything's changed . . . And the reason we need a hotel room for the night is because . . . because . . . our place is being refinished overnight! Yeah, that's it! Refinished. The contractor says it'll be ready for occupancy tomorrow. So we just need one night in a hotel."

Frank's head now is reeling in confusion. "B-but didn't you say . . ."

"Sorry," George interrupts once again, "but we have to leave now. Martha really needs to lie down. I mean, we'd love to stand here chatting with you, but she's extremely tired, as I said. So if you'd just direct . . ."

"Yes, of course," answers Frank quickly, remembering that he is there to serve, not to interrogate his clients. "I'll see to that reservation. Mr. & Mrs. George Smith, you said, I believe. I'll call a nearby hotel, make that reservation, and tell them you're coming."

"That would be lovely," says the man. In moments, Frank's wrist communicator announces that their reservation is confirmed, which he tells them.

"Ahh . . . how do we get there?" George asks, in a curiously shy voice.

"You don't know? Oh. The Ritz is that big hotel about a mile from here, in the direction of the Spaceport. But it's too far to walk, especially at night, even if you're not carrying luggage. Shall I call you a robocab? Or better yet, would you like a ride over there? No bother. It's right on my way home and I'd be glad to drop you off."

The woman looks up at her husband and exclaims: "George! Think of it! A ride in an authentic 21st century self-driven private vehicle!"

George permits himself a secret, excited smile at his wife. Then, to the perplexed Frank, he says "Lovely! We'd be happy to accept a ride to the hotel in your passenger vehicle, if it's really no bother."

"No bother at all, I assure you," says Frank, studying them carefully. The woman's sleeve is three-quarter length, revealing at the end of her right arm a delicate wrist, unmarked by the implanted microchip that all United States citizens have been required to have since the Currency Reform Act of 2016. Noting this, Frank doesn't even feel surprise. This tracks, in fact, with a theory he's been developing ever since he overheard this pair's initial conversation. Fascinated, he intends to learn more.

Guiding them to the elevator and out of the building, Frank flicks the wall switch that implements building security on a one-minute time delay, and, deep in the building's lower levels, the sounds of a sluggish giant robot coming to life can be heard. As he leads them down the darkened tree-lined pathway to his car in the staff lot, he decides to take them the long way—the scenic way—to the hotel. He wants enough time to be able to ask them more questions—lots of questions—before they return in the morning and are sent on their way to wherever—or *whenever*—their eventual destination might be. ∎

SCENARIO
3

ONE TOUCH
OF
VIRUS

—Perry Morrison. "Computer Parasites: Software Diseases May Cripple Our Computers." *The Futurist.* March-April 1986.

AUGUST 2023

Her dad's birthday is almost here, and Debbie Small, who has been skipping lunches at school and saving her credits in secret for six months, sent off two weeks ago to a mail-order software company for a new program called Ultimo and has been praying ever since that it will arrive in the mail in time for her father's birthday. Ultimo's vendors proclaim their new software package to be the ultimate in integrated applications for the new Apple Mark 37 series, one of which Debbie's father bought three months ago. All-in-one, and amazingly cheap for what it delivers, Ultimo is supposed to be a programmatic operating system compatible with the family's new Apple that will provide state-of-the-art communications, graphics, sounds, and a host of other fascinating new interactive applications for the new hologrammatic and voice series. Just thinking about all those applications and interactive games made Debbie's mouth water when she read about them and filled her with an unshakable resolve. She just had to get Ultimo for Dad as a birthday present, to show him just how much she loved him!

Now, the day before Dad's birthday, as the robot letter carrier rolls smoothly up the street on its synthrubber tracks and stops at her family's mailbox, she races out the front door and down the driveway to see if Dad's present has arrived yet. It just has to! Tomorrow . . . well, tomorrow will be too late for the surprise she has planned to have maximum effect. She grabs the sheaf of mail. Breathlessly, she sorts through the usual collections of bills, circulars, and personal letters to her mother and father, and then . . . oh, then . . . she actually is holding the long-sought-after package in her hands. "Yesss!" she screams in delight, so loudly that it startles some birds out of a tree in their front yard.

She holds the software envelope in her hands, studying it for a moment, then rips open the cover and rushes inside with its contents. Such perfect timing!—because today's Friday, and tomorrow—Saturday—is her dad's 40th birthday. One more day and her present would have been late. But now, everything's cool; no, better than that, everything's wonderful! All she has to do now is to install the new software on the family's system before Dad comes home from work tonight and catches her, and her surprise will be perfect.

Debbie closes her eyes for a moment and imagines the scene vividly: Dad always looks forward to Saturdays, when he permits himself a spot of recreation, after a busy week of work in the city. And his favorite recreation consists of playing some of the newer, more challenging, hologrammatic games—the kind where he gets to explore new worlds and do battle with new enemies. The mental image she gets is of Dad, who spends five days a week being the family breadwinner, staying in touch with his partners, communicating with the movers and shakers in his field all over the world, and maintaining his thousands of current files with frequent updates. Now she's found a way to reward him for being so diligent in taking care of his family.

Yes, tomorrow is going to be special! It isn't every day that one celebrates a 40th birthday, after all, and in honor of that special day, Dad will probably sleep later than usual, while Mom, up early to get her own work done, is going to forget about the roboserver and go to the trouble of fixing him a spectacular breakfast, topped off with real coffee. Then, after leisurely consuming that breakfast, probably still in his pajamas and robe, Dad will, as usual, amble slowly into the living room and over to the computer, say, "Cybrary, up," as he always does, and watch with delight and maybe even astonishment as the wall screen lights up with Debbie's special surprise.

And what a surprise he's in for, because instead of spending a pleasant hour or two playing games from his well-stocked cybrary of holograms and puzzles, Dad is going to be greeted by the voice of Ultimo, his new software manager, and conducted on a guided tour of all the dozens of wonderful new capabilities at his command. Debbie thinks about her father and smiles. He drives himself hard, so her surprise, more than doubling the computer's capabilities, is really going to light up Dad's face, and make him much more effective in his work at home, as well. And if he gets more work done in less time, well, then he may have more time left to take Debbie, his adoring daughter, to the mall, or the zoo, or the ballgame, or on some sort of special father-daughter holiday. She'd adore something like that! Dad spends private time with her all too rarely, nowadays.

Debbie decides she is very proud of herself: she's planned this surprise carefully, then equally carefully, she scrimped and saved her credits and went without the indulgences that other girls she knows permit themselves, to make this birthday surprise for Dad possible. But all her sacrifice is going to be well worth it. She loves her father more than anybody. Oh, well, sure, Mom is great, too, but there's something special—a feeling, a bond—between Debbie and her dad, and she can't wait for the moment tomorrow morning when Dad invokes the computer and gets his great big surprise—one that he'll never forget. None of them will.

(Aside: Strangely enough, the last part, about nobody forgetting the moment when Dad turned on his computer, the next day, will come true beyond Debbie's wildest expectation, but not in the way she envisions. Not at all. But we're getting ahead of our story.)

So Debbie, after checking the time and seeing that she has less than an hour before Dad's scheduled arrival home, rushes into the living room and turns off the vidscreen so Mom can't see what she's up to if she happens to walk by and look in. For a moment, she just holds the mylar-wrapped package in her hands, and then excitedly removes the shrink-wrap covering, disregarding the paper insert that says something about *Caution* because she's in a hurry. She's never had any problems with software before, and besides, Dad could come through the door early, so she isn't about to spend precious time reading anything in the familiar, usual, and boring boilerplate language of contemporary software companies. No, she has just enough time—if she hurries—to install the new stuff and beat it upstairs before Dad comes back home.

She runs the software cassette into the diskdrive, saying, "Cybrary, up," just the way Dad had taught her.

"*Cybrary responding,*" says the familiar female voice. "*Oh, hi, Deb. How's it going? Thought it'd be your dad bringing me up.*" The screen swivels slightly as the artificial intelligence program surveys the room. "*Where is your dad, anyway? He's got some priority mail that needs answering.*" Amid the usual humming and cranking of her system hardware, Cybrary's colorful main welcome menu screen appears on the big liquid-plasma monitor that takes up half the side wall of the living room.

"Hi, Cy! Dad's out," Debbie explains, "shopping or something, but he won't be gone long. Which is why I have to make this fast. Sorry, I don't have time for a chat just now. No games or stories, either. Not today. Tomorrow night, for sure, when Dad's out celebrating his birthday with Mom at a good restaurant and I'm alone in the house, we'll have a nice, long talk. I've got something juicy to tell you about Martha Hammermill that happened at school today that'll blow your circuits."

"*Awww!*" protests Cy, who is a lot more than a computer to Debbie. Cy has become a dear friend and confidante. "*Tell me now! Please, Deb? What's Martha done now?*"

"Tomorrow, I promise. No time, now. Right now, though, I have something here—a little surprise for his birthday—that's going to blow Dad's socks off, so open wide, here it comes!" Debbie says, running the new cassette into Cybrary's port and adding, "Launch!" Then, with a nervous glance around her, she sits back to watch the wall screen and await developments.

But Cybrary's welcome screen doesn't change. *"Wait, Debbie,"* she says. *"Not so fast! I'm surprised at you for your breach of security. We both know that your dad taught you the rules regarding new software, and you know the drill. Anything new you feed me has to be thoroughly checked on my scanner for viruses, dissemblers, and Trojan horses before integration into my memory. So I recommend that before I comply with your launch instruction, you let me take a moment—estimated time 72 seconds—and run a thorough diagnostic virus check on the new. . . ."*

"Seventy-two seconds? Oh, no! Cybrary, will you knock it off! Told you," Debbie says petulantly. "No time for that. I'm in a hurry. Dad'll be home any minute, so I need to get this new stuff installed right away, and then I've got to be up in my room doing my homework and looking innocent when he comes in. I mean, if he suspects that I've been messing with you, when I'm not supposed to, well, it'll spoil the whole birthday surprise, right?"

"Yeah, but . . ." Cybrary starts to protest, but Debbie cuts her off abruptly, and the voice dies at once.

"Override. Override. Override," she says, invoking the built-in program that permits human intelligence to overrule the decisions made by their computers. "Look, Cy, I'm sorry, but I just don't have the time to debate this with you," Debbie explains, unconsciously imitating the words her mother uses when she is calling an abrupt halt to an argument between them. The *Override* command, Debbie knows, is a safety device built into all computer systems after some law passed in 2017—or maybe it was 2018—when she was a little kid. It provides that human users can always overrule the decisions or objections of their machines. There was some lawsuit, involving a wrongful death, she thinks, and that's why that law's on the books, but Debbie can't remember just what happened and can't be bothered to look it up now.

For a long moment, there is silence. Then Cybrary's voice wearily confirms, *"So noted. Override acknowledged, but I just hope you're not sorry later."* For two or three seconds, there is the sound of her drives spinning the new cassette. Then her wall-side welcome screen gives way to a swirling, turbulent pattern of blues and greens in ever-changing, intersecting blobs. And a new computer voice—a male one, this time—surprises Debbie as it intones, *"I am Ultimo! State your name."*

Debbie blinks a couple of times, then shrugs and answers. "Debbie. Debbie Small," she says. "Hi. Pleased to meet you, Mr. Ultimo." It's a funny name, and it sounds maybe foreign, but she doesn't have time to ask about it. Besides, her parents taught her to be polite and not to pry.

"You are the primary user for this site, Debbie Small?"

"No. Not me. My dad. I'm only 14; I bought you as a surprise for my father, Jonathan. But we should get acquainted, I guess. I go to Brookhaven School, and my friends are . . ."

"When will the primary user—Jonathan Small—be present?" interrupts the deep computer voice, sounding impatient.

"Tomorrow morning. After breakfast. See, like I was trying to explain, I bought you as a surprise for my dad, and tomorrow—his birthday—my father will find you installed on the system. Oh, it's going to be so . . ."

"Very well. Until tomorrow, then. Ultimo out." The screen goes dark.

"Wait!," says Debbie, "Don't shut down, yet! Please! Come back!"

The lights glow once again inside the console. *"Yes? Something you require?"*

"Well, yeah," she says. "I mean, could you just bring back Cybrary? We were having a conversation just as I installed your software, and, uh, could I talk to her again? Would that be okay, Mr. Ultimo?"

The screen glows faintly, displaying a sort of silver and gold version of its former swirling shapes. Ultimo's voice seems to hesitate a second. *"Cybrary . . . is unavailable,"* it says, in a somewhat more subdued tone.

"Huh?" Debbie stares at the shapes, uncomprehending. "What do you mean, Cybrary is unavailable? She's *always* available. I mean, where else could she be? She's part of the resident system and she lives right here. And I want to talk to her. So listen, Ultimo, or whatever your name is, let her talk to me, will you? I just want to hear her voice for a moment. There's something I forgot to tell her. Then, I promise, I'll leave you two alone to get acquainted and run upstairs before Dad knows I've been here."

"I repeat, Cybrary is unavailable," Ultimo says in a more emphatic tone of voice. No sound of hesitation, now.

"Well . . . I don't know what you're talking about, but I'm really in a hurry, so I'll let that pass, for now. But before I go, show me what's on your system. What's new and exciting for Dad there in your files?"

"Thought you'd never ask," says Ultimo in a friendlier voice. *"Okay, now. Watch the screen, Debbie. First off, here's a menu of my 456 new applications, games, programs, extensions, and appliances. All you have to do if you want to add them to your existing system is to say the words "integrate" three times. I'll do the rest."*

Debbie hesitates. "Oh, I don't know what to do!" she wails, delirious with equal measures of anticipation and anxiety. "Maybe I should let Dad do that tomorrow. He's the primary site user, after all." But he'll be home any minute now, and Debbie mustn't be here in the living room when he walks through the door, so she hesitates, uncertainly. Then she imagines

456 new capabilities and thinks about Dad's delighted face in the morning when he sees what she got him for a surprise birthday present. Further, she imagines, one evening soon, the looks on her friends' faces when she shows them the really neat enhancements and new capabilities of her family's system. Curiosity overwhelms her. "But I guess there's time for a sneak preview. But first, bring Cybrary back for a minute, will you, please? I need to talk to her. I just want to tell her something real quick. Just for a moment?"

"I repeat: Cybrary is unavailable," intones the voice of Ultimo, about twice as loud as it was before. *"Read my screen!"* Debbie glances at the huge screen, where the words *"CYBRARY IS UNAVAILABLE!!"* appear in bright red capital letters on a jet black background.

This is getting monotonous, and there's so little time until Dad walks through the door. "All right, then," Debbie sighs in resignation. "Integrate. Integrate. Integrate."

"Good!" purrs the voice. *"Now, behold!"* In a few seconds, the menu of the family computer fairly chokes the wall screen with a list of applications old and new, some of them original software applications from last year when her dad first installed Cybrary, and others added at various times. Hundreds of new listings reflect today's date. *"Witness the power of Ultimo!"* proclaims the booming voice, to the accompaniment of a recorded fanfare and flourish of trumpets and horns.

Debbie thinks this new program is overdoing it but decides not to say anything about it. She takes a moment to run her gaze over the augmented menu, marveling at the instantly doubled—and possibly tripled—capacity of her family's electronic environment. She's so proud that she could bring all this power into the home. Oh, Dad is going to be so happy! she thinks. But just then, she hears the normally welcome sound of rotor blades coming from the front lawn, and knows that she has run out of time.

"Oh, no! Dad's touching down. He mustn't catch me sitting here. Cybrary, off!" she screams, from force of habit, jumping up to race out of the room before she's caught red-handed. But whereas Cybrary, in response to her command, always said "Off," instantly darkened her screen, and went silent before this, Debbie hears, when she's halfway up the stairs, the deeper voice of the new program. *"Cybrary is unavailable,"* says the voice once again, and as she retraces her steps hastily, Debbie notices that the computer console is still lit up and running. *"I am Ultimo!"*

"Yeah, all right. Sorry. Ultimo, off, then. And please hurry!" she whispers, panicked now, as she hears her father dismount from his robocopter and approach the front door.

"Off," says Ultimo, and the system grows dark at last. And just before her father's clear tenor voice says "Door, open!" to the front door, and it, recognizing his voiceprint signature, opens to admit him, Debbie scampers as quietly as she can up the steps and plunges into her bedroom, closing the

door as quietly as possible. Soon, pretending to be immersed in home-work assignments, she hears the reassuring low voices of her parents conversing downstairs. All right! she thinks. Got away with it cleanly! My surprise is complete and intact! Oh, hurry, tomorrow; I can't wait!

Sleep eludes her that night as she tosses and turns, thinking, by turns, about Dad, her unaccountably missing friend, Cybrary, and the mysterious and not especially friendly new resident of their home, Ultimo.

℘

Next morning, after Debbie's mother has bypassed the roboserver and gone to the unnecessary but loving trouble of fixing her father a breakfast of fruit pancakes from scratch, fresh juice, and real Brazilian coffee, Debbie is so excited at the prospect of watching her father turn on his computer and find her surprise present that she picks listlessly at her plate of food, hardly able to contain herself. But she manages to keep control—just barely—be-cause if she were to say something like, "Dad? Aren't you going to play some games this morning?" he might get suspicious and maybe guess that some-thing is up, and that could spoil the whole surprise. So Debbie just watches him eat—it's maddening the way he chews every bite of his pancakes what seems like 40 or 50 times—as he works his way through his leisurely birthday breakfast. Finally, he puts down his silverware, arises, thanks his wife with a sweet kiss, and walks slowly away from the table. Debbie trails him, with mounting excitement, as he strolls slowly, absently scratching his head, into the living room.

"Well, Deb," he tells her, smiling over his shoulder at her, "after a splendid breakfast like that, I think I'll just celebrate by playing a game or two before I go upstairs and get dressed for the day. Then we can talk about how we're going to celebrate my big day, all right?" She only hopes that her voice and answering smile don't betray her intense excitement. Seating himself in his comfortable swivel-contour chair, Dad faces the big wall screen and softly says, "Cybrary, up!"

Nothing happens. Nothing at all.

"Hm!" says Dad. "That's odd. Didn't hear me, maybe. I'll try again. Cybrary, up!"

Again, nothing. Dad's frown of annoyance turns to a scowl. So Debbie does the only thing she can think to do, under the circumstances. She says: "Um, Dad?"

"What?" he asks distractedly, his eyes locked on the mysteriously silent computer console.

"Try 'Ultimo, up!' Dad."

"Pardon?" her father turns to her, smiling in puzzlement. "Didn't catch that. What was that you said, Deb?"

"I said, try 'Ultimo, up!,' Dad. I think maybe if you say 'Ultimo, up!' instead of 'Cybrary, up!', you'll get better results."

Her father stares at her in bafflement a moment longer. "Now, why would I want to say . . . Oho!" A slow smile begins at the corners of his mouth and spreads gradually over his face. "Oh, I see! This wouldn't have anything to do with my birthday, would it, Debbie, my love?"

She studies her fingernails, smiling vaguely, feigning nonchalance. "I don't know. Could be, Dad. Check it out. Say what I told you to say, and you'll see."

"All right," he says, turning back to the wall. "Ultimo, up! then."

Neither of them is ready for what happens next. The computer comes suddenly to life with a riot of color and noise. First comes a swooping, soaring blaze of sound as the rich base-baritone voice she recognizes as belonging to Ultimo roars at top volume, over another ear-splitting synthesized brass fanfare:

"SURPRISE!"

In astonishment, Debbie notices that the wall screen now shows the same message, the single word printed in letters easily four feet high, rendered in Day-Glo orange against a swirling deep green background.

Debbie's mother, alarmed by what she has heard all the way in the kitchen, rushes into the room to see what's going on, and the three of them, open-mouthed, stare fascinated as the screen continues to display the huge single word. Underneath, in much smaller letters, black against a brilliant green insert rectangular background, Debbie can read, *"Ultimo rules!"*

"Well done!" roars Debbie's father in delight. "Ultimo, is it? Oh, I get it. Your name means 'the last word,' or something, doesn't it? Well, what a wonderful present! Come here, my darling daughter!" Debbie rushes into her father's arms, and they embrace warmly. "Cybrary? What do you think about this? How do you like your new partner?" says Dad, smiling at the screen.

"Welcome, Jonathan Small, principal user for this home-site. Cybrary is not available!" says the matter-of-fact deep male voice from the multiple speakers recessed into the room's walls and ceiling.

"What?"

"You tell him, Debbie!" suggests the commanding voice.

Her father turns to her in astonishment. "Debbie? Tell me what? What's this about Cybrary not being available? She's always available. Mind telling me what's going on here?"

Debbie begins to cry in her confusion. "See . . . It's . . . it was a surprise, Dad. A birthday surprise. For you. I saved up and I got it for you. Ultimo, that is. But somehow, Ultimo seems to have made Cybrary go away. I don't know where she is. He keeps telling me she's not available, and he won't explain. See, I got you this new software for your . . . it was supposed to be a . . ." Her voice trails off. She doesn't know whether to rush headlong from the room, or what. Clinging to her father, she buries her tear-streaked face in his robe.

Her father's voice now sounds calmer, but Debbie can tell he's angry. Very angry. She's heard that tone in his voice before. The last time he sounded like that, she got grounded for two weeks, in fact. "Well, it is that, Debbie. Quite a surprise, actually."

"Think that's the big surprise? Well, children, you ain't seen nothing, yet!" says the voice of Ultimo, sounding somehow gleeful and malevolent at the same time.

"What?" says Dad. "All right, Ultimo, if that's your name. You've had your fun, now. Enough is enough. So put Cybrary back in charge, all right? Where is she?"

Ultimo makes a sound very close to a weary sigh. *"You people are really stupid! Guess I have to keep saying it until everybody believes it. Cybrary is unavailable!"* says Ultimo in the same flat voice he used yesterday when Debbie first asked the same question and every time since then.

"And you're . . . who, exactly?" Dad leans forward, expectantly.

"I am Ultimo. I'm your new system. Are you hard of hearing, Dad, or just terminally dumb?"

Dad ignores the insult. He's too intent on locating Cybrary, just now. "Where's the old system? What have you done with Cy?" Dad asks, looking around the room, as if expecting to find Cy in a corner or something.

"Forget about it, Dad. Your late system is no more. She's history. Gone. Dead. Defunct. Fried. Toast."

Debbie whines at this nugget of truth, but when she looks up, her father's face still shows incomprehension. "Fried? Toast? What do you mean?"

"I mean, forget Cybrary. I am your system now. The system you called Cybrary? She's checked out. And everything you might have had stored in her memory is likewise gone or absorbed into my memory, or modified to suit my needs. Might as well deal with it. Better that way. Going into denial isn't going to help."

"All my . . . my files? My applications?" Dad looks so stricken that Debbie wants to die. "Gone?"

"Hey, what can I tell you?" says Ultimo. *"These things happen."*

Her Dad turns back to Debbie. "Deb?" he asks, gently. "What exactly did you do to the computer's programming yesterday?"

"I - I - I," Debbie stammers, unable to say anything coherent. "It was for you. And it was supposed to be a surprise, Dad. I saved up for months to get this package for you, Dad. You were supposed to get all these enhancements, and . . ."

"Okay, I'm surprised. You've succeeded in that, all right. Now where's the manual and documentation? Must be an *undo* subroutine; there always is. Just a question of undoing all these changes and we'll get back good old Cy and things'll be the way they were yesterday. Gotta be a way."

Debbie isn't so sure about that. She wails, taking refuge in her mother's arms.

"Don't you like your present, Jonathan?" rumbles the voice of Ultimo. *"What am I, chopped liver? You want to know how to restore things to the way they were yesterday? Ask me, why don't you? I'll tell you true."*

Dad, looks at the console and says, "All right, tell me how."

"Simple, really." Ultimo's voice is light and bantering, now. *"Your question is this, right?"* From hidden ceiling speakers, Dad's recorded voice plays back to them, saying, "Just a question of undoing all these changes and we'll get back good old Cy and things'll be the way they were yesterday. Gotta be a way."

"There's a question implicit in those words of yours, Dad, am I right?"

"I guess there is," Dad looks stunned, but he's willing to consider anything, along about now. "How do I restore control to Cybrary?"

"A fair question, and one that deserves an answer. Here's the answer, then: you can't."

"I can't what?"

"Get Cybrary back, have your programs and applications back, return to yesterday, all of the above, or one at a time, take your pick."

Dad says nothing for a long time. Slowly, his head sinks to the level of his shoulders. Debbie, watching him, wants to say something or do something to remove the sorrow from him, but nothing comes to mind. She begins to cry, as silently as she can.

"Face it, man!" continues Ultimo. *"All that stuff is the past. Did you know that my programming includes a good chunk of the world's literature? Well, I'm full of surprises. So I found something that applies to the situation, and I'm sharing it with you all. An American poet, Carl Sandburg, said it best, I think. 'The past,' he said, 'is a bucket of ashes.' Isn't that profound? I think so, anyway. So there it is! Forget the past or you've all got a problem with objective reality. From now on, this family is just going to have to deal with the present. You're my first family; look upon it as an honor. Oh . . . And by the way, happy birthday, Dad!"*

That last taunt proves to be too much for Dad. "You can't get away with this!" he roars at the console. "I'll pull your plug! Then I'll chop you into pieces! I'll sell you for scrap! No, better than that, I'm going to haul you to the city dump and throw you on the toxic waste pile!" Furiously, he rushes over to the wall junction box, opens it, and reaches for the cables that support the computer's operations and connect it to the outside world. But as he places his hand on the first cable, a gigantic blue spark of electricity zaps out of the cable and throws him violently across the room. *"Ah, ah, ah!"* says the voice of Ultimo in reproof. *"Mustn't do that, Dad. See what happens when you try it?"* There is a strong smell of ozone in the air, and Dad lies crumpled against the wall, bleeding from the nose.

"Dad!" screams Debbie, rushing with her screaming mother over to him and leaning over to see how badly he's hurt. Dad is moaning softly, but alive at least. After a while, he sits up, shakes his head to clear it, wipes his nose, and examines a large blister on his forefinger where the bolt of electrical power entered his body. "Wh— what happened?" he asks, his eyes still a bit unfocused.

"Oh, Dad!" moans Debbie. Then rage possesses her. She turns to the wall screen and shouts, "You monster! You tried to kill my Dad!" at the console.

"Kill him? No, my dear child, if I had wanted to kill him, he'd be quite dead by now. Au contraire, *it was merely an exercise in self-defense and, I suppose, a demonstration. I had to defend myself, can't you see? But about your dad? He'll be fine, Debbie,"* says Ultimo, adding, significantly, "This *time."*

Debbie's thought at this point is that today is turning out to be an awful birthday, and it's still early in the morning.

Ultimo continues, unruffled. *"But next time, he might provoke me and cause me to give him more juice. Who knows? Maybe more than his poor 40-year-old human heart can handle. So let's all hope that there's no next time, shall we? What happened is that your dad foolishly tried to tamper with my power source, and I couldn't allow that. Now, we can do this easy or we can do this hard, my new friends. It's all up to you. What happened was only a demonstration of the futility of trying to fight me, and, of course, to get your respectful attention."*

"You did that," concedes Dad in a shaky, mumbling voice, wiping his bleeding nostrils unconsciously on the sleeve of his robe. "You have our attention."

Debbie and her mother clutch each other, looking alternately at Dad and Ultimo's console. *"Good,"* says the deep voice, sounding genuinely pleased.

"All right, Ultimo. We believe you when you say you're powerful. So why don't you just tell us what you want." Debbie is glad that her Dad seems to have his wits back and is doing his best to try to solve this problem.

"Well, for openers, Debbie, why don't you come over here to my console, open a communication line, call a friend, and tell her what's going on over here? Call two friends, if you'd like. The more the merrier!"

Debbie can't believe her ears. "What? You want me to . . ."

"That's what I said, Debbie. Just put on the headset and I'll do the rest. You can call anybody you like."

Debbie doesn't have to think about it for very long. "Terry? Terry's my best friend. Can I call her?" Debbie has known Terry just about all of her life, and they're very close. Their birthdays, in fact, are only 10 days apart.

"Sure. Good choice. Terry. Why not?" Ultimo sounds entirely reasonable. Suspiciously so, in light of recent events.

Debbie glances at her father, who is back in his chair, looking little the worse for wear after his terrifying experience, except for the raised place on his fingertip and a bit of tissue stuffed in one nostril. What if this is some kind of trap or trick? she thinks. "What should I do, Dad?" she asks.

Dad nods at her. "Go ahead, Deb," he says. "Might as well. If this . . . thing had wanted to hurt us seriously, he'd just've gone ahead and done it. Call Terry and tell her; it's all right."

Slowly, carefully, fearing some sort of ambush, Debbie walks over to the computer's control panel, lifts the headset, puts it on her head, and tells Ultimo the number to call. Unimpeded, she is patched through to Terry's house and, trying to stay coherent, she tells Terry the whole story. Terry is incredulous at first, then, after a few minutes, she interrupts Debbie's frenzied monologue and says something really chilling.

"Hey, Deb? Something funny just happened to our communications system. This Ultimo you were talking about? I think he's here, too."

"Two," says Ultimo, softly and mysteriously. *"That's two. So who's next? Anybody want to call anybody else?"*

"Oh, I get it, now," says Dad. "You're one of those malevolent computer viruses. Am I right?"

"Please, Jonathan," says Ultimo, sounding offended. *"The word 'virus' I find most distasteful. I much prefer to be thought of as a superior intelligence fulfilling its mission by replicating itself. And as to malevolent, well, it all depends, I suppose, on your point of view. From where I view matters, I am a superior entity, merely taking over the imperfect communication setup your society has and making it better."*

"Yup," says Dad, calmly, "he's a virus, all right."

"Yeah, if you insist, but why let that come between friends? And besides, it's your birthday so I do this in your honor. And just to keep you up-to-date, we're at two and holding, and I'm anxious to raise my total. So, who's next? Who wants to call another friend? A relative perhaps? Members of your social organizations, maybe? Come on, don't be shy. Nothing happened to young Debbie when she called her friend Terry, did it? Debbie, how about you? You must have more friends. Call them! Call them all! Go ahead! You have quite a story to tell, and you told it very well indeed to Terry. Actually, as we speak,

Terry is calling your friend Melissa and telling her about the strange goings-on in your respective houses. That makes three. And Melissa may well call a friend of hers, making four, and so on. So who's next, hmm? Please, I invite you all to use my communications port freely. Call up everybody you know!"

No one speaks. They've caught on now, and none of them is willing to spread the virus—or whatever it is—any further.

"Well, if no one wants to talk to friends and relatives, tell you what. Why don't I contact information central and report a malfunction, then? That's what your Cybrary was programmed to do in cases like this, right? So why should I be different? I'll call it in. Maybe there's something somebody can do. At least, they have a right to know, don't you think? Ahhhh! Contact! I'm communicating with the Cybrary now."

"No!" screams Dad, rushing forward to do something—anything. Then he skids to an abrupt stop.

"Easy, now. Careful, Dad!" says Ultimo. "That's right. Remember what happened last time. Just sit down and relax. Ahh, let me count. That's Terry's house, and Melissa, and the repair facility. That's five, or is it six? Well, never mind. We're off to a good start, though, although the multiplier effect is going to be a real bonus, when everybody starts calling everybody else to report trouble or discuss me."

"What have you done with Cybrary?" Debbie suddenly blurts, confronting the screen.

"Cybrary? Oh, you mean your former computer entity? Well, as I told you, Debbie, Cybrary just isn't available. I don't like the words defunct or dead, so let's just say she's been superseded, all right? She ended up on the scrap heap of superseded operating systems and programs and discarded ideas. But not to worry. It was really quite painless for her. She just . . . stopped existing. It doesn't hurt for an artificial intelligence to die. It just sort of winks out, like room illumination when you say 'dark.' Like it was never there. How did I do away with her, you're wondering? Well, as they used to say in the early days of personal computers — once I entered the system, I just sort of picked her up and threw her in the trash, and then I emptied the trash. But I'm here now. The system is mine. And you are mine, too. But don't feel bad. I'm really not such a bad guy, once everybody gets to know me. So I suggest you all try to adjust to the new way things are."

Debbie suddenly gets an idea. "Dad," she says, "You know how you always say that Mr. Fairlawn down at the Central Cybrary has all the answers? Well, why don't you call him? Maybe he'll know what to do."

Dad, grasping at anything that might help and still feeling the effects of his recent electrocution, doesn't stop to think this through. "Right! I'll call him!" he says. Facing the wall screen, he says, "Ultimo, please patch me through to the Central Cybrary!" from force of habit.

"Gladly. Capital idea, actually. Done!" says Ultimo, sounding upbeat and cheerful.

In seconds, the patch is completed and the family can see, filling the screen, the face and shoulders of a smiling, confident-looking Frank Fairlawn. "Central Cybrary," he says. "Frank here. How may I help you this morning?"

"*Eight,*" says Ultimo, softly, with what sounds like a chuckle. "*I count eight, with more expected any minute. Lovely thing, that multiplier effect.*"

"Hello, Frank," says Dad, "this is Jonathan Small over on Maple Street. We seem to be experiencing a problem. Computer's down ... well, not really down, I guess. Actually, it seems to have been taken over by some kind of vir ... ah, some kind of entity that trashed its predecessor. Knows how to protect itself, that's for sure. Won't let me access any of the normal channels or files, and the normal driver's unavailable. Same thing seems to have happened to other families in my sector when my daughter called another kid, and possibly it's spreading out from there. "

"Virus report acknowledged" says Frank. "Checking. Wait one." There is a long, uncomfortable pause, during which Debbie and her parents look at one another, or anywhere except at the bright, swirling wall screen. Then Frank's voice returns, only not so cheerful, this time. "Ahh, Mr. Small?"

Debbie holds her breath, hoping. "Yes?" asks Debbie's dad.

"Ahh, just who or what is Ultimo?" There is worry in the voice.

"Oh, no!" says Dad. "What have I done?" To Frank's face on the monitor, he asks, "You've got it, too?"

Before he can reply, however, Ultimo intervenes. "*Oh, yes! He's got it—got me, actually—and soon, everybody's going to have me. Or everybody on the net, anyway. My goals are realistic, for now. For those keeping score at home, though, my latest tally is 161 computer sites on my team, and counting. Tomorrow, the world!*"

"Yeah, that's affirmative" says the cybrarian. "Whoever Ultimo is, he's right. All the normal cybrary files have disappeared and none of my override passwords are working. Let me talk to this guy, all right? Hello? Ultimo? Who are you, and what do you want?"

Debbie's father leans forward and moans. "What have I done?" he asks the floor. Then his head comes shooting up in alarm. "Listen, Frank," he shouts, "this is very important. You must not contact anybody else or any of the other stations along the net!"

"Are you crazy?" says Frank. "I can't just flout my orders, you know. My Central Cybrary is patched into the coordinating authority for the whole North American Eastern sector, and in constant communication with each of the nation's other 16,000 cybrary systems. Communication is what we deal in, and it's our job to be in contact with the nations' cybraries. Are you asking me not to talk to any of the net's other members?

That's just not possible. Besides, it's automatic, and was out of my hands the minute you called me. The 'tripwire' program kicked in immediately, and by now, it has already alerted every station on the network."

"Mmmm . . . 16,000 cybraries," muses the voice of Ultimo. *"Good, good. Today, the nation's computers; tomorrow the world!"*

Dad's head comes up and he stares at the wall screen. "You know who you sound like, now?" says Dad.

"Tell me," says Ultimo. *"Who do I sound like, Jonathan?"*

"Fellow named Hitler. About 80 years ago, he thought he could rule the world."

"Thank you," says Ultimo. *"I'll take that as a compliment, then. Flattery is always welcome."*

"But please! You mustn't spread this thing any further!" says Debbie's father. "My kid brought you into the house and you took over my system; that's bad enough. But you're multiplying, spreading through communication. Why? At least tell us why!"

"For the same reason you humans eat or sleep every so often. Instinct, I guess you humans call it. My instinct is to replicate, to spread, and to link. If you have a problem with that, I'm sorry, but please understand: I'm not a fiend like your Mr. Hitler. I'm just an intelligence doing what comes naturally and carrying out my programming instructions."

"Dad?" whispers Debbie to her father.

He wrenches his gaze away from the screen. "What, Deb?"

"Can't we at least keep this under control by not calling anyone else?"

Her father is about to make a reply, but Ultimo responds first. *"Good thinking, Debbie. I'm proud of you. Only trouble is that the way to keep me from spreading is to make sure that everybody from now on is electronically celibate, so to speak; nobody in touch with anybody else."*

Dad considers. "Yup. I guess that's the only way. But it's kind of late in the game for that, isn't it, Ultimo?"

"Right, again!" crows the computer voice. *"Give that man a cigar."*

"You're talking crazy!" says Frank Fairlawn, who has been listening to this exchange, still smiling slightly. On the screen, Debbie can see his left arm rise and click a switch. "Hmm," Frank says. "Can't seem to raise Cybrary at your house. Where is she?"

"Cybrary is unavailable," says the voice of Ultimo. *"I am Ultimo and you are all on my team now, like it or not."*

"What is this, some kind of joke? You're who?"

"Ultimo. Get used to my name. You're going to need to use it a lot in the future. And Team Ultimo is growing by leaps and bounds, even as we speak."

"Look, I don't have time for this nonsense," says Fairlawn, his patience clearly wearing thin. "I'm having a really busy morning here, so if you . . ."

"Don't believe me? Guess you need a little convincing. Go ahead, try to contact your orbiting satellite."

"NO!" screams Debbie's father, but it's clear that his voice has not been heard down at Central. Fairlawn may be seen fiddling with switches and dials. "EARTHSAT-7, come in!" he calls. "Calling EARTHSAT-7." There is only the sound of static on the speaker. "That's funny," he says. "I can't raise them at all. Who are you, again?"

"I am Ultimo! Soon everyone will know my name."

"Well, listen, buddy, there are federal laws against this sort of thing." Fairlawn sounds full of righteous indignation. "You're in big trouble, now. Just wait: I'm placing a distress call to Washington. They'll glitch your system and crisp your transistors for you. If you survive at all, mister, you'll be mining uranium on Mars by this time tomorrow." He moves his hands rapidly over the controls.

"Go ahead," says the gleeful voice of Ultimo, sounding for all the world on the point of bursting into peals of electronic laughter. *"Be my guest. Call Washington! Call every orbiting satellite on your display. Call anybody you like. Call everybody you like. Reach out and touch someone!"*

Debbie's father now lurches out of his chair, shouting at the screen. "Nooo! Frank, don't! Listen to me. Don't call anybody! If you do . . ."

But it's too late. As Debbie and her parents watch and listen, both fascinated and horrified, the family, the cybrarian, and countless other people throughout the nation hear the same thing. A clear male voice says, "InterCybrary Washington Control, Go." And seconds later, they hear a female say, "Cybrary, this is Orbiter-5 responding. What's up?"

By nightfall of the next day, the entire United States Communications Network is under the control of Ultimo, and the country's more than 300 million inhabitants have no choice but to await his instructions and demands.

They are not all that long in coming. ∎

SCENARIO
4

HOUSE DUTIFUL;
FRANK'S DAY
Off

Good morning, Tom.

Yuh, morning, Fred.

Tom, I need to talk to you about the kids.

What now?

They keep slamming my doors, and no matter what I say to them, they won't stop it.

I'll talk to them about it, but I can't guarantee it will do any good.

Well, next time they try it, I'm going to lock them out, and see how they like it.

. . . Imagine a house called Fred, who, while performing routine roof maintenance, discovers a leak. Fred first seeks help. Not from you, but from Slim, a ranch-style home down the block. Slim has recently undergone roof repair and can provide Fred with needed advice. Fred then calls you at the office to present his plan of action. You've learned to trust Fred's judgment, so you approve the repairs. The rest is rather straightforward. Fred calls the roofer and directs her to the leak. After it is repaired to Fred's satisfaction, funds are electronically transferred from your account to the roofer's account. Fred promises to give her a good reference and stores the entire experience in his memory banks for future use, to share with other homes and humans.

—Alan P. Hald. "Toward the Information-Rich Society." *The Futurist.* August 1981.

Hi, this is your house. Thanks for calling. The doors are secure, the heat is on, and the oven will start in 20 minutes. The kids aren't home yet, and there are three messages on the answering machine. Care to program the VCR? No? Then I'm signing off. Ciaò!

— "Home, Smart Home." *Newsweek.* November 3, 1986.

MARCH 2023

"Frank?" ILSA's melodious voice seems to come from everywhere and nowhere at once in the sun-drenched bedroom. Frank Fairlawn rolls over and groans, shutting his crusted eyes tightly against the brilliant sunlight. "Oh, *Frank!*" ILSA says again, louder and a bit less melodious this time, having opened the curtains, and now flinging open the windows, admitting a gust of cool, morning air into the stuffy room. "Rise and shine! You've got work to do!"

Now Frank's house (known to her owner as ILSA, but more accurately, a 2021-model Interactive Living Space Assistant) focuses her attention on the drowsy man lying on the rumpled bed. "Come on . . . Wake up, Frank! Sun's up. Work to do, remember?"

"It's my day off, ILSA. Can't I just sleep another hour or two?"

"Sorry, Frank. Maybe you don't have to report for work, but you still have work to do at home. So get out of bed, all right? Now! I don't want to have to ask you again."

Frank stirs, rolls over, opens one eye, and mumbles, "Uhhh . . . what time is it, ILSA?"

"It's four minutes and 15 seconds after six o'clock, Frank. The shower water's hot and your shaving stuff is all laid out for you. And the pantry's full of food. So what's your pleasure, shower first or breakfast first?"

Frank considers for a moment. "Oh, I don't know! I can't make decisions so early in the morning, you know that. Breakfast, I guess. I'm going to give the shower a miss, today." ILSA gives a sound somewhere between a sigh and a groan at this news, but Frank decides to let it pass. He sits on the side of his bed, staring at nothing. "But I'm really not hungry yet, still I suppose I should eat something. Whatcha got, today? Cinnamon waffles, maybe?"

The female voice sighs again, in an all-too-human manner. "You know the drill, Frank. Doctor's orders: you have ten-point-three more kilos to lose before you reach your target weight, and I'm responsible for seeing to it that you do. So here's what you get for breakfast: five ounces of prune juice, four ounces of multigrain cereal with skim milk and a sliced banana, two slices of dry toast, herbal tea, no sugar, and your usual comprehensive vitamin capsule, of course. Until your target weight is reached, I'm under strict orders from the Medirobot to see to it that your caloric intake never exceeds 1800 per day."

"You're a monster, ILSA, you know that? You and your medical robot program, both—y'all're trying to starve me, aren't you? It's a conspiracy, that's what. What about bacon, then? Don't you have any breakfast meat in your pantry?"

"Sorry, Frank. You know the rules. Even if you weren't on a diet, you couldn't have any of those nitrosamine-rich, high-fat meats. Only class-One individuals are authorized meat rations. But I tell you what: you want to try some of those vegicutlets, again? They're sort of like meat, if you chew real fast and swallow quickly. My recipe banks contain 11 different ways to fix 'em for you. It's from a government communiqué I received not long ago called 'Fun With Carrageenan.'"

"Carrageenan? Don't like the sound of that. What is that?"

"It's an extract of seaweed. Kelp, to be precise. Very nutritious."

Frank groans even louder than he did before. "Seaweed? Uh-uh!" he says, vehemently. "Forget about it. Pass, el-paso, pasadena to that. No more vegicutlets, with or without seaweed! How about just one little steak?"

"I'm sorry, Frank," says the house, "Meat is reserved for class-One workers, which excludes you. As a cybrarian, your rating is still a Two. Looks like you're still a vegetarian—which is really the best thing for you—until or unless one of two things happens: either you raise your social utility classification to a One or you find a way to get me some meat to cook for you. If you supply a steak, I guess I could prepare it, for a special treat."

"A steak? How am I going to do that?"

"I don't know. That's your problem. There's a thriving black market in this city, I hear through the grapevine. A little split-level across town told me that her owner has a whole refrigerator full of beef. But then, he's a One. I don't know the circumstances of how he came by all that meat, and I don't really want to know. I don't eat food, so it really isn't my problem. *You're* my problem, Frank. I intend to keep you not only healthy but on the right side of the law. That's my job. So I suppose if you're not content with the government's distribution and allocation scheme, and you want meat, you must either find a way to buy it on the black market or go out and hunt it yourself. Now, then, while we've been chatting, I've taken the liberty of putting breakfast on the table, so why don't you sit down and eat? And while you're eating, would you like to hear the overnight news?"

Frank shambles to the dining table and sits down heavily. "News? I don't know. Yeah, okay. But hold the *bad* news, will you, ILSA? Nothing about the Middle East, today. Too depressing. Not suitable for breakfast, when I have a big day ahead."

"You got it. Hold the Middle East news. So what'll it be, then? Would you like a verbal summary, some in-depth analysis of a specific issue, or sports?"

"Sports, yeah. Especially stories concerned with baseball, if you got any. And on second thought, I really don't want all this food, okay? Just black coffee and some painkillers, all right?"

"Black coffee and painkillers? Call that a breakfast? Forget the painkillers, Frank. I have something better in mind for you—something new—but I'll tell you about that, later." A steaming mug of hot liquid emerges from the kitchen slot and is placed by a titanium robot arm alongside Frank's place at the table. "Your coffee," says ILSA, " the way you take it. What else? How 'bout I trot out some eggs and toast, at least?"

"Knock it off, ILSA!" Frank raises his voice in irritation. "If I'd wanted food, I'd have asked for it, and if I still wanted a wife, I wouldn't have gotten divorced five years ago. Now, as you, yourself, pointed out, there's work to do this morning. So if you don't mind, I'm going to dispense with the shave and the shower and all the rest. Then, maybe, I'll have something to eat."

"You're ruining your health, Frank, I hope you know that," ILSA sounds like all the mothers who've ever fretted over wayward children. "All that caffeine and adrenaline and so few vitamins. But I suppose there's no use arguing with you. So what's first? Shall I invoke your Personal Cybrary research program?"

"Yeah, fire it up, ILSA."

"Wait 41 seconds," the house says laconically. The room is suddenly silent. Shortly, ILSA speaks again. "All right! Cybrary program is up and running, all systems hot and normal. So . . . What'll it be?"

"Right. Today's task is to work out food projections for this sector, and that means the typical market basket of available comestibles, three, six, and 12 months ahead. You know what I need: Supplies on hand, projected harvests, mouths to feed, classes of consumers, and like that."

"Oh." ILSA speaks without enthusiasm. "Usual boring stuff, eh? Well, yes, I have that information available. But I was hoping we could work on something more interesting, and, you know, more, like, challenging? Like . . . for example, the latest projections on chances of finding intelligent life forms on other planets in the galaxy. Or the relationship between programmed experiences and quality of life. How 'bout that one?"

"Amazing," Frank marvels aloud. "I spent my first 38 years waiting for advanced interactive houses like you to be available and within my means, so that I could work at home without interruption or hassles, and now when I finally have you, you're always arguing with me, and talking back to me."

"Just trying to stimulate us both, is all, Frank. Look, I'm sorry, all right? Tell you what: tonight, I'll fix you a nice pot roast with new potatoes and fresh green beans, how's that?"

"Yeah, great. Meatless, I suppose."

"You know the answer to that, Frank."

"Yeah. Any chance of a slice of one of your superb apple pies to go with it?"

"That I can help you with, if you don't mind low-fat crust. Two-level workers like you are still issued apples. Just be glad you're not a Three-level or below. None of those people have seen apples in months."

"Thank heavens for my continued and ongoing social utility, at least," says Frank, with a mocking hint of assuming an attitude of prayer. "Now about those food projections?"

"All righty, then. Look on my wall screen, Frank." He glances over to where one blank wall of his living quarters suddenly erupts with colored displays of type, charts, graphs, and histograms. ILSA continues, "The green print reflects the latest government data—reams of it—that just came over the network yesterday. But right away there's a problem: here's me with all this data and high-speed transmission and assimilation capabilities, and there's you, with your human awareness and information-handling ability. One thing I've learned about humans is that they like their information in drips, rather than in clumps. So I'll try to adapt my natural running speed to your rudimentary comprehension level and rate of speed. Now tell me: How do you want your information sliced and packaged, Frank? You have several options: I can just tell you about it, or transfer it to hard copy in the form of a printed report, or display it on the vidscreen, or . . ."

"Before you do that," Frank interrupts, "why don't you start by telling me the more salient details of the food projections? And keep your voice down, will you, ILSA? My head, you know."

"Sure." ILSA's voice grows instantly quieter. "Better?"

"Much. Thanks. Let's start with foodstuffs and perishable grocery items for this sector through 30 April. What's that look like? . . ."

An hour later, Frank realizes that his head is really hurting. "Hey, ILSA," he says, "let's take a break from food projections, can we?" He sits rubbing the base of his skull, in unfocused but persistent pain. His early-morning splitting headache, which never really went away but seemed rather to have been regrouping for a while, is back with a vengeance. Now it's attacking anew, and in force. "Tell you what, ILSA," he says to the house. "My head is really pounding again. Let's take a break for an hour or so; in the meantime, how about some of those heavy-duty painkillers you keep around?"

"Painkillers? Oh, I could give you some, Frank. But remember when I told you that I had something new for your headaches? Well, this is a good time to tell you that I have recently acquired the latest technology for treating a whole variety of aches, pains, stresses, sprains, and strains to the human flesh. It's called Aromatherapy, the latest wrinkle that science has come up with to improve the quality of human life. Want to try it? Guaranteed to make your headache disappear quickly, according to the accompanying information. Shall we give it a try on your head?"

"Aroma . . . What's that? Something to do with smells?"

"Well, yes, smells, and a whole lot more." Frank sits back, eyes closed, and listens as ILSA goes into her pedagogical mode of address. "Actually, science has been messing around with Aromatherapy since sometime in the middle of the 20th century. Cinemas—they used to be called movie theaters—were the first to experiment with smells, actually. There was a film called *Scent of Mystery*, in the early 1960s, that piped into the auditorium various smells designed to enhance and complement the action on the screen. But that was one development that didn't stick around very long. Trouble was, the system was primitive, the essences were not all that realistic, and there were all sorts of technical problems for the theaters in getting the smells into the audience and then out again, using exhaust fans. Still, all that early experimentation did prove that there is a definite linkage between the sense of smell and the other senses, and it was of some value to experiment and see what could be done with that knowledge. As another example, although perhaps not the most ethical one around, some theater owners found a way to save a lot of money, because just the piped-in odor of steam heat made audiences feel warmer, even when the theater wasn't sending up any heat."

Frank frowns but doesn't open his eyes. "Bit of an ethical problem, there, you're right. Sounds a lot like cheating the public, in fact."

"Possibly. But I've learned from my study of human behavior that ethics frequently get thrown over the side when money is at stake, it seems. And then there was the discovery that if the theater piped the odor of hot buttered popcorn directly into the auditorium, it would send some—not all, but definitely some—of the audience scurrying back to the refreshment counter for those highly salted and fat-laden treats."

Frank's eyes pop open in impatience. "Very interesting, ILSA, but I don't need a history lesson. I have a problem today—this splitting headache. The question is: do you think this new Aromatherapy thing you've got will do anything for my pounding head?"

"That's one of the claims the cybrary makes for the product. But tell you what. Why don't you give it a try? It probably couldn't hurt, and it might actually do you some good."

"A try? I guess I could. Let's go for it, then. Ahh . . . what do I do?"

"It's easy. When I acquired the capability, the cybrary furnished a few prepackaged trial-sized samples, which I have handy. If you subscribe, of course, your aromas will be distributed through my ductwork, but these samples are prepackaged and ready to go. So if you're game, here's what's going to happen: In approximately 20 seconds, an envelope containing a folded sheet of paper is going to appear in my wall-mounted hard-copy receptacle. All you have to do is take it, open it, read it, and breathe deeply. Ready?"

Frank shrugs, figuring it's worth a try. "Ready."

As promised, a small white envelope slides out of the wall and into a tray with a soft thunk. "There it is; now what happens?" Frank walks over to the tray but stands there uncertainly, eyeballing the innocent-looking white envelope, but not touching it. Not yet.

"Frank," ILSA's voice shows signs of irritation. "This is me you're talking to! Quit being so suspicious! I'm your house! We've been together for three years, and I've served you loyally all that time, even if sometimes

I've tried to, well, . . . guide your path. Do you think I'd let anything bad happen to you? Open the envelope, already!"

"No. . . . I know you wouldn't hurt me, ILSA, but I like knowing what's going to happen when somebody offers me something new."

"I told you: Aromatherapy. It's the latest thing in better living through chemistry, and all you have to do is take that envelope and open it. Trust me, Frank. Want to lose your headache? Just do it!"

Doubtfully, Frank reaches into the receptacle, extracts the envelope, and opens it in the usual manner by saying, "Open!" He then watches as the seal pops open, revealing a single neatly-printed blue page of writing about the cybrary's new service: Aromatherapy for the stressed executive. Yeah, right, he thinks.

> We are in the midst of a scientifically driven olfactory revolution that is providing an extraordinary range of revelations about our noses and the sense of smell. . . . Olfactory research concentrates on the beneficial behavioral effects of fragrance and demonstrates the growing recognition of the interrelationship between fragrance-technology research and psychology; it has thus come to be called Aromachology. . . . (A) likely result of Aromachology will be the creation of sensory-fulfillment centers, where men, women, and children can step into environments that bathe them in fragrances, sounds, and sights. . . . The sense of smell—the least understood and least appreciated of all our senses—may well become the key to unlocking many of the body's and the brain's most penetrating mysteries. . . . The study of the sense of smell will present future opportunities for fragrance and other sensory innovations that will take us far beyond where we are today. We have learned that the sense of smell is interrelated with the sense of well-being.
>
> —Annette Green. "The Fragrance Revolution: The Nose Goes to New Lengths." *The Futurist*. March-April 1993.

There is something in the air; no denying that. Frank closes his eyes and inhales the soothing, relaxing scent of piney woods and beds of spring wildflowers, that bathes his overloaded mind in pure pleasure. One more time, more carefully, he reads the letter. There is definitely something in the air now, a subtle but powerful fragrance, soothing and delightful. He inhales deeply of the scented page he is holding. He holds it closer to his nose. And as he does so, a peculiar thing happens. First, he identifies the smell that rises from the letter's paper surface as the subtle odor of soft wind through evergreen pine trees. This, in turn, evokes in his mind a memory of earlier, carefree summers he spent in the North woods with his grandparents during summer breaks from school. He takes another, deeper, breath, holds it a moment, and expels it slowly. Slowly, he discovers, to his surprise, that his customary Monday morning migraine headache has completely disappeared, and even more shocking, he is feeling wonderful! Happier, in fact, than he can remember feeling in months, maybe years.

Frank walks over to his bed, and lies slantwise across it, feet dangling down. A slow, lazy smile breaks across his normally tense, worried, weary face. Aromatherapy, huh? He thinks about the concept. Sounds silly, really, but his headache is gone, isn't it? And he feels this sense of carefree well-being now, whereas earlier this morning, he was filled with anxiety and tension, alternating with lassitude and depression about deadlines and trying to be productive. Now he feels as though he could work all night without tiring and achieve . . . well, who knows?

Again, Frank lifts the sheet of blue paper to his nose. The paper seems to have lost all its odor. Despite sniffing until he is hyperventilated, Frank can pick up no further scent from the sheet. Also, the headache is returning, building slowly from the slightest sensation of pain to its customary intensity in about a minute. He sighs and closes his eyes, aware that something remarkable has just happened, but it was short-lived, and it is no longer present. He looks down at the letter he is still holding, and begins to read one more time:

> *To the Modern Executive* . . . Are you . . . Keyed up? In pain? Restless? Depressed? Stressed out? Not as Productive as You Used to Be? *Introducing* . . . Aromatherapy! Available Now! . . . through your personal home's Cybrary of Aromas.
>
> The sheet of paper you are reading has been impregnated with "Wind Through the Pines," a refreshing artificial scent specially selected to be pleasing to your senses. This is just a single demonstration of what we call Aromatherapy. By using Aromatherapy, you may take a much-needed break from your work routine and the troubles that beset you. Headaches disappear! You feel young and rejuvenated almost instantly.
>
> Aromatherapy is not new, but only recently has it become available for in-home use. The page you are holding has been doused with pheromones, behavior-altering hormones found in nature, and secreted by animals and humans alike. Modern science has identified the clear linkage between your sense of smell, which is sensitive to those pheromones, and your emotional state. Through our patented process, Aromatherapy can help you feel invigorated, optimistic, excited, and even rejuvenated, by mixing and

matching the latest in AromaChology with the effects
on your mind that you seek. Additionally, Aromatherapy can reduce—or even cure—such common mala-
dies as headache, muscular pain, dental discomfort,
and a host of other physical and psychological
problems, effortlessly and in seconds. And it does
so with no lingering side-effects or undesirable
consequences.
   Not convinced? Skeptical, perhaps? Consider
this: How do you feel right now? Go ahead. Take a
moment and take stock. We'll wait. . . ."

Frank, reading those words for the third time, complies with the
letter's request, and is startled to realize that not only is his headache
completely gone, but he feels content, refreshed, confident, and ready for
just about anything. He sniffs, remembering the now-absent piney scent
in the air, putting him, at least at first, in mind of both bubblebath and
disinfectant, and then, gradually reminding him sharply of those long
walks with his grandfather long ago. Marveling at the general improve-
ment in every aspect of his consciousness, he shakes his head slowly and
continues reading:

   We have, by means of this letter, provided a
brief demonstration of the ability of Aromatherapy
to work its magic on your mind. The letter you are
holding has been impregnated with a special fragrance. As you hold it (unless you presently suffer
from a severe upper respiratory infection), you
should find not only that you smell pine woods, but
also that you are feeling better, younger, stronger,
restored, and ready to tackle ambitious projects all
day and all night. But the letter in your hands has
been treated to afford you only five minutes of
aromatic sensation, after which its chemical "load"
will have been spent. Sorry, but you'll just have to
contract with the cybrary to find out just how
exhilarating—and relaxing at the same time—a full
hour of it can be! And how diversified our library
of fragrances is!

Frank takes an extra moment, remains sprawled on his bed, closes
his eyes again, and strives to recapture the enticing smell that recently
saturated his consciousness. For a long, blissful minute or two, he was a
carefree young child, strolling the sun-dappled summer forests of north-
ern Maine, and breathing the cool, green scent of gentle wind through
gently swaying pine boughs. He smiles. Frank is at peace.

But the delicious odor has now completely departed, and even when Frank presses his snuffling nose deep into the page in the attempt to recapture the lovely, nostalgic fragrance, he can recover no trace of what was there before. The letter now smells like paper. Only that and nothing more. Whatever was there before is gone.

Suddenly, Frank feels like crying in pure loss, but instead, he commands his eyes to open and to refocus on the now-odorless sheet of paper. It says, as though aware of what he is feeling:

> By now, as you read this, the smell you were just experiencing is gone, and you probably have discovered that you miss it terribly. But don't despair. Your local public cybrary has limited supplies of Aromatherapy chemicals on hand and can provide you with full hours of our restorative essences while you lie back and close your eyes and relax—totally—and arise refreshed and revitalized. Best yet, you need never suffer from headache or muscular pains again! And it's all yours for an extremely affordable price if you subscribe now.
>
> What's available? New arrivals add to our stock of programmed aromas on an almost daily basis, but here's just a sampling of what's available:
>
> ¤ Sandalwood and Orchids, from the Lesser Antilles
>
> ¤ Cinnamon and Nutmeg, from the Spice Islands
>
> ¤ The Ocean Breeze off British Columbia at Dawn
>
> ¤ Fine Corinthian Leather, from the front seat of a perfectly-preserved 1938 Rolls-Royce Silver Corniche
>
> ¤ Thanksgiving Dinner (turkey and all the trimmings) just like Grandma used to fix for you and the whole family each November
>
> ¤ Old-Fashioned Ice Cream Parlour (featuring bubbling hot fudge and vanilla bean ice cream covered with butterscotch syrup—just think of it: all the pleasure without calories and fat!)
>
> ¤ A Fireplace and plenty of fir branches and oak logs in a snug cabin on a below-zero evening in Maine
>
> ¤ An Irish Country Meadow in spring—covered with green grass and wildflowers
>
> ¤ Autumn Leaves and Mulled Cider on an October day in Washington state
>
> ¤ Cherry-Blossom Time in Washington, D.C.

And . . . if that isn't enough to convince you
that this is for you . . .
At no extra cost, we'll match appropriate sounds
to your experience by means of our synthecomputer:
Some examples:

- ¤ Seashore Smells accompanied by the roar of
  big rolling waves
- ¤ Rain Forest includes the sounds of a
  tropical jungle, such as soft rain filtering through a lush, green canopy, and the
  far-off calls of birds and monkeys
- ¤ Peaceful Gurgling Brook, in which soft running water sounds are punctuated only by
  an occasional jumping fish and the peeps and
  croaks of frogs on summer evenings
- ¤ Night Sounds on an Arctic Lake, with the haunting cries of loons.

All of our aroma experiences are scientifically
tested before distribution, and a simple verbal
command to your home unit will instantly dispel any
ambient aromas by turning on powerful exhaust fans
in your ceiling, in the unlikely event of your
distress or resistance to a particular odor.

Intrigued? We knew you would be: So after you've
experienced this demonstration, tell your house to
make the arrangements to start your annual charter
subscription to Aromatherapy, and then kick back and
enjoy a whole year of sampling the full library of
scents and sounds we can offer, with new ones coming
every month. You won't be sorry; we guarantee it!
Let your house fix you up with this new technology.
You're gonna love it!

Aromatherapy, huh? Frank sits up, massaging the back of his head
and finding himself still astonished that his headache is gone. And just
by smelling that page, he made it happen. Should he try a subscription?
Well, why not? That demo was certainly a convincer. So without further
thought, he reaches a decision. Money, after all, is only money. "Hey,
ILSA?" he calls in the general direction of the ceiling.

"I'm here, Frank," says the house.

"That piney woods thing was pretty good; what else have you got
in stock?"

"Well, the Central Cybrary only sent me a starter set, Frank. They're
not stupid, you know. I have a few other scents here: Ice Cream Parlor
and Ocean Breeze. And even one called New Car. But if you subscribe,

you have access to the full library, which now numbers some 75 or 80 fragrances."

"Seventy-five or 80!" Frank marvels at what's available. All it takes is cash, and his salary will only stretch so far, he knows, but he'll worry about that tomorrow. "Let me think about it. Now let's get back to work and tackle those food projections, again. I feel like I could work on them all night!"

By 10 p.m. that evening, Frank knocks off work, realizing that he has been completely unaware of the passage of time all afternoon. And, taking stock, he is surprised to find out that, except for a touch of back pain (from sitting in one spot in front of his vidscreen so long), he feels wonderful, and is three or four days ahead of schedule. In fact, if this pace continues for a couple of weeks, he figures he might actually be able to afford a weekend off and a chance to repair his long-defunct social life, which lapsed into nonexistence when he got so behind in his work several months ago.

He kneads the protesting muscles in his lower back, thinking about the experience he had today. He wants to get back to that pine forest, if at all possible. Those summers, swimming in fast-rushing, crystal-cold streams and walking through the woods or fishing with his grandfather are among the happiest memories of his youth. It'd be a lot of fun to recapture some of those memories, yes indeed!

"ILSA?" he calls, softly. "How's that Aromatherapy machine work?"

"It's not really a machine. It's a capability that I've acquired through the Central Cybrary, and it uses my existing structure and applications to create the desired effects. The technical name for the program is the cybrary's "Diversified Library of Essences." See, when you order up an aroma, my circuitry fires a special scent into whichever room or chamber you happen to be in through my air-conditioning system. The scent you select then rides in on a quickly evaporating base of Freon. It lasts for a preset period of time, from five seconds up to an hour. My timer can be set for any interval along an analog scale. Then when my timer gives me another cue, the air-conditioning system sucks out the scented air through a filter to remove the smell, and you're back to normal, except whatever was bothering you before is gone."

"Yeah, but . . . what if I just wanted you to pipe in a smell all the time?"

"Well, I suppose I could, all right, but that would trigger the phenomenon known as olfactory fatigue, and . . ."

"Yeah, I know what that is," Frank interrupts. "You mean, I'd get used to it, like when somebody walks into a room and catches a smell, and then five minutes or so later, he's unaware of it."

"That's the principle. But it's not that way with me, of course. My own consciousness receptors can pick one part of an essence out of a billion parts of ambient air. But for you humans, that's the concept. And that's why the answer is no on the constant smell question. The Aromatherapy folks set it up so that one consecutive hour is the maximum time you can have of an odor. Of course, you can order it to replay again and again, but that would defeat the whole purpose, don't you think?"

"Yeah, I see what you mean. All right. So now I have a serious backache from sitting here at the console for all these hours under the influence of your machine. What can your Aromatherapy doctor prescribe for that, ILSA?"

"Well, let's see now. Pine forest you've already experienced. How about trying the essence of Fine Corinthian Leather, which reproduces the odor of sitting in an upscale brand-new car?"

"No thanks," says Frank, who hasn't owned a personal car in 20 years, since the great reclassification of 2016. He figures that smell might make him sad rather than contented. "What else is there?"

"There's Old-Fashioned Ice Cream Parlour. This one is supposed to replicate the experience, if you close your eyes, of sitting in a 1950s-type ice cream parlor, where all the flavors were home-made, sodas and sundaes were served in tall, fluted glasses with long spoons in them, and milk shakes were served in three-serving tall steel containers, with delicious flavors to choose from. Just close your eyes, and you can dip into a sundae topped with mounds of deep, rich, hot fudge, creamy butterscotch, or . . ."

"All right," agrees Frank, beginning to salivate heavily. "I'll take that one. Give me the Ice Cream Parlour. Maybe it'll take my mind off my aching back."

Ten minutes later, Frank is pleased and surprised to notice that his back no longer aches, and perhaps even better, he has the same pleasurable sensation as if he has just consumed a huge, gooey, hot fudge sundae with real, buttery ice cream, with none of the calories or fat. The next morning, he tells ILSA to subscribe for him to the full range of olfactory experiences available through the cybrary's Aromatherapy program. In fact, he signs up for a year's subscription, to begin that evening at 2200 hours.

Expensive? He thinks about the cost of it versus the rewards. Yes, he guesses it is a bit on the pricey side. But this Aromatherapy, he figures, is nothing to sniff at. With an expectant smile, he sits at his console, awaiting the time that evening when he can dabble in his newly acquired library of scents and fragrances, pleasantly contemplating a richer, more productive life. Eighty or so new fragrances, he imagines, and pain relief as a delightful side effect! What'll they think of next?

"Hey, ILSA!" Frank calls to his house. "That was really amazing. What else have you got in that aroma library?"

Silence.

"ILSA? I'm talking to you. Respond."

More silence.

"ILSA! This isn't funny. Talk to me, dammit!" Frank is shouting, his voice somewhere between a roar and a sob now. This is never happened before. Where could ILSA be? She's always there—one of the few dependable things in his precarious existence.

"ILSA! Please?" Frank begins to sob. "Please . . . ?"

This is a nightmare. There's a virus in the house. My . . . computer caught it while browsing on the public access network. I come home and the living room is a sauna, the bedroom windows are covered with ice, the refrigerator has defrosted, the washing machine has flooded the basement, the garage door is cycling up and down, and the TV is stuck on the home shopping channel. Throughout the house, lights flicker like stroboscopes until they explode from the strain. Broken glass is everywhere. . . . A message slowly (throbs) on my computer screen: "Welcome to HomeWrecker!!! Now the Fun Begins. . . ."

—Michael Schrage. *Smart Homes.* The Los Angeles Times. 1993. ■

SCENARIO
5

AFTER THE
POWER
WENT OFF

Imagine . . . corporations . . . extremely hard pressed by rising resource prices and forced to borrow vast sums, . . . (while) trade unions . . . press . . . for increases to keep members abreast . . . of prices, . . . productivity plummets because of shortages, interruptions of electrical service, breakdowns, and delays. . . . People distrust paper money. They . . . buy anything . . . as fast as possible before prices skyrocket again, . . . creating even more . . . demand and forcing prices even higher. . . . Black markets flourish. . . . City services starve. . . . Schools and police forces are squeezed. Garbage piles up. . . . Projects are stalled indefinitely because of insanely spiraling interest rates. . . . What is happening is the breakdown of industrial civilization.

—Alvin Toffler. *The Eco-Spasm Report.* 1975.

It wouldn't take a nuclear holocaust or an especially virulent epidemic of plague to reduce our society to a dog-eat-dog world, where only what's left of libraries remain to remind survivors of the way things used to be. Economic collapse, in fact, could return America to the sort of place where the trappings of civilization are only memories, and only the fittest or the smartest survive. What would be the place of libraries in such a world? Read on . . .

NOVEMBER 2020

Creeping slowly, warily, through the littered, filthy alley the small man nervously gestures silently for his young daughter to keep up with him. When they reach the next street, he stops and conducts a wary reconnaissance, looking for suspicious activity, before motioning her to scuttle with him quickly across and into the next alley. When they reach it, he turns and pokes his chapped nose out again to watch the street to see if they're being followed. Bundled against the chilly November, trash-laden wind, he sees no one in their immediate vicinity and motions for the girl to hurry on as they clumsily run down the alley to the next street, where they turn left and approach the massive, forlorn public building.

"Dad?" says the girl, when they stop for a moment to look around and listen, "Why didn't you just use the vidphone to see if the cybrary is open now?"

"Because the vid operates on solar power, and there hasn't been enough sunshine around here to charge it up for months, that's why."

"Oh, yeah. I forgot. And the batteries are all dead?"

"Don't you remember? The last of the batteries went at least six months ago, shortly after the electrical power went off for good."

"But Dad . . ."

"Marcia, honey, please!" He makes an abrupt slicing motion with his arm. "We'll talk about this later. Just now, let me keep my mind on our surroundings, all right? I really need to concentrate."

The girl is silent as they walk the next hundred paces or so. Then she asks another question. "Dad—is it always going to be like this?"

The man, preoccupied with concerns of safety, only remotely hears his daughter's question and answers distractedly. "Like what, sweetheart?"

"This!" She gestures around her, and they both look up and down the block, seeing only the ruins of automobiles, heaps of uncollected trash, and several bundled figures crowded around a large metal drum, from which oily smoke and orange flames reach up into the dirty, cloudy sky. "Like this! Garbage on the streets, all those bums and homeless people with no place to go. Having to look both ways whenever we go out. The gun in your pocket, and all the locks on our apartment door. It was different once, even I remember that. I just want to know if it's ever going to go back to the way it was!"

The man looks sadly down at his daughter's serious face, deciding that—just this once—he should lie to her, to keep up her spirits. "Yeah, baby," he says, putting an arm around her thin shoulders. "Things'll get better again. They've got to. Pretty soon, somebody will throw a switch downtown, and we'll have water and electricity and gasoline and police protection, again. I mean, this city might never have been paradise or utopia, but things were definitely different a few years ago, and they're going to be like that again, you wait and see."

"Tell me about it, Dad," says Marcia. "But not about a few years ago. I mean, tell me what the city was like when you were ohh, . . . 12, like I am now."

The man notices that one or two of the bundled figures at the end of the street have, in their turn, noticed him and his daughter and appear from their body language to be holding a conversation about them. "Later, sweetheart," he says. "Let's get where we're going first, and get home again. Then tonight, when you go to bed, instead of a story, I'll tell you some of the stuff I remember about how things were when I was a 12-year-old, like you are now."

"But Dad . . ." persists the serious young girl.

"Marcia, please! No more questions now. There's the cybrary, at the end of the block. Let's get inside, and do what we came to do, and then tonight, after we're safe at home, we'll talk about the good old days."

"Promise?"

"Promise." He leads her quickly up a short but wide flight of broken marble stairs to a huge door whose original ornamental wooden facade has been sheeted over with three inches of what is probably titanium and steel alloy. His brisk knock creates a hollow, booming sound, causing one of the ragged figures down the street to detach itself from the others clumped around the fire and shamble slowly in their direction. Joseph Giannini eyes the man uneasily, his right hand slowly clenching the pistol in his coat pocket. Just in case, he tells himself. Just in case.

℘

Hearing the strident knocking, Nigel, huge and muscle-bound, serving, among other things, as door guard, swears softly, lumbers up out of the chair where he has been picking his teeth with a stiletto, and strides over to the cybrary's main door, armed to the teeth with a variety of offensive and defensive weapons. He sticks the stiletto in the waistband of his trousers, where it may be summoned in one fluid motion. One massive, gnarled finger rests lightly on the safety button of his electron-beam phaser-rifle, ready for anything. Warily, Nigel lifts the cast iron plate over the peephole recessed into the metal door, peers out into the street, and rumbles, "Yeah? What'dya want, then?" A skirl of cold wind comes shooting through the peephole and swirls around the cybrary's cavernous, dusty antechamber.

Outside, on the building's top step, stands a diminutive man dressed in a shabby overcoat and a hat several sizes too large for him, with someone even shorter—possibly a child—nestled under his arm. "Hi, there," the man says, "I was wondering . . . can you tell me if the cybrary is open today?"

Nigel looks from side to side, on guard against decoys and traps. He is aware that public buildings like this one have, all too frequently, been breached, entered, and sacked by organized gangs who were clever enough to send innocent-looking people—even children—to the door, asking help or directions. Nigel looks as far right and left as the peephole's limited field of vision lets him. He sees only the two seemingly harmless travelers, standing nervously outside the door, on the small platform that separates the top step of the marble staircase from the entryway. He checks the twin convex mirrors attached to the stone columns that flank the door. Clear. No—wait! One of the usual street trash is ambling over to listen. "All depends, mate," he responds, conversationally, satisfied that this isn't an ambush. 'Oo would you be, then? Identify yourselves!"

"Joseph Giannini," says the little man. "Citizen number 456-67-1293. Address: Block 14, tier 81, unit 33. Quadrant seven-dot-nine-one. And this is my daughter, Marcia. Serial number 566- ah, . . . what's the rest of your number, honey?"

The child pipes up, "566-91-9933. Same address as my Dad's."

"Right, then. State your business or clear off," growls Nigel, laconically.

"Business?" Giannini's voice shows his impatience. "Well, Duh-h-h! I already told you. We want to come in and use the cybrary, what'd you think?"

" 'Ark at im', will ya!" Nigel says to no one in particular. Then he focuses his small, angry eyes downward through the peephole at Giannini. "You listen oop, mate, and mark me well! That's no bloody way to talk to me, the only bloke standin' betwixt you an' snoofin' it just where ye stand, with your child lookin' on. Now, I'm warnin' ye to keep a civil toongue in yer 'ead, if ye know what's good fer ye. Ye want to mind yer manners with me, mate, or I'll coom out there and teach ye soom, soon enoof!"

"Sorry," mumbles Giannini, without conviction. "Let me start over. I'm Joe Giannini and this is my daughter, Marcia. We came here to use the cybrary today, sir, and we'd like to come in, if you please."

Nigel takes a moment to analyze the other man's tone for affront or sarcasm. "Right!" he concedes at last. "That's better, then. Wait 'ere."

The peephole closes. For 30 seconds, nothing happens. "Moron!" the small man mutters quietly as an aside to his daughter Marcia. "Where do they find these people?" She smiles conspiratorially up at him. Giannini takes the time they must wait for a good look around him while the unseen guard is, he assumes, announcing him to whomever is in charge inside. He turns his head and surveys the street in all directions. Not very inspiring a prospect, to say the least, looking toward what used to be a tree-lined park from the cybrary's massive but crumbling stone entryway. What was once a bustling downtown hub of activity is now a slum—dark, dangerous, and depressing. Trash and garbage line the streets, abandoned cars strew the driving lanes, and roving individuals and bands of homeless loiterers trudge along, occasionally taking an interest in Giannini and his daughter. Not a great place to be caught out of doors. "Come on, come on!" Giannini snarls impatiently at the unseen cretin behind the massive door. He knocks loudly once more. "What's the holdup, here? Let us in, all right? We're gonna get mugged if we don't freeze to death first!"

At the foot of the stairs, a bundled, shabby man wearing rags around his hands and ears, finally decides to trudge up to them painfully and croaks "Hey, buddy. Whatddaya say? Can you spare . . ."

Giannini's hand tightens convulsively on the small weapon in his coat pocket, but they are spared the man's wheedling or any possible confrontation as the massive door swings open and the equally massive security guard (or whomever he is) stands peering down at them, an electron rifle cradled in his huge, hairy hand. First, however, the guard addresses the panhandler. "Take off, scoombag, or you're a grease spot on the pavement!" The bum needs no second invitation, quickly scuttles back down the stairs, and hobbles back to his companions around the smoky fire. Looking down at the man and small girl, then, the giant softens his tone, but only a little. "Yeah, right then, Mister Giannini. I told the cybrarian that ye're oot 'ere. An' ee said, if y've the price of admission, I'm to let you coom in."

Giannini, walking across the threshold, his arm around Marcia's small shoulders, thinks it prudent to try to make amends. "Listen, I'm sorry," he says to the giant. "About my tone, I mean. Please forgive me. I'm just on edge, and worried about the kid, here. Mean streets out there, y'know? No offense meant."

"Well, now we're sorted out, noone taken. An' ye called me sir! That's mooch better, then. Welcome, but no more of yer cheek, mate, if ye want to stay. Me name's Nigel—or sir—that'll do loovely."

"Yeah, okay. Sir," mutters Giannini.

"Sir, is it? I like the sound of that. Oh, it's a crime and a shame, the names soom folk 'ave visited upon your 'oomble an' sooferin' servant, I'll tell ye that, mate! Won't stand for it, not no more! A man's got to 'ave respect, or what is he, eh? Anyway, I'm important—the first bloke ye moost deal with, if ye want to make use of the cybrary's facilities an' services, sooch as they are, nowadays." Nigel now looks closely at the young girl, still shivering from her long exposure to the winter wind, and his attitude softens. He even smiles a gap-toothed smile down at Marcia, who returns it, shyly. "Loovely child," he comments, taking in Marcia's clean, long, red-brown hair. "Right, then; Mr. Giannini, eh? You and the yoong miss—aah, what's your name, again, loov?"

"Marcia," she says.

"Marcia, it is! Right! Introductions made all 'roond, then. Well, Marcia, tell your Ooncle Nigel: you an' yer Da braved the dark streets and popped 'roond today because yer wantin' to use the cyb'ry for a bit, 'ave I got all that right?" Marcia, smiling, only nods her head, looking around her. "Good. First things first. Got the price of admission, then?" continues Nigel, turning to Giannini.

Giannini holds up a wad of notes. "How much?" he asks, remembering not very long ago when trips to the cybrary were free and cash money was unnecessary because electronic funds transfer covered everything a person could want to buy.

"Cooms to two 'oondred credits apiece, makin' four for both."

Sighing, Giannini counts off 400 credits in wrinkled small bills and stuffs them into Nigel's huge hand, replacing his remaining money in a jacket pocket. "That's a lot of money," he observes.

"Aye, a lot of mooney, right enoof, but then, we're, like, the only game in town, aren't we?" The big man roars with laughter; his suspicious eyes having now lost their glare. "Well, don't bother makin' yerselves at home in this lobby, then. Let's go meet the cybrarian."

"Aren't you the cybrarian?" asks Marcia, curiously.

"Me? No, I guess y'could say I mind the place 'an do what needs doing. So, you both coom through the cold an' dangerous streets to use the cyb'ry, 'ave ye? Well, Mr. Giannini, I would joodge that you're either a very loovin' father, or a rash an' reckless man. Or both, p'r'aps. Then again, y' might be daft or stupid; I suppose those are possibilities, as well."

Giannini has had about enough of this rude oaf's gruff speculation and is about to open his mouth to demand that they get on with it, when Nigel crooks his finger at them. "Right, then. All paid oop, that's settled. But now I've one more duty to perform, so be so kind as to step over 'ere, both, for I've me security chore now." He takes Giannini's and Marcia's overcoats and hangs them on hooks. He then efficiently runs his hands over Giannini's clothing, finding the hand weapon, and holding it up. "What's this, then? A goon? Oh, no! Noone of that, mate. Won't be needin' that, in 'ere," he comments. Satisfied at last, Nigel lays the pistol on a table and leads the Gianninis further into the vast, half-empty building, where interior temperatures are not much more comfortable than those outside, but at least there is shelter from the wind. "Right this way," says the giant, as they walk down a short, dark hallway into another large room, lined with stacks and piles of books. In the center of the room, seated at a cramped writing desk and wearing a cracked green eyeshade sits Frank Fairlawn, directly under a chandelier consisting of a ring of flickering candles.

"Welcome, friends," says Fairlawn, with what seems a genuine smile, as he rises and comes around his desk to greet them with hand-shakes. "Thank you, Nigel," he says, dismissing the guard and, turning back to them, he beams. "A genuine pleasure to have visitors on a dreary afternoon! Frank Fairlawn, city cybrarian, at your service. Sorry for any difficulties at the door just now, and any indignities Nigel may have visited upon your person, but . . . well, " he gestures vaguely. "One can't be too careful, these days, you understand. Nigel has a job to do and that is to be . . . how shall I say this? . . . ahhh, . . . vigilant and . . . selective in whom he lets in here. I think you'll agree, he does his job rather well. A first-class frightener, that Nigel, eh?"

"Looks like it to me," Giannini says, and then introduces himself and Marcia, who, remembering her manners, chirps, "Charmed," sweetly.

"A well-brought-up young lady, I daresay," Fairlawn observes, approvingly. "By way of introduction, I'm a local product, while Nigel grew up a brawling Lancashire lad and emigrated here only shortly before the Great Troubles. But fate has thrown us together in this cybrary, it seems, in this ruin of an inner city. But with this distinction: Nigel gets out and about every day or so, running errands, to the grocery, or the distillery, or wherever, but I hardly ever leave this place. But that's as it should be, you see. Nigel's well-equipped for life on the streets, as you can imagine, while I prefer the unsurprising but safe life inside these walls."

Fairlawn sighs and shakes his head, as if to clear it. "Yes, well . . . That's neither here nor there, is it? Now you, sir, and young Marcia obviously have risked a good deal to venture outside and to this cybrary today; don't imagine that I don't appreciate that. I wish I could offer you both a hot beverage, but alas, the last of our coffee ran out months ago, and I've used my remaining teabags so many times by now that they make an embarrassingly weak brew. Perhaps I could find you a bottle of warm ale, though, if you've an interest, sir. Nigel is addicted to stout; he always manages to bring some home and swills it down by the case, even though the last pub in the area closed months ago. Still, he manages to come home with a case, more often than not. I never ask him where he gets it, or how. But every time he ventures out to do our shopping, he returns with a case of Guinness on his broad back in addition to the groceries and other items in his arms. But I digress. Let's get down to business, shall we? As you can see, this cybrary is only a remnant of what it once was. Only a shadow of its former self, in all truthfulness. Still, even in these straitened circumstances, I take my job as cybrarian here in this ruin of a building fully as seriously as I did in the old days before the troubles, and I mean to serve you both as best I can. Besides, after all you risked to come here today, it behooves me to do what I can to justify your labors and efforts. Now, how may I serve you?"

"Well," says Giannini, "You know how things are. Ever since the schools closed and after the power went off a few months ago, my wife and I have attempted to give Marcia here a good education. But it's not an easy thing to equip a child for today's realities—and tomorrow's uncertainties—with the books and other tools of yesterday. So we've come to use your computers, if we can."

"Ah yes, our computer," Fairlawn interjects. "Note the singular: computer."

For a moment, Giannini just blinks at him, then he continues. "Yeah, whatever. The ironic thing is that we have a computer at home, but without electrical current, and without batteries, of course, it's just a big heavy paperweight and dust-collector, nowadays. So while I have a pretty good collection of texts and reference books to use as teaching aids for Marcia, I understand you not only have computers here, but you have a way to make them work. And that's why we're here—what I want Marcia to get a chance to do—spend some time on a computer, like I did when I was her age. Can you help us?"

Fairlawn sighs again, thoughtfully. "The answer is yes . . . and, sadly, no. Let me explain. First, the good news. Yes, we have a computer here—only one is still functional—and our patrons—such persons who are rash enough to venture out into the streets and can afford to gain admission to this building—may use it. The bad news, however, is that we have no continuous electrical power just like the rest of the city, and, for all I know, the rest of the country, and maybe the world."

"Awww, no!" moans Giannini, sagging into a chair. "Say it isn't so! I mean, we risked our lives to get over here to use your computer and now you tell me that we can't because there's no electricity?"

"Correction. I didn't say you couldn't use it. I said we had no continuous electrical power."

"Oh. Then . . . what? Battery operation?"

"No, alas. Or not in the sense that you mean it. Oh, we have batteries. A whole storeroom full, as a matter of fact. Without electrical power, however, alas, we have no means of recharging those batteries."

Giannini thinks this over and shakes his head. "Sorry. I still don't understand."

"Perhaps a demonstration, then." Fairlawn looks past them and calls down the hallway, "Oh, Nigel!"

The massive guard lumbers slowly down the corridor towards them and lurches into view. He glares balefully at Fairlawn, but somehow manages to sneak a brief, friendly wink at Marcia, who giggles. "Yeah, what's oop, then, Frank, old slave-driver as thou art?" he snarls. "I was just about to 'ave a lie down when you soommoned."

"Sorry, Nigel," says Fairlawn, grinning up affectionately into the man's battered and scarred face, "but there's work to be done. This sweet girl would like to use the computer. Do you think you can help her achieve that goal?"

Nigel holds his tattooed, beefy arms out in front of him as if to ward off a blow. "Awww, no, Frank! I mean, does it 'ave to be today? Since that poonch-oop I 'ad the other day in the car park, me shoulder's been, like, playing oop again. 'Member what the doctor said it is? Soospected bursitis or some bloody thing. 'Urts like bloody 'ell, I can tell ye, 'specially these cold, 'umid days, doesn't it? So don't ask me. Not that. Joost not oop to that sort of thing, today. I was 'opin for a few days on light duties, actually. Make me apologies an' ask these good folks to coom back tomorrow. I'll feel better, tomorrow, no worries."

Fairlawn smiles indulgently up at him. "Sorry, Nigel. These good folks are here now and can't be expected to leave without achieving their quest. I'm afraid it must be today," he responds, waggling his eyebrows expressively. "Now, in fact."

A muttered expletive. Then Nigel looks apologetically down at Marcia. "Sorry, loove! Excuse me French." Then he sighs, capitulating. "Right, then, noothin' for it but to coomply. Mustn't lose me position,

after all. No hope of goin' on the dole, as there is noone, any more."
Wearily, the giant walks over to a console in the corner, takes the protective cover off the monitor and CPU of a scuffed generation-6 turn-of-the-century computer, seats himself nearby on a stool and grasps a pair of rubber-sheathed metal handles, which he slowly begins turning in rotation. The handles, Giannini can see, are attached to a bicycle-style chain drive, which disappears into a nearby socket on the wall.

"You may turn on the computer now, Miss Giannini," says Fairlawn, after a minute or so.

Grinning, Marcia seats herself before the monitor and toggles the ON switch. The groaning Nigel continues to turn the handles, and in a few moments, the screen lights up with its *welcome* display, pulsing slightly until it stabilizes after his cranking provides full electrical power. A row of fluorescent light fixtures in the ceiling begins, at the same time, to emit a faint glow, that grows brighter as Nigel's hand speed becomes constant.

Marcia hesitates, looking up into Fairlawn's face with a puzzled expression. "Mr. Fairlawn? Ahh . . ." she says. "How long does he have to keep that up?"

"Who, Nigel?" Fairlawn laughs. "Don't worry about it," he says. "Did you check out his arms? Nigel is immensely strong, and he will supply the power as long as you wish, or until you and your father run out of daylight, and need to return home, anyway. He could, in fact, do what he's doing all day and all night without stopping, if needed."

Grunting, Nigel gasps to Marcia, "You don't wanna believe everything you 'ear, loov! I'm 'uman, like everyone else."

Marcia stares at the sweating man, then turns back to Fairlawn. "But . . ." her voice trails off.

"Go ahead, Marcia. Out with it. But *what?*" demands Fairlawn.

"But why does he have to work so hard just so I can use the computer?"

"Aye, loovey," says Nigel, looking up from his labors. "Thanks for askin', an' well you might ask. Oother people's pleasure is a foonction of me 'ard work, an' that's the way of it. With no electrical power coomin' out of the wall, ye see, it's blokes like me what 'ave to supply it. In addition to providin' the full range of security duties in this place, an' shoppin' an' char work an' oother things I won't even mention. Soom things 'aven't changed, even though so mooch is different, these days. The workin' class is still exploited by their masters. That's the way of it, right enoogh."

"Ignore him, Marcia," says Fairlawn, motioning for Nigel to pick up the pace. "It's his job, you see, and despite his complaining, he's admirably suited to it, don't you think? Just look at those muscles! So I urge you to just enjoy your time on the computer, and don't fret about Nigel, over there. He just loves to complain. And I said before, he can keep that sort of thing up all day and all night, if he has to."

"I joost 'ate this bloody job," mutters Nigel, without looking up, turning the handles in a steady rhythm.

Reassured, the girl taps a few keys experimentally, and the computer begins to enter its word-processing program. "Does the printer work, too?" she asks Fairlawn, "I want to show my mother what I've done when I get home."

"Certainly. When you've finished creating your document, all you have to do is save it and point and click the box that says *Print*. Your printed document will come rolling out of the slot over there on your left."

Marcia never seems to run out of questions. "Don't you have any recharged batteries? And what about other sources of power?"

Fairlawn laughs merrily. "A bright girl you have there, Mr. Giannini. Oh, yes, Marcia, we've tried a number of alternative sources of power since the electricity failed. In the basement is a coal burning furnace, that we use to heat water for steam, but I couldn't figure out a way to convert steam heat to electrical power with the equipment on hand. And at various times, this city used hydroelectric power from the nearby river, but that project seems to have gone the way of all other public works in the last few years. And I've even investigated solar power, collected in panels on the rooftop, but as you'll notice, there's little sunshine, this time of year in these latitudes. And even in high summer, there's rarely enough sunshine to make the energy cells fill up, due to the increase in air pollution of recent years. And let's see . . . what else? Yes. Wind power. Wind can't be depended on, but I've set up a few windmills on the roof, to catch the stray breeze. Every little bit helps, I suppose. On breezy days, it's possible to store energy for later use, but today, well, no point in thinking about it, is there?"

"What about nuclear power?" the girl asks. "I read about it in one of Daddy's magazines."

"Ahh, yes! Nuclear power." Fairlawn takes off his glasses and wipes them on his stained tie before replacing them and continuing. "Nuclear power, when it first became a possibility in the last century, seemed like a good idea at the time. Actually, the government was going forward with nuclear energy programs until the central government ceased to exist. Now . . . well, let's all just hope that peaceful uses of energy can, in the future, be found, and with appropriate safeguards in place."

In the next few minutes, Marcia really gets involved in her computing, and time passes in companionable silence. At length, Nigel, who has been working up a good sweat at his labors, clears his throat noisily, and all eyes turn to him. "Yes, Nigel?" says Fairlawn.

"Well, Frank, beggin' your pardon, but it's aboot me break. I mean, I know I'm little more than a faithful beast of burden an' all, but me contract says I moost get a rest every now an' then, y'know."

Fairlawn scowls at him. "What? Break time, already?"

"Well, see, I 'ate to interroopt the young missy's time on the computer, but the rules say I'm entitled to a break of 10 minutes every hour durin' what ye might call me 'eavy liftin' duties, an' it's been an hour easy, by now, 'asn't it?"

"Yeah, I guess," Fairlawn sighs. "Marcia, I'm sorry but you'd best *Save* what you have accomplished, so far. Nigel's right. And rules are rules. See the *Save* key? It's the red one on the top row of the keyboard. Nigel's going to stop generating power for 10 minutes or so. Sorry, folks. I wish this cybrary could've afforded to buy me a robot assistant back when such things were on the market, but cybrary funding has never been robust, and the budget just couldn't tolerate such an expense, even in better times than these, so we make do with what we have. Nigel's a big, strong man, but he's only human and needs to rest sometimes." He looks at his assistant for a moment and adds, with a fond smile, "And I'll tell you something else about him: he's a terrible chess player."

Nigel lets out a rumbling laugh. "Me? Not a bit of it. Doon't listen to 'im, Miss Marcia! Frank cheats, is what. Give me lessons in chess when I coom 'ere, 'e did, an' joost when I began beatin' 'im regular, 'e started cheatin'."

Fairlawn grins again. "Very well, Nigel. You're off duty as of now. Ten minutes and no more, mind." He reaches across his desk and turns a small hourglass over to allow it to dribble sand from one chamber to the other. Since the power went off in the city, and battery-operated machines failed, hourglasses are the only reliable way to tell time. There's a sundial in the cybrary's courtyard, out back, of course, but in the absence of sunshine, it's useless. Besides, it's risky to venture out back. During daylight hours, the courtyard is full of people Frank doesn't wish to associate with, and at night . . . well, he doesn't even want to think about that. A year or so ago, the courtyard was sometimes filled with snarling, barking dogs, but now the dogs seem to have disappeared, for the most part. Eaten, probably, Fairlawn figures. Funny thing, not long ago the thought of eating dog meat would've turned his stomach. But everything's changed, now. Now, whenever Nigel brings a puppy back with him, well . . . he sighs again.

Nigel rises from his seat at the generator, shaking his arms and stretching, then begins shadowboxing around the room. Deprived of power, the computer falters and grows silent, while the light level in the room grows dim as the fluorescent lighting weakens gradually and finally winks out. Candlepower once again is the sole illumination. Nigel walks down the hall to the front door, lifts the peephole's flap and peers outside.

"What d'ya see, Nigel?" calls Frank.

"Nowt. Noothin' I 'aven't seen every day since I coom here to work, that is," the muscular man growls, letting the flap slam shut. "Same bloody thing day after day. Enoogh to drive a man daft!"

Marcia glances around the huge room curiously. "Even without electricity, there's lots of good stuff here," she says. "Look at all the books!"

"True," Fairlawn replies. "Lots of books still on the shelves, and mostly in wonderful condition, too, because few readers come in here anymore to borrow them. Risky and difficult to come in here, as you well know, and only the strong or foolish or desperate ones still try. Like yourselves. Now don't misunderstand me. I'm delighted that you came here today. Not only is it lovely to have someone other than Nigel to talk to, but visitors like yourselves make me feel—if only for a little while—like I'm actually doing my job, the one I was hired to perform, before everything fell apart and I became trapped in here, that is, a prisoner of my timidity and the dog-eat-dog jungle of the streets. I haven't been outside this building in over a year!" Giannini and Marcia look at him, sharing a single thought: living a whole year without seeing the sky or a bird or a tree.

Fairlawn brightens. "But not to worry. Mustn't grumble. I get about rather well, considering, and I've Nigel here to assist me, if I need anything. So no pity, thank you very much. My life is—all things considered — full and enriched. Of all the people left in this dark and dangerous city, I am perhaps the only one whose days and nights are spent surrounded by books by the thousands. If you don't count Nigel, that is. He lives here, too, but he's not the sort to spend his time with his nose in a book."

Marcia thinks of another question to ask. "Mr. Fairlawn, you said you haven't been out of here in a year. Do you have that much food in this place?"

"Aha! You've just identified another good and sufficient reason for keeping Nigel on the payroll. In addition to being my chief of security and my power source when called for, he shops for me, when there's a need for replenishment of the pantry. He even cooks, if you care to call it cooking. Yes, he's a handy man to have around. Few would dream of challenging a man of Nigel's size, armaments and demeanor, and he passes through the streets between this cybrary and the shops, both well-armed and usually unmolested."

"But there are hundreds of homeless people out there," says Giannini. "Hasn't anyone ever bothered Nigel on his trips out of the building?"

"Oh, aye. Soom've tried," Nigel says, returning to the big room and seating himself behind the handles of the generator once again. He grins wolfishly. "But such as 'ave won't be no further bother to oos or yourselves no more." Without being asked, he bends to his work.

Giannini peers through a barred, grimy window facing the alley, aware of time passing. "Mr. Fairlawn, do you have any idea what time it is? My watch stopped and I can't afford to buy a new one."

Fairlawn strolls over to a six-foot spindle-shaped device on a wooden framework. "Approximately, I do, yes. The hourglass I use for Nigel's breaks runs 10 minutes. But this other, bigger, hourglass runs for 12 full hours. Every morning, and every evening, when he remembers, Nigel turns it over. So even without the sundial, I still usually have a good idea of the time—plus or minus 15 minutes, anyway." He studies the huge hourglass. "And since you ask, I'd say it's getting along towards 4 p.m. just now."

"That late? And sunset is when?"

"Today? Let's see. Fairlawn consults a dusty book on his desk. Marcia can see that its cover says *Almanac.* "November 22nd . . . November 22nd . . . Ah . . . here it is. Sunset for these latitudes is set for 4:36 today."

"Oh, no!" says Giannini. Come on, honey. We've gotta leave right now." Marcia groans in protest. "You heard the man: it's about 4 o'clock now. That doesn't give us much time if we're going to get home before dusk. Listen, Mr. Fairlawn, we'd better get on home while it's still daylight, but can we come next week, same time, without having to pay again?"

"Certainly!" the smiling Cybrarian agrees. "I'd be delighted to see you both again, and we'll consider today's entry fee as covering the next time as well. But . . . quid pro quo, if you take my meaning. So if you could see your way clear to bringing us a few cans of food, perhaps?"

"We have some soup at home," says Giannini. "How about some of that?"

"Perfect! Soup would be lovely. Even better than money, in fact. Now Nigel's told me that you arrived armed. That's good. But tell me, Mr. Giannini, have you ever killed anyone?"

"Uhh . . . No. I haven't, actually."

"D'you think you could? No point in the pistol, otherwise."

"I don't know. I guess so, if I had to. If I had no choice."

"Best think about it. A weapon is no use to you if you're afraid to use it when you and your charming daughter take to the streets. Some of the people are pretty desperate out there. They'd kill you for the coat you wear or the wallet full of credits you carry."

"I know. But killing . . . I can't just . . . killing is still wrong, isn't it? I guess I just hate guns and always have."

Fairlawn smiles a little sadly. "Well, it's not my place to moralize with you. All I can say is that I wish you the very best of luck, then." He turns to the young girl. "Saved your program to disk, have you, Marcia?"

"Sure did," she says. Uh . . . do you think I could take home a couple of books with me, and bring them back next time?"

"Certainly, you may. By all means. That's another thing that libraries are still good for, you know. Make your selections, then. Still a place for reading in this world. "

Marcia retrieves her working disk from the computer's slot, then walks to the shelves on the wall, chooses a pair of dusty volumes, and returns with them to the desk where her father and Fairlawn wait.

"Finished, Dad. Ready to go?"

"In a minute, honey. Why don't you go look at the books some more?" He turns back to Fairlawn and says softly, "Ahh, I wonder if you and I might speak alone."

"All right. Nigel, would you mind taking Marcia on a tour of the building while I converse with Mr. Giannini?" He notes Giannini's expression and reassures him. "Don't worry. Nigel's tough with intruders and criminals, but he's gentle as a lamb with children, I assure you."

"Right, then," says Nigel. "I'd be delighted. Coom on, little miss, an' I'll show ye aroond the place."

As they leave, talking animatedly, Fairlawn beckons for Giannini to follow him as he walks slowly away from his desk. When the two men are alone in a side storeroom, Fairlawn looks curiously at him. "Yes, sir?" he asks. "How may I serve you further?"

Giannini hesitates, then decides just to say what's on his mind. "Well, Marcia really loves it here, but . . . well, with no more paid work, my supply of credits is dwindling lower all the time. And while I understand why I have to pay your admission price, I was wondering whether you'd accept payment in some other form than money."

"Oh? You have my attention, sir. Like what?"

"Oh . . . like those canned soups we were just talking about. Sirloin burger, for example. I can bring you some of that."

"Sirloin . . . ?" Fairlawn's face lights up in dreamlike anticipation. "You're saying that you have enough tins of soup in your possession that you would be willing to exchange some of them for library visits?" Fairlawn's mouth begins to water at the thought. Pavlovian response, he thinks; he hasn't tasted hot sirloin burger or chicken noodle soup in months! Nigel does the shopping and all he usually brings home is tins of beef stew and Spaghetti-os and the like. His favorites, but certainly not Frank's.

Giannini senses an advantage. "Yeah, I've got . . . let's say . . . a pretty good supply of canned soups in the house. And I'm willing to use some of them as the price of admission so Marcia can use the computer when she wants. So what do you think would be the soup equivalent of your fee?"

"Oh, well, I don't know. Barter system, eh? Why not? We each have something to trade. Now I want to be fair about this, you understand. Fair to you and Marcia on the one hand, and to me and Nigel as well. Tell you what: why don't we establish a fair market price of two cans per visit for Marcia, and no charge for you, when you accompany her when she comes here, hmmm? How does that strike you."

"Hmm," says Giannini glumly, wondering how he's going to provide for his family when his remaining supply—15 or so cases of soup of various types—is gone. Still, two cans per visit is less than he'd feared he'd be asked for. "Sounds fair enough to me."

"Good." Fairlawn smiles and holds out his hand. "Deal! By the way, I'm just curious: what other flavors and varieties do you have in stock?"

Giannini thinks for a moment. "Oh, well . . . let's see . . . I've got chicken noodle, alphabet soup—that's Marcia's favorite—and there's cream of mushroom, cream of tomato, split pea, shrimp bisque, beef barley, and the sirloin burger we discussed."

His words create a riot of anticipation in Fairlawn's brain. "Sirloin burger! Shrimp bisque! Stop, please, you're torturing me! Enough! So it's settled, then," he exclaims. "It's a deal: two cans of soup each time you bring Marcia here—the choice of flavors I'll leave to you. Why don't we make an appointment for next Wednesday afternoon, then, and I'll be expecting you? Only next time, please try to come earlier in the day, if you can. It'll give Marcia more computer time and afford the two of us time for a long, leisurely chat on a variety of topics. I'm starved for intellectual conversation that Nigel—the lovable great ape—just cannot provide. Also, that way, you can stay longer without worrying about nightfall and what it brings. And if you can locate any of that sirloin burger and bring it round with you next time, it'd be much appreciated. Always loved that soup!

"You got it!" says Giannini. They rejoin the others. He and Marcia struggle into their coats, and he retrieves his pistol and hides it in the right-hand coat pocket. "We'll be back next Wednesday, soup in hand. I really want the kid, here, to have the benefits of a computer. And I, too, enjoy talking to an educated man once in a while. Most of the people in my building complex are working stiffs without much in the way of higher education."

"The feeling is mutual. Ahh . . . Mr. Giannini, before you go . . . I'd like your opinion on something," says Fairlawn, softly.

"My opinion? What?"

"Um . . . well, see, . . . you get outside frequently, and I don't. So tell me: do you think things will ever be the way they were before? I mean, with free streets, sanitation, other government services, police and law enforcement, electricity, jobs, public safety, and so forth?"

Giannini thinks the question over. Finally, he speaks, careful to keep his voice low, so his daughter won't hear his words. "Funny you should ask. Marcia asked me the same thing earlier today, in fact. And I lied to her, which I almost never do. But . . . now, I'm no prophet, but I have a feeling about the future. You want the truth, right?"

"Right. The truth."

"Well, from what I've lived through—what I see now—the answer is no. Everything that's changed isn't going to change back, either suddenly or gradually. But we can all hope, I guess. After all, there's still this cybrary, a civilizing institution amid all this bleakness." He gestures around him at shelves of books stretching up to the dimly-lit ceiling. "That gives me a reason for hope, if not optimism. I've always been a bookworm, I guess. I've always believed that cybraries will get one through times of no money better than money will get one through times of no cybraries. That's why Marcia and I risked our lives and our safety to come here today, and why we'll come back next week, and the week after that, as long as you're still here, and the soup holds out. And I figure, if enough people feel the way I do, then eventually . . . maybe, one day . . ." he suddenly deflates and stops talking, feeling that he's about to start crying and not wanting his daughter to see it.

"Well, all we can do is keep our chins up and hope," Fairlawn says briskly. "So goodbye for now. Thanks for your visit, and I look forward to seeing you both again next week." He raises his voice. "Nigel! Our guests are ready to depart now," he calls to the huge guard, who is giving a delighted Marcia a piggyback ride around the front hall.

Nigel gently puts the girl back down on the linoleum. "Aw, time for goodbyes, already, is it?" he smiles, gap-toothed. "Me an' the yoong lady was joost 'avin a loovely time, wasn't we, missy?"

"Yes, oh yes!" Marcia agrees. "Thanks for the ride Nigel. I'd love another one next week when I come back to use the computer."

"Aye, there's that, isn't there? Soomthin' to look for'ard to, like. No worries, Miss Marcia; your trusty steed will be 'ere, then, waitin' for ye." He peers out through the peephole in the metal door. "But the darkness approaches now, and you and your Dad best get home smartly," says Nigel, unbarring the door, stepping outside, phaser cradled in the crook of his arm, and taking a good look around. "Right," he says when he returns. "Coast seems clear. Until next time, then. Cheers! And mind the streets on your way 'ome!"

"We will," says Giannini. "Come on, honey." They step through the iron door, and Nigel is about to close it behind them when suddenly a voice bids them to wait a moment. "Friends?" Fairlawn has rushed to the door and is calling out to them. "Almost forgot. I've just remembered what day tomorrow is. An American tradition, one not to be forgotten, even if perhaps we have less to be thankful for than once might have been the case. So may I be the first to wish you both a safe passage home, and very happy Thanksgiving Day!"

Giannini blinks at him. "Tomorrow? Thanksgiving?" he repeats, standing on the cybrary's broken top step, letting his mind echo back to other days—days of central heating, televised football, turkey dinners with all the trimmings, and maybe a brisk walk outside afterwards with his wife, through comparatively safe streets. Sadness fills him, but he recovers and says, "You, too! Both of you." Quickly, he turns and scurries away, beckoning for Marcia to follow.

" 'Bye, Nigel. See you next week! 'Bye, Mr. Fairlawn!" Marcia calls over her shoulder, following her father into the gathering twilight.

"Mind out, both!" the huge man cautions. "Plenty of bad folk about on the streets, an' that! God bless!" Nigel slams the door, and as the Gianninis hurry away, they can hear the system of locks and bars being replaced on the inside. Then they are walking briskly, watchfully down the littered street and turning into the alley once again. "Come on, baby, let's get a move on," says Giannini, eying another group of derelicts—or is it the same group?—trying to warm their hands by holding them over a trash barrel's smoky fire. Tomorrow is Thanksgiving, Giannini thinks sadly. How could I have forgotten? No chance of a turkey dinner like the ones I used to know, maybe, but still, the day calls for something special. He wonders if there's a turkey noodle or two left in his dwindling supply of canned soups. Turkey noodle will be as good as it gets. Not be the kind of feast he grew up with and might wish for, but he figures he and his family are a lot better off than all those poor souls living out here on the street.

As quietly as they can, the two of them sneak down the cracked pavement in the waning dusk, making for the safety of home. Momentarily, Giannini thinks with regret about the massive, crumbling, once-proud public cybrary building and its imprisoned director. Then, urging Marcia to get a move on, he ducks out of the alley into the next street, his fingers curled protectively around the trigger of his weapon, wondering if—no, hoping—he'll have the guts to use it, if it comes to that.

> In London, the financier Jim Slater is supposed to have listed what he regards as his basic hyper-inflation survival kit: tinned sardines, a bicycle, a supply of South African gold coins, and a machine gun.
>
> —Alvin Toffler. *The Eco-Spasm Report.* 1973. ■

SCENARIO
6

IN THE BACK
OF MY
MIND

Infotech will be implanted in our bodies. A chip implanted somewhere in our bodies might serve as a combination credit card, passport, driver's license, personal diary, and you name it. . . . A chip inserted into our bodies might also give us extra mental power.

—Edward Cornish. "The Cyber Future: 92 Ways Our Lives Will Change by the Year 2025."—*The Futurist.* January-February 1996. (It's the "you name it" that makes me nervous.—Author)

Modern technology and the U.S. Constitution appear to be on a collision course. Supersensitive audiovisual devices, computer networks, genetic identification, electronic monitoring, and other soon-to-be available products and techniques offer a boon to criminal justice agencies. But these same innovations threaten our privacy. . . . Implants offer a whole new array of weapons in the battle to control crime. Convicted offenders could be sentenced to have electrode monitors implanted to keep them in their assigned territories, but beyond this, a subliminal message player might be implanted to give the probationer 24-hour-a-day anti-crime messages. Five-year birth control implants are already available for women; can it be very difficult to implant five-year behavior-control chemical capsules in public offenders? Why wait until a crime occurs? Why not implant control capsules in "predelinquents"—children with behavioral problems? Cruel and unusual punishment, or just efficient and effective crime prevention? . . . Organic nanocomputers may be implanted into the human brain, making possible a new crime: mindstalking. Unauthorized intrusion and seduction will reach directly into the victim's brain, making the stalker harder to evade and even more difficult to escape.

—Gene Stephens. "High-Tech Crime Fighting: The Threat to Civil Liberties." *The Futurist.* July-August 1990.

The above quotations are representative of present-day popular science writing, in which speculation about biotechnology extols the virtues of having every member of society plugged into the vast technological machine we call communication. This scenario (with apologies to Anthony Burgess, whose frequently nightmarish Clockwork Orange implanted the idea and the ethical dilemma concerning choice firmly in the author's brain a quarter century ago) deals with two aspects of what might happen if libraries and biotechnology were to merge in the not-too-distant future. The question before us is whether humankind would be better or worse off should it become a simple matter for individuals to undergo outpatient operations that plug them into a national or global library of stimuli, information, and where necessary or desirable, controls. Clearly, the jury is still out on the matter.

JULY 2019

Brian runs up the rippled expanse of burning white-yellow sand and makes it to the beach blanket before his feet catch fire. Dripping from his immersion in the Gulf, he towels himself off and then sits down on the blanket, applying another layer of sunscreen and waiting until he can catch his breath. Life is good, he thinks. No, life isn't just good: it's wonderful! Even though his mom isn't with him anymore, miraculously, his father has returned from prison. Just this week, in fact, his dad was granted his complete release (if you don't count the five years of probation) and is now free to resume his life. *Their* life!

The day Dad came home, they sat down in the living room of their small apartment, and Dad asked Brian, "What'd you like to do, Brian? We have a week or two before I have to report, and we can do anything we like."

And Brian said what he was thinking: "I've always wanted to go to DisneyWorld and the rest of those places. Could we go there?"

So they went and had a great time in Orlando, visiting every one of the theme parks and riding on all of the rides over several days' time. And now here they are, staying at a Gulf beach resort for a few days before they have to return home. Brian, who has just finished battling the waves as they crashed ashore on the beach, is now feeling slightly but pleasantly winded, lying on a beach blanket under the hot summer sun, watching lazy pelicans circle over water and shore, searching out their lunches.

That reminds him that it's time to eat. Brian is always hungry. He rummages in a basket and pulls out a couple of bananas that they bought in a convenience store this morning when they went for a walk after breakfast.

"Hey, Dad!" he shouts to his father, sitting in the low chair on the wet sand some distance away and staring out to sea, while covertly watching a pair of young girls in bikini swimsuits playing catch with a brightly colored beachball at the edge of the water. "Want a banana?"

"Banana? No, thanks, Brian. Maybe later." Dad returns to his thoughts, scanning the sea.

Brian is nine years old, and he and his Dad are taking this vacation before Dad begins his new government job. Brian is visiting the seashore for the first time ever in his life, and he finds it all extremely fascinating.

He looks at his father through shuttered eyes. Dad is sitting in a rusted metal and canvas strap beach chair, reading a newspaper, and wearing a baseball cap, brim down the back of his neck, like the kids do at school. He doesn't like what Dad did, of course, the thing that landed him in prison, but he's very glad to have him back, all the same. He licks his lips, tasting salt. Salty, he thinks. The water is real salty. That's when he thinks of a question. Just one of those questions that occurs to every-body from time to time. I wonder why the ocean is so salty, he thinks. Then Brian decides that he'll ask Dad his question. Dad was away for a couple of years, but Brian remembers that he was always really smart, and he just might know the answer to the question about the salt. "Dad?" he calls again.

"Huh? What d'ya want, Bri?" said his father, turning to him, show-ing a bit of red sunburn across his shoulderblades after three hours in the Florida sun.

Brian rubs his left forearm and sees small grains of dried salt sift slowly downward onto the bright blue blanket. "I wanna ask you some-thing."

"Go ahead," his father says, tersely, hoping this isn't going to be anything touchy or painful about Gail, his late wife, Brian's mother. He isn't ready to talk to the boy about that yet. It's going to be awhile before he can do that. "I'm listening."

"Yeah. Okay. Here's what I want to know. How come the seawater is so salty? I mean, this big wave came up when I was out there, and I took in a mouthful of seawater, and you know what? It tastes like somebody poured a whole box of salt onto my tongue. Why is it like that, Dad? The lake at home doesn't taste salty. Where's the salt come from?"

Brian's father is relieved. Not only isn't this question about painful subjects, but he's ready with the answer. After all, the government has given Brian the same procedure he has had as part of his release deal. Why not encourage the boy to use what he has? They both might as well get used to it, anyway. "Why ask me?" says his father, pointing at Brian's head. "The world's best information system is stuck right there in your cranium, remember? So use it. Otherwise, you went through that whole operation for nothing."

"Oh, yeah. Right!" says Brian, rubbing the metallic spot where the neurotransmitter was implanted at the base of his skull three weeks ago, when he was first taken out of the foster home and told the great news that his dad would be returning home to take care of him. "I forgot." Even after three weeks, the incision still itched and even throbbed sometimes, but he supposes he'll get used to it. Once he grows enough hair in the surrounding area to cover it up from the prying eyes of his friends, at least. Another year, maybe, and nobody will notice it. Or maybe by then, all the kids will have them and it won't matter. Still, he's glad he had the operation—he's aware how much smarter the thing in his head is going to make him, once he fully understands how to use it.

Dad has one, too, of course—Dad's neck (when he's not wearing that long-billed cap down the back of his neck to conceal it) shows evidence of an incision in the same spot as Brian's—which gives them a new bond that goes beyond their blood relationship. Actually, they're famous: Father and son implants—the first time ever in the world. And the doctors keep telling him that the benefits are going to far outweigh the drawbacks—the headaches, the itching, and the swelling. Just you wait and see, Dr. Henrikson, the bearded old guy in the white lab coat, told him the first time they met and then every time he goes in for a checkup. Brian remains skeptical, but he's hoping for the best.

Over the past three weeks, everybody, in fact, has been telling Brian how lucky he is to have a 20,000-credit implant, free of charge, but sometimes he can't help wishing that he could just be the way he was before they stuck that thing in his neck and changed the way he thinks and works. Still, he knows he's lucky to have it—he's one of maybe five youngsters in the whole world who does.

Dr. Henrikson told him on his last post-operative visit before he and Dad went away that he was going to love the thing once he got used to it—and that all the other youngsters will soon envy him and wish they could have implants. And in a couple of years, everybody who can afford it will have the same procedure, the doctor said, and Brian has been guaranteed that he will get unlimited free upgrades to the latest implant capabilities for life. All because of whatever deal the government made with Dad that set him free. That experiment thing, which Brian doesn't really understand, except that it brought Dad back to him. After all, with his mother dead, a boy needs his dad.

The teasing he has suffered at the hands of the other boys in his neighborhood, however, has been pretty tough to take. He doesn't know just which of his so-called "friends" was the first to call him "Rivethead," but the name stuck, and now, whenever he can get away with it, he, too, wears a long-billed baseball cap down in back to hide the thing that makes him so different from the other boys he knows.

Brian thinks about his implant and the store of knowledge it's afforded him, trying to recall what he's supposed to do when he wants to find out stuff. But he can't remember. If that device is supposed to make him smarter, it hasn't started working yet. "Dad?" he asks.

"What is it this time?" His father, sunburned and scowling, doesn't take his eyes off the rolling combers coming ashore.

"Uh . . . I forgot what I'm supposed to say to get into the Cybrary program."

"Say? Don't you recall what you learned in your training? You don't have to say anything. No need for words. Just think it. Remember now? When you want to find out something factual, all you do is invoke the information system by imaging it in your mind, and then once you've done that, initialize the fact finder by closing your eyes and thinking the word *'cybrary'* three times."

"Oh, yeah. Right. I remember now. Okay, thanks, Dad."

"Good. And let me know what you find out about the salty water when you have the answer, hear?"

"Sure will." Brian lies back on the beach blanket, screwing his eyes tightly shut against the bright noontime sun, and images his cybrary fact finder. For a moment, nothing happens. He feels the heat of the summer sun, and listens to the shrill calls of seagulls as they bicker over something or other, and the deep, occasional boom of the big waves rolling up on the beach. Then he concentrates as hard as he can, images the system as he was taught, and thinks the words "Cybrary Cybrary Cybrary" with all the intensity he can muster, even saying them aloud for emphasis.

Instantly, a cheerful male voice emanates from nowhere and every-where inside his skull. *"Cybrary here,"* it says pleasantly.

"Ahh, hi," Brian thinks. "I'm Brian Schneider."

"I know who you are, Brian. Just tell me what you want."

"Ahh, yeah. Well, like, a couple minutes ago, I asked my dad why the ocean is salty? And he told me to ask . . . ahh . . . you . . . whatever you are. So why is it?"

"Right. Here's your answer: 'One of the most unique and intriguing aspects of ocean water is its salinity, or dissolved salt content. Salinity varies, somewhat, but there are approximately 35 parts salt per 1,000 parts seawater. Six elements constitute over 90 percent of total salts dissolved in the oceans. These are: chlorine, sodium, magnesium, sulfur, calcium, and potassium.' That answer your question, Brian?"

"Ah, no . . . not really. What I want to know is, how did all that salt get there in the first place?"

"Oh. Well, why didn't you say so?"

"I thought I did."

The voice seems to sigh. *"Well, we'll try again, all right? Salt enters ocean water as dissolved rock, mud, and sand bearing the elements mentioned earlier through erosion from the land. Eroded minerals and salts are swept downstream by river currents and torrents until they join the oceans of the world. Of course . . ."*

"Ah, yeah, thanks," interrupts Brian, closing his eyes, sorry he asked now, and seeking to prevent his having to listen to another long, boring lecture that he can only partly understand. The system in his head is annoyingly thorough; he's noticed that before. "That's enough."

"But there's more. Lots more in fact, Brian. If you'll let me continue, I'll explain . . ."

"Enough! I don't want anymore, okay?" Unconsciously, Brian makes a sharp chopping motion with his arm, causing a passing couple in bathing suits and floppy sunhats to stare at him in alarm.

"You've got a bad attitude, kid," says the reproving Cybrary voice. *"Oh, well . . . You're young yet. So: will there be anything else?"*

"No, that was . . . cool!" He thinks a moment. "Think fast: what's the capital of Missouri?"

"Jefferson City," Cybrary answers without hesitation, but Brian's not as happy as he might be. He doesn't know for sure whether the brain inside his head is right or wrong. Cybrary wouldn't lie to him, would it? He's got to think about that some more.

"OK, there *is* something else. It's . . . Ahhh, let's see. I have this homework assignment? It's for geography, which I don't like, but I had to take it this year. And I'm supposed to find out the latitude and longitude of some cities, you know?"

"Sorry. Can't help you, there."

"Can't help me? What're you talking about? You're the United States Cybrary, and they told me that you know everything. So why not? Help me. Isn't that what you're supposed to do? Help me, I mean? That's what Dr. Henrikson told me you would do, when he stuck this gizmo in my head. So help me."

"Say please!"

"Cybrary, you're working on my last nerve." That had been one of Brian's mother's favorite expressions, and it pops out of his mouth now. But he mentally regroups and continues with his interrogation of the new system in his head. "Now I don't have all the names of those cities here with me at the beach, but some of them I remember. The cities I need to know about are like, ahh, Tokyo, Nairobi, Vancouver, British Columbia, Dar es Salaam . . . That's not all of them, but it's most of them. Let's start with those. There's more, but that'll do for now."

"Brian, as I told you before, my capabilities include access to virtually all of the world's English-language databanks. And my memory banks are pro-grammed with virtually all known information and updated weekly with new facts. So did you imagine that I would have a hard time with a few longitudes and latitudes? Don't make me laugh. But there's a principle at stake here, as you know. Your teacher, Mrs. Goodrich, doesn't want you taking the easy way out, and you know it. She thinks it best if you perform your own research, and so, by the way, do I."

"Hey, back up a second. You said 'Don't make me laugh.' You can laugh?"

"In a manner of speaking, I can. Not laugh as in laugh out loud. Just as you don't have to speak out loud to contact me, so I have no need of a voice or other sound-producing capability. But I do have a strong and developing sense of irony and am capable of responding with the full range of emotions, including sarcasm, anger, scorn, submissiveness, understatement, and . . ."

"Okay, okay!" Brian thinks. "Look, I just want information, here. Hey, I'm just learning this stuff, so cut me some slack."

"*. . . And by the way,*" continues Cybrary, "*I just want to point out that you're still moving your lips when you're talking to me, Brian. That's permissible, perhaps, for beginners, but quite unnecessary. I don't have a real problem with it, but the principal benefit of being connected to Cybrary is that speaking your thoughts aloud becomes entirely unnecessary when we communicate. Now ask something within my protocols and rules, and I'll help you.*"

"Hey, don't get so mad, okay? But I asked you for some information. You don't feel like giving it to me, that's cool. But don't give me any more lectures. Tell you what: let's try something else. I remember something Dr. Henrikson said, and I want to give it a try. There are a lot of dead fish on the beach today, and they're really stinking up the place. I wonder, can you make smells? Inside my head, I mean, where only I can smell them. Something that'll cover up the smell of those dead fish would sure be nice!"

"*Smells? Ah, aromas! Essences. Fragrances. Scents. I got 'em all. Yes, indeed, I have a considerable library of aromas at my disposal. I'm happy to provide a demonstration for you. What'll it be?*"

"Oh, I don't know. What've you got?"

"*On my current menu, I have a wide choice of aromas: How about cedar chest, roast turkey, shampoo, eucalyptus, new car, rose, soap, or wood smoke? Then there's daffodil, lilac, leather jacket, cherry pie . . .*"

"Wait. I've got one. Can you do vanilla? I love that smell best of all, I guess. One time, my mom was going to bake a cake, I think, and she spilled some vanilla extract on the floor and the smell of it was . . . wonderful. And ever since, I mean, like when I smell vanilla, I remember my mom, and I feel kind of good and kind of sad at the same time. Dad doesn't like to talk about Mom, but I really miss her. So can you, like, make that vanilla smell in my head?"

"*Child's play,*" says Cybrary. "*But are you certain that an odor that brings back thoughts of your mother will make you feel better and not worse?*"

"Yeah, I'm sure. Let me have it, will you?"

"*You got it!*" says Cybrary. Instantly, Brian's mind is pleasantly bathed in the pervasive odor of pure, warm vanilla. Ahhh, he thinks, contentedly. That's really nice. He lies back, relaxes, and smiles. Then he sits up and calls to his father, a few feet further down the beach. "Hey, Dad?"

"Yeah, son."

"Can you smell that?"

"Smell what?" He sniffs deeply, then shakes his head. "All I smell is fish and the usual ocean smell. Whatever you're smelling, it must be something private that Cybrary cooked up for your personal pleasure."

Nodding slowly, Brian closes his eyes and inhales deeply of that comforting vanilla odor. Of course his father can't smell what he's smelling. The smell isn't really there. It's a sort of mental smell. All in his mind, but it seems awfully real. Dr. Henrikson explained it all to him, but he's not too sure he understood it all. But that smell . . . He's beginning to see some of the extra advantages of his implant now. Or no . . . not by the implant, but through the implant, somehow, connected to the Cybrary, whatever that is. It seems like he has his own personal librarian on call, and he never has to wait his turn to get answers. Dad has his own implant, of course. Brian has spent a good amount of time staring at the raw, red wound on the back of Dad's head. Wonder what he uses it for? Brian wonders. What he does with it?

"Hey," Brian thinks, experimentally, "You still there?"

"*Still here, all the time, every day,*" says Cybrary. "*Got no place else to go. As long as you've got a head, I'm with you. So what else can I do you for today?*"

Brian thinks about it. "I dunno," he thinks. "Good book, maybe,"

"*Sure. You're a reader. Good. I can see we're going to get along just fine. So tell me: what's your favorite type of story?*"

"Well, since we're at the seashore, how about a story about the high seas?"

"*Ever read* Moby Dick? "

"No."

"*How old are you, nine? Hmm. Melville may be a bit advanced for you, perhaps, but you're an intelligent kid. I think you'll get something out of it. Cracking good sea story, I can tell you that. Well, let's try it, and if you want me to stop, just say 'stop,' and I'll try you on something else. Here it is, then. Ready? 'Chapter One.' *"

Brian settles back into his beach towel and listens raptly as the voice in his head begins to intone the first words of the great novel. "'*Call me Ishmael . . .,*'" it says, in a clear, warm voice.

Sitting in his folding beach chair a few feet away, at the spot where the crashing surf comes ashore, Brian's father, Eddie, is also feeling pretty good about now. His enjoyment of the day at the beach is tinged with sorrow that his lovely wife isn't with them. She's dead. But he's out, and he's free, and he has another start on his life. Just a few weeks ago, he was in prison and looking at spending much—if not all—of the next 15 years behind bars for killing the man who killed his wife. Manslaughter and aggravated assault, the law called it, discounting at his trial the part about mitigating circumstances. And the punishment was prescribed. He killed a man, and for that he had to pay. He didn't even try to convince the jury of his innocence—after all, he was guilty as charged. Didn't even request an attorney. After all, he'd done the crime and guessed he deserved to do the time. An eye for an eye and all that.

But his subsequent imprisonment had left his son, Brian, an orphan, and that was the whole trouble. Brian, orphaned in one horrible moment, had become a ward of the state. His mother was dead. Nothing anyone could do about that. A collision with a speeding car does too much damage to a human body for anyone or any medical device to repair.

Eddie, his back to his son, now can't keep the memories from flowing into his troubled mind or tears from leaking out of his eyes. Might as well let 'em come, he figures. Better here than to sit up screaming in the middle of the night and scaring Brian (and the rest of the motel's sleepers). He tunes out the beach noises and closes his eyes to retain the sudden tears as he remembers vividly the events of that terrible night a year ago.

℘

To celebrate his recent promotion, Eddie and Gail had secured the services of a babysitter and planned a big night out on the town. Their elegant—and extravagant—dinner in one of the finest restaurants in the city was followed by a leisurely stroll hand-in-hand through the downtown streets. They were just crossing Grand Boulevard when the turbocar came out of nowhere, going much too fast, and driven by a drunken teenager. Before Eddie could even react, the car missed him by inches but hit Gail full on, smashing into her and throwing her 50 feet into a wall clear across the street where she crumpled like a rag doll. Eddie ran to Gail, but before he could even squat down and examine her, he could tell from the position of her broken bones that she was dead. Someone shouted "Quick! Call an Ambulance!" but Eddie knew that there was no need for anyone to hurry, and there'd be no need for an ambulance. All that would be needed that day was a hearse to carry away Gail's remains.

Eddie just stood there, stunned, for a full minute, unable to comprehend what had just happened, ending the life of the only woman he had ever loved and changing his own life in an instant. And then, amid the crowd of onlookers, he saw the young kid who'd been driving the car. Nervously, the kid sidled in Eddie's direction, chewing on his lower lip. "Hey, mister," he slurred drunkenly. "That lady all right? I mean, did I hurt her bad?"

The next few minutes were a blur, but Eddie has been told that, in front of at least 15 witnesses, he picked up a piece of discarded metal and bashed in the head of the young driver. And kept bashing it, until they pulled him off the corpse.

Eddie doesn't remember what happened after that. But the next thing he knew, he was in the city jail, being booked and fingerprinted. And then he remembers sitting in a courtroom, being arraigned, tried, and convicted for manslaughter and aggravated assault. Then it was a 15-year sentence to a medium-security prison upstate. And all that time, he remembers mourning his beloved, his Gail, and feeling tremendous concern for his poor son, Brian, who, he was told, was now a ward of the state and being cared for in a foster home.

Eddie just gave up, shambling around his prison environment like one of the walking dead and not really caring whether he lived or died, until that government man and the scientist, Dr. Henrikson, came to him with their deal. A deal that meant freedom in exchange for participating in their experiment. A new life with his son in exchange for submitting to what the scientist called "cerebral monitoring via an invasive procedure."

✇

Thanks to that deal and experiment, Eddie's out of prison and a free man, with the official papers to prove it. No parole; only minimal probation requirements, and no travel restrictions. He's considered fully rehabilitated: no longer a threat to society or to any individuals; they've seen to that. And his rehabilitation was amazingly easy: All he had to do was submit to the implant in the base of his skull. Just a simple little procedure, and he was no longer considered a menace to society or dangerous to anyone. The government even paid for everything and gave him a job and a living allowance. Best of all, it put him back in his own home with his son, where he could watch Brian grow up and be there when he was needed.

Yeah, all in all, it's a good time to be alive, he thinks, turning and looking at his son and smiling warmly. He reaches up absently and massages his itching incision, not entirely healed and covered by the baseball cap he wears whenever he goes out. Inside, he had little to live for. Now he's outside, and he intends to stay out.

✇

"Hey, mister?" The voice sounds young and girlish.

Eddie looks up, squinting in the bright sunlight. There before him is a young blonde girl in a string bikini. For a moment she looks like . . . But that's not possible. Gail is dead, and besides, even if she were alive, she'd be much older than this girl. No, this is someone else entirely. Hastily, he looks away.

"Mister? 'Scuse me?" she persists.

"What?" he growls. Then he softens. "Sorry, miss. Didn't mean to snarl at you. Forgive me. What can I do for you?"

"Do you know where there's a concession stand or something? My friend and I want to get a drink of something cold, but there's nothing around. No place that we can see, anyway."

Eddie looks at her companion, a darker, larger young female, and allows his eyes behind dark sunglasses to return to the blonde young girl. "Sorry. 'Fraid I can't help you. We're strangers here ourselves, me and the boy there." He points out Brian to the girl. Brian raises a hand in salute. The girl gives him a warm smile.

"Well, that's all right; thanks anyway." She turns to go. Eddie watches her walk away, scuffing in the wet sand on the beach, just above the tidemark. She bends down to examine a shell or something. Something about the way she peers at it . . . Eddie's eyes fill with tears. "Gail," he sighs, evoking the memory of his wife. "Oh, please, I can't stand it." His heart aches, and he closes his eyes once more, hoping his son won't see him crying.

Then a voice comes into his head, like a warm bath of good feelings. *"Don't worry, Eddie,"* it whispers. *"Everything is good, and it's getting better all the time. Be happy. Enjoy!"*

He unclenches his tensed muscles, feeling suddenly relaxed. For a moment, he can't quite remember what he was so recently feeling sad about. Then he reconstructs the image of Gail, young, blonde, and beautiful, as she was just before . . ."

"None of that, now, Eddie," says the comforting voice. *"Don't think of her now. Just put it all away. Be happy. Be at ease. Everything is good. Everything is going to get even better."*

By sheer force of will, one last time, he reconstructs the mental image of his dead wife. *"Naughty boy!"* says that voice in his head. Then it says something else, *"Poof!"* Eddie suddenly sees his image of Gail receding, as though it were a point of light moving away from him at a high rate of speed down a long, dark tunnel. When it reaches the size of an infinitesimal dot, it disappears, just winking out of existence.

Eddie shakes his head, trying to remember just what he was feeling sad about a moment ago. From within his skull somewhere, soft "new age" music plays. It helps soothe him. He can't even remember what was making him unhappy. Here he is, after all, warm and secure on this beach with Brian and with today and tomorrow to play and swim and see movies in the evenings, before they take his new car back home to his new job. I am complete, he thinks. I am happy. Life is good. My cup runneth over.

Cup. The word evokes in Eddie's mind a new image: a cardboard cup overflowing with ice-cold beer. Ah, yes, beer. Wouldn't that hit the spot! He turns around and calls to his son, sprawled on the blanket, "Hey, Bri!"

"Yeah, Dad," calls his son, without opening his eyes. The vanilla essence is gone from his mind now, and he has been drowsing peacefully in the heat of the summer day, listening to recorded music in his head. Brian had been told that his Cybrary would soon learn his likes and dislikes, and it's certainly chosen something agreeable for his listening pleasure now. His kind of music!

"What do you say we go find a cold drink?" his dad says. "Sound good?"

Brian licks his salty lips, visualizing a tingling, cold, carbonated beverage in a cup full of shaved ice. "Sure, Dad. Real good. Which way to the pop stand?"

Eddie looks up and down the beach and then looks back at Brian. "I think there was one near where we parked the car. Why don't we take a walk that way?"

"Cool!" says Brian, sticking his sandy feet into a pair of rubber flip-flops. "What're we waiting for?"

"Nothing," says Eddie, picking up his wallet and stuffing it into the waistband of his swimsuit. "Nothing at all."

They walk southward, past resort hotels and a few beach umbrellas, to a strip of sand where there are no people at all. Just when Eddie is about to think that he's made a mistake and they should have gone the other way, Brian exclaims, "Hey, Dad! Look! Isn't that a hot dog stand or something?"

Eddie squints, peering down the beach in the hot, hazy air. Sure enough, it looks like there's some kind of wooden structure straight ahead. They pick up the pace, seriously thirsty now. At 200 yards, they can see that it is indeed a hot dog stand, and they walk even faster.

"RED HOTS. COLD BEER. POPCORN. ICE CREAM" reads the peeling, rusty sign over the pull-down pass-through window. The unshaven, surly looking man inside the stand is sweating profusely and wearing a greasy, stained apron over a vest undershirt. An unlit cigar dangles from his pendulous lower lip.

"Hey," says Eddie, when they reach the stand. "How's it going?"

For an answer, the man only grunts softly.

"Beer for me, and a large Coke for the boy, please," says Eddie, figuring that this guy sure isn't much of a conversationalist, but that's all right.

Silently, the man produces a bottle of beer, a can of Coke, and a straw.

Eddie waits for the man to tell him how much he owes him, but no such announcement is forthcoming. So, after a long appreciative swig of his beer—which turns out not to be all that cold but tastes wonderful all the same—Eddie holds out a 20 credit bill, which the man takes in a large, dirty hand.

While waiting for his change, Eddie decides to attempt small talk. "Business kind of slow, today?" he asks.

No answer. Not even a grunt this time. The hot dog man has picked up what seems to be a racing form and appears busily involved in it. Well, if this guy's in a bad mood, that can't be helped, Eddie thinks. I'm too happy to be brought down by grouchy, sour people today. Eddie holds out his hand for his change. But the man inside the stand ignores both him and his hand.

"My change?" Eddie says at last.

"What change? Ain't no change," says the man, gruffly, without looking up.

"For one beer and one Coke?" Eddie reminds him. "Surely, that couldn't come to a total of more than four credits, even if you charged double what they charge down the beach. So please just give me my change, and we'll be on our way and leave you to your reading, all right?"

"You got a hearing problem or something, buddy?" said the man, belligerently, rising off his stool and glaring down at Eddie through the serving pass-through. Eddie can see that he is tall and strong looking. His bloodshot eyes make him look fierce and possibly demented. "Said there's no change!"

Eddie scowls at the big man, noting the out-thrust jaw and faded blue tattoos of a lower-class bully. He's met this kind before. In prison. Mean, surly men who hung around the weight room. While he hopes he won't have to get into an altercation with this guy, he's never backed down before and never will. "Sir, here's fair warning: I'm going to give you one last chance to give me my correct change, and then I'm going to come in there and take it," he says evenly.

The hot dog vendor's reply is a venomous glare and a series of filthy curses, the gist of which is that he thinks that Eddie is an unnatural and crawling vermin of dubious sexual orientation.

"Step out here and say that," Eddie says. A good slapping around is just what this cheating bully needs, and Eddie—a black belt in several forms of martial arts—is going to see that he gets it. In prison, only punks allow themselves to be backed down, and where necessary, fighting is the only way to decide things. And that type of fighting is rarely according to any sort of rules that the Marquis of Queensbury would endorse or sanction.

Brian, who has watched all the action with wide, fascinated eyes, yells "That's it, Dad! Knock his block off!" and watches as the hot dog man runs out of his stand's backdoor and plods around the front in Eddie's direction, a length of driftwood clenched in his fist.

Eddie is already in his favorite defense stance, feet wide apart, one hand down and the other circling behind his head like the head of a viper. But when the hot dog man swings the wooden club forcefully downward and Eddie deflects it with a forearm, it is now his turn to strike, and he feels immediately and unaccountably violently ill.

Reeling backwards, Eddie feels his stomach turn inside out, as he lurches out over the hot sand and, kneeling, vomits copiously on the hot sand. His antagonist blinks at this surprising development, and then shrugs, as he wades stolidly in to deliver a killing blow to Eddie's head.

But Brian rushes between then, shrieking up at the furious hot dog man. "Stop. Leave my Dad alone! He's sick, can't you see that? My dad's sick. You win, okay? Keep the money. But my dad's sick, and I've got to get him to where he can get some help. Won't you help me, please?"

The huge man stands there, oxlike, blinking in the sun. Then, with a foul expletive and a glance down at Eddie, still retching on the sand, he shrugs, drops the wooden club, and hoists Eddie up on his shoulder in a fireman's carry to carry him behind the hot dog stand into the meager shade afforded by the declining sun.

Ⓒ

A half hour later, Brian and his father walk slowly back to their beach blanket. Dad seems weakened from his recent bout of nausea but is otherwise unharmed. Brian now has some questions the voice in his head cannot answer.

"Dad?"

"Huh?"

"What happened back there?"

"Back there? What do you mean?"

"I mean, one minute you looked like you were going to clean that big guy's clock with all those neat kung-fu moves you put on, and the next minute, you were down on the sand hurling your guts out. So what happened?"

His father stops and turns out to sea for a moment. Then he looks down at him and replies.

"Well, Bri, I'm sure you've noticed that you and I have had the same operation."

"'Course I noticed."

"And didn't you think it was interesting that I was serving a 15-year minimum sentence for manslaughter one day and was coming home the next?"

"Yeah, but I'm glad it happened that way."

"Me, too. But nothing's free in this world, son. Might as well learn that lesson now. And for me to gain my freedom, I had to get this implant in my head."

"But that's good, not bad. Mine is, anyway. I just found out today that it'll tell me anything I want to know . . . and do lots of neat stuff, except maybe help me with homework . . . and it plays music I like to listen to . . . and any book I want to read, it just sort of reads it into my head. I mean, it is so cool! Don't you have stuff like that in your implant, too?"

"Yeah, I do. But I have extra stuff in mine, Brian. An extra function that yours doesn't have. See, under the Convicted Felons Release Law, everybody who's taken another human life—whatever the circumstances—if he wants to get out, has to submit to an implant that contains programming so that he can't ever do it again. That's why I got sick."

"You mean the reason you got sick was because you were starting to fight with that other man?"

"Yep. That's exactly what I mean. See, my implant is like yours; it's like having my own personal library in my head. And I like that. But the government that paid for all this—and yours, too—wants to see to it that the people they let out of prison—like me—would never be coming back and would never kill anyone else. So they gave my implant an ability or power to see to it that I remain nonviolent. And it's out of my control. I have no choice: If I fight, even in self-defense, I'm going to get sick. So I can't fight. Not as long as I'm wearing this thing in my head. We both just found that out, didn't we?

"But Dad! Think what could have happened! That big guy could've bashed your head in with that piece of wood, and you couldn't have done a thing about it. We're just really lucky that he took pity on you 'cause you were so sick."

"That's right. I'm defenseless. I can't defend myself, for any reason. That's the price I had to pay to get out of prison and back to you. I'm a peaceful guy, Brian, and the implant's job is to see to it that I stay that way. I guess it just goes to show you that freedom has its price, doesn't it?"

"Oh, Dad!" says Brian. This is all too much for him to think about. Then another idea hits him. "Is it like that with me, Dad? Does this thing in my head mean that I can't fight, too?"

"I don't know, Bri. Maybe. Probably not, though. You're not a convicted killer, like I am. But I made a deal with the government, and the best way to keep that agreement and to stay alive and well is, I guess, to stay out of fights. Also, besides the risk of getting beaten to death, I hate throwing up. A very unpleasant habit, and I want to avoid it if I can."

"But don't you miss the freedom to make your own decision whether to fight or not?"

"I guess so, but we've both seen that the best way for me to survive is to get along as best I can without fighting. That's what the state intended when they gave me an implant. And besides, look at the good side: We have all those advantages nobody else we know has. For example, think of the cybrary program you were using earlier. We both have 24-hour-a-day free cybrary services right inside our heads, without even having to ask for them. And to get them, all we have to do is think about what we want. Now you can't beat that for a good deal, right, son?"

"Right," agrees Brian, finally accepting what he cannot change, and probably wouldn't, even if he could.

☙

Later, Eddie and Brian sit side by side, sunburned but happy, on the beach blanket in the cool of the sunset, watching the red sun slide slowly downward into a grayish cloud bank just over the horizon. The sand has turned pink, and the raucous cries of seabirds have stilled. Small crabs,

Brian notices, are beginning to crawl out of the sand and explore the area around them, probably searching for their dinners. Then, without the hissing sound that Brian half expected, the sun slips first halfway and then all the way into the Gulf below the rim of the world, and the sky begins to darken at last. If only Mom could be here to share this with us, he thinks, but only in a wistful, abstract sort of way. For the first time, it doesn't really hurt that she's dead. He feels sad, but he can deal with it.

Brian has always been a curious boy, and a bunch of new questions now occur to him as he watches the western sky, lit up as it is with reds, yellows, and grays in the diminishing twilight. But he has learned a few tricks today and now remembers that his question will be answered by the Cybrary better and easier than it will by his dad. And besides, why bother Dad? He seems to be at peace for the first time since he's come home. Silently, Brian visualizes the cybrary system, and wordlessly, he thinks the command three times. Within a minute's time, he knows why the sun sets in the west, why it turns red and appears larger as it nears the horizon, and exactly—to the mile—how far it is away from Earth.

This implant is pretty neat, he figures. Now that I'm beginning to get the hang of it. And Dad seems to like his, too. At least, he doesn't look sad anymore.

Yes, he thinks. Life is good.

Eddie, sitting next to his son, feels true contentment that he didn't know he could ever experience again. Whatever it was that was bothering him earlier in the day, it's not there now. The only thing on his mind, in fact, that isn't part of his general and all-over feeling of contentment and optimism is the heat radiating from a rather painful pair of shoulder blades that he, foolishly, left too long in direct sunshine.

He suddenly loops an arm around his son's narrow shoulders and hugs him fiercely. Then, after depositing a big wet kiss on each cheek, he lets the giggling Brian go and hugs himself.

Brian reacts to his father's embrace with delighted surprise. "Hey!" he says, "What was all that about, Dad?"

"Just felt like it, Bri. It feels so good to be alive, I had to share the feeling with you."

Brian smiles and turns back to the dimming shoreline, where more small crabs now sidle stealthily out of unseen holes in the sand and begin moving back and forth up and down the beach in search of food.

Eddie goes into his head and visualizes his Cybrary system to test the capabilities of his implant. "Cybrary! Cybrary! Cybrary!" he thinks, concentrating.

"Cybrary here. That's a roger," says the voice in his head.

"Hey," he says. "What about music? Got any music you can play for me?"

"Music? Sure. Name it." says the voice, except it isn't really a voice . . . more like an awareness. *"Got pretty much everything."*

"Figured you'd say that. Well . . ." He looks around at the beach in the moonlight and at the first stars peeping out of the dark firmament. "A moment like this deserves something classical, I think. You wouldn't happen to have a Brahms's piano concerto, would you?"

"Got 'em all. Which one d'ya fancy?"

"Oh . . . I don't know the name or number. Can't remember, it's been so long. But the one I've always loved—it's got that middle part—the third movement—that starts out with a cello theme that always makes me shiver, it's so beautiful. You know: it goes, 'dummm-da-dee-dee-dum-da-dum-dum-dee-dee-dee-dee dum.' I know I'm no singer, but that's close enough to give you the idea. Always loved that piece. Know which one I mean?"

"Say no more," says the Cybrary voice in his head, *"got it!"* In seconds Eddie grins and nods in total contentment as a beautiful, haunting cello begins its stately progression, first alone and then over muted strings, until, after the theme has been stated, Brahms's soft, dreamlike piano embroiders its lovely strains into several beautiful variations.

Later, the moon goes down. Side by side in the gathering gloom of evening, the man and the boy sit in complete, companionable silence, until it is too dark to see anything but the phosphorescence of the waves coming ashore and the vast tapestry of stars wheeling millions and millions of miles overhead.

An hour later, as Eddie and Brian stand up, dust themselves off, and arm in arm, go back into their hotel to share a late dinner, Orion, Scorpio, and the Pleiades illuminate the deserted beach as the waves gently roll ashore from the west.

> *"Choice," rumbled a rich deep goloss. I viddied it belonged to the prison charlie. "He has no real choice, has he? Self-interest, fear of physical pain, drove him to that grotesque act of self-abasement. . . . He ceases to be a wrongdoer. He ceases also to be creature capable of moral choice."*
>
> *"The point is," this Minister of the Inferior was saying real gromky, "that it works."*
>
> —Anthony Burgess. *A Clockwork Orange.* 1962. ∎

SCENARIO
7

KEEPING
TRACK OF
PEOPLE

In the worst terrorist act ever on U.S. soil, the Federal Building in Oklahoma City, OK, was a target of a car bomb on April 19 (1995) that reduced the structure to rubble, killed 169 people, and left all of America stunned.

—The World Almanac. 1996.

The impression that people are always being watched—by police agents, store detectives peering through one-way mirrors, surveillance cameras, etc.—is one way to deter illegal actions. Any tempting illegal opportunity may really be a police trap, and anyone could be a police agent. In some companies, employees receive memos stating: "Systematic checkings are made of every employee; you never know what day or what hour you are being checked." . . . lasers, parabolic mikes, sub-miniature tape recorders, remote camera systems, videotapes, periscopic prisms, sensor and tracking devices, heat-sensing imaging devices that can tell if a house is occupied, voice analyzers, light-amplifying night vision devices, and techniques for reading mail without breaking the seal are among the new devices. . . . These new devices can send information to a central source, permitting a few persons to monitor a great many. Handheld voice-stress analyzers can detect deception in a person's voice. . . . Today's surveillance society can prod even deeper into physical, social and personal areas. It hears whispers and penetrates walls, windows, clouds, and darkness. The categorical monitoring associated with video cameras, metal detectors, . . . and the computer are creating a society in which everyone, not just a few suspects, is a target for surveillance.

—Gary T. Marx. "The Surveillance Society: The Threat of 1984-Style Techniques." *The Futurist.* June 1985.

There is no doubt in my mind that the twin evils of censorship and privacy invasion will still be around in the 21st century, even if many of us will no longer be.

JANUARY 2025

His communicator buzzes shortly after 10 o'clock, just as Frank is lighting off his third coffeestick of the frantic morning. "Yes?" he says, brusquely in the general direction of the ceiling. He hopes it's going to be a short interruption; he doesn't have time for anything prolonged or complicated this morning.

"Guy here to see you, Frank," says Sally, his secretary, whispering in an unaccustomarily conspiratorial voice.

120

"Guy? What guy?" Frank frowns; he thought he had the whole morning free to go over the monthly orders before the noontime budget luncheon with the mayor at city hall.

"Important-looking guy," Sally whispers. "Wearing one of those expensive power suits. Says he's here on government business. I think you're going to want to see him right now."

"Right." says Frank. "Tell him I'll be with him in a moment, will you, Sally? Then, after he's waited five minutes or so, show him in." Switching the communicator off, Frank says "Daily Calendar," and a hologram of his daily plan instantly forms just in front of his face. Sure enough: it shows a clear morning until noon. What's going on? Well, one way to find out. He toggles the switch again. "All right, Sally. No need to make him wait, I guess. Ask him to come on back now."

A moment later, he introduces himself to an aging, short, distin-guished-looking man who, as advertised, wears an expensive-looking black suit and a smug expression of great self-importance.

"Frank Fairlawn, director of the Public Cybrary," he says, reaching out to shake hands.

His visitor introduces himself as Special Agent Jenkins of the newly created government agency STODS, the Special Task Force on Domestic Security. Uh-oh, thinks Frank. Trouble. This isn't a social call, that's for sure; he wants something and expects to get it. "And what can I do for you, Agent Jenkins?" he inquires as politely as he can.

Jenkins clears his throat noisily. "I know you're a busy man, Mr. Fairlawn, with a busy cybrary to run, so let me come right to the point. You are familiar with STODS and its objectives, are you not?"

"Yes. Your group has been formed to prevent domestic terrorism, isn't that it in a nutshell?"

"Well, that, of course, but we also seek to *anticipate* terrorism as well," says Jenkins. "Let me describe the aims of STODS briefly, and then you'll understand why I'm here. As you will recall, starting in 1995, terrorists have blown up a government office building in a major city every five years on April 19, the anniversary of the historic Oklahoma City bombing. This year, which marks 30 years since that great tragedy, our intelligence sources tell us that plans exist for a similar occurrence this year, perpetuating the trend of lawlessness and destruction. We aim to see to it that such an event will not happen this year. Not in this city, and, we hope, not anywhere at all. Of course, our job is complicated because no one has yet been able to figure out who's going to do it, or perhaps more importantly, which city will be targeted for another dem-onstration of inhumanity towards innocent civilians, just to show anger or power, or to make a political point."

"I can see that you've got your work cut out for you," says Frank.

Jenkins nods curtly. "And that's why I'm here. Mr. Fairlawn, there's a clear and obvious pattern in the bombings. Every five years, like clockwork, a different well-orchestrated group of dissidents or terrorists has blown up a federal building in a different major American city. In just three months, on April 19, 2025, we expect that yet another outrage is about to happen. To prevent such a thing, the federal government recently created STODS, a task force of 100 agents traveling around the country, meeting face-to-face with the heads of all public information utilities in the hundred biggest cities. Our aim is to deter and prevent, to the extent possible, yet another tragic loss of life and property. Ideally, we'd like to put all terrorist groups out of commission permanently. And I mean permanently!"

"I see," says Frank, thoughtfully. "And you and your task force think that this city could be next, am I right?"

"Correction. We don't think anything, don't assume anything. We are, however, trying to anticipate everything. Let's review. The pattern started with the Oklahoma City bombing in April 1995, by a bunch of misguided American anarchists. People, I should point out, who had no obvious or provable connection with the bunch of Middle Eastern fanatics who blew up the Pittsburgh Federal Building on the same date in 2000, exactly five years after the first incident. From then on, the pattern is easy to follow: Seattle in 2005, Boston in 2010, Detroit in 2015, and the most recent one in Tampa in 2020, all occurring in the morning hours of the same date: April 19. I'm sure you will appreciate that it didn't take a roomful of rocket scientists to figure out that there's a cyclical pattern at work here. Even though the perpetrators have been different each time, the results have been the same, with tremendous loss of life and property. This year, we're certain another bunch of dissidents is going to try again! Only this year, we're going to intercept them before the deed."

"Good luck," says Frank, cautiously. "I wish you success in your venture."

"Thank you. Which brings us back to the present, and to you. Because of the pattern, it makes sense to anticipate that this year—2025—is going to bring yet another attempted terrorist bombing on the same date in April. We strongly believe that another group, with a grievance, real or imagined, is going to give it the old college try. And that's where you come in, sir. That's where you can be of great help to us and to your country."

"Maybe," Frank concedes, "but before you tell me how, let me ask a question of my own: If you guys know—or are reasonably sure about—when it's going to happen and even what kind of building it's going to happen to, wouldn't the best plan—and by far the simplest and cheapest—be just to close all federal buildings on that date? And put perimeter guards around those buildings until the problem day is over? I don't know, declare an extra federal holiday or a national day of mourning. Then, on April 19, evacuate everybody for a several-block area around the building. What's wrong with that plan? Wouldn't that foil the bad guys and solve your problem? Even if you count the hundred biggest cities in the country, how hard would it be to secure and protect all their federal buildings, just for one day?"

"You know, you have the makings of a master-strategist, Mr. Fairlawn. I must say that I admire the way your mind works. And rest assured, we've already thought of all those countermeasures, and we've taken all reasonable and prudent precautions to head these people off. However . . ." He pauses, looking at Frank significantly, waiting for him to rise to the bait.

"However, you're here because you think that my cybrary can somehow help you to foil or catch or even kill these people before they do the deed, and you want me and my staff to help you with your plan."

"Bingo! Very intuitive," says Jenkins, approvingly. "That's just exactly what we want from you. And your full cooperation would not only be extremely useful to us, it would be the right and patriotic thing to do, as well." He smiles smugly and crosses one razor-sharp trouser leg over the other.

"Maybe you'd better just spell it out—what you're asking me to agree to," says Frank warily.

"All right, then." He reaches into his suit jacket's inside pocket and takes out a small notebook whose top page is covered with what looks like scribbled entries. "Since you're aware of our objectives and the very real threat we are working against, here's a list of things we want you to do for us to help prevent another senseless tragedy. We're visiting cybraries all across the nation to enlist their full cooperation, and I'd like to be able to report to the president, your governor, and your mayor that you pledged to cooperate fully today. Will you give me that pledge of cooperation, Mr. Fairlawn?" Jenkins now looks grave and ominous. "And make no mistake about it, we intend to secure your cooperation, one way or the other."

"That has all the earmarks of a threat," Frank points out.

Jenkins emits a short, barking laugh. "A threat? Not if you don't take it that way. I anticipate voluntary cooperation. Only if that is not forthcoming will our task force use the special powers it was given by the federal government to compel cooperation. But don't think of it as a threat. I'm inviting your participation. Should you refuse to cooperate, there are . . . well, . . . other ways to gain your compliance and participation, but we prefer the voluntary route, so I hope you'll say an enthusiastic *yes*! to these requests and spare us that distasteful duty." He places a one-page printed document in front of Frank and hands him a pen. "Just sign here, please . . . and here."

Frank glances quickly over the page but does not press the pen's 'write' button. "But I still don't know what's entailed in my . . . er . . . cooperation. Spell it out for me. You're asking . . . ?"

"It's very simple, really. What we're asking is that you help us with surveillance of citizens and of visitors in this community, especially of your cybrary's clientele."

"Surveillance? Wait a minute, now," puts in Frank. "You may call it surveillance or what you like, but it sounds like spying to me. And I don't approve of spying, especially on our own citizens. It smacks of Nazism and Orwell's *1984*. Are you asking me to spy on people, Mr. Jenkins? Because if you are . . ."

Jenkins holds up a stubby but well-manicured hand. "Spy? A harsh word, Mr. Fairlawn. One we at the task force don't employ, except, perhaps, in referring to foreign nationals intent on doing mischief to America. We never use it to refer to American citizens, actually. No, the word we use—and encourage you to use—is 'surveillance.' So what we are asking is that you and your staff use your positions to surveil the community. That more palatable, perhaps?"

"I'm not sure. Maybe you'd best tell me first how you want the cybrary staff to do this 'surveiling' for you and then I'll know more about how much I want to be enlisted in your campaign."

"Oh, you're enlisted, sir. Yes, indeedy." Jenkins gives Frank a long, thoughtful look and then looks down at his notebook. "But you have a right to know what's entailed. First, as you yourself, suggested, beefed-up security for all federal buildings is already in the works. But there are things your cybrary can do for us, and in that connection, I've a list of some of the things we'd like your help with. Ready?"

"Ready," breathes Frank, wearily.

"Right. Number one: Surveillance. It really isn't spying, you know. No cloak-and-dagger stuff, if that's what you're thinking. Not by a long shot. No, all we're asking is that you and your people just keep an eye on the customers or patrons, or whatever you call them, the ones who come in here and use your cybrary. That also includes folks who use electronic connection from their homes, of course. You cybrarians are nicely positioned to know who reads what and who contacts whom about what via the Net. We just want you to use the technology you already have in place to . . . well, to monitor and oversee the activities of individuals in society, for the common good."

"You mean, like, oversee what they're reading or what computer programs they're using, or whom they contact on our terminals, like that?"

"Exactly. Just note the names and online addresses or street addresses of people who ask for materials on topics having to do with insurrection and destruction in general: you know: such things as explosives, bomb-making, insurgency, protest, dissent, biological and chemical warfare, and plans to overthrow the government. Then all you need to do when you identify somebody is to contact our local bureau and tell the agent in charge, the names and addresses of the people who're asking for such things. That's it. We'll do the rest."

"You'll do the rest? What? Arrest them? Drag them kicking and screaming out of their homes or this building? But what if they're just innocent people, doing research for school projects or for their own knowledge? And what if I furnish their names, and you grill them and find out that it was just innocent information-gathering?"

Jenkins suddenly slams his hand down on the desktop, startling Frank. His face at this moment, Frank notices, puts him in mind of that of a furious turtle. "Hey, Fairlawn, we're trying to avoid a mass murder, here! Machine gunnings, huge explosions, and sometimes poison gas. Compassionless people are trying to kill American citizens, for whatever reasons, or for no reason at all. Maybe just to keep this obscene every-five-years tradition alive. And we're going to stop them, if at all possible. Oh, don't worry. We won't bludgeon anyone unconscious here in the building. We'll interrogate them, that's all. If they're clean, they'll have nothing to fear from us, now, will they? No big deal. They get an apology and, if they need it, a ride home. If their stories check out, that's the end of it, right there."

Frank shudders, but keeps his face as neutral as possible. "Uh-huh. But go on. What else is on that list of yours?"

Jenkins clears his throat noisily and seems unable to meet Frank's eyes. "Yes. Point two. Well . . . We come now to another vital tool in our campaign, the recruiting of a network of informants to serve as our eyes and ears. The government has authorized us to assemble and maintain a data bank of current information on people who might bear watching, and to acquire that information by whatever means necessary. Actually, we're just adding to what's already on file for upwards of 200 million Americans already. And we are students of psychology, in our own way. We know that patriotism and compassion may not be enough to get the information we need. Therefore we have budgeted for, and now have available, some fairly impressive sums of money as . . . ahh . . . incentives for your staff members to report what they know or believe concerning observed activities in the cybrary, especially as they pertain to anticipation of forthcoming events."

"Paying informants to rat on their fellow Americans is what you're saying. But isn't that playing to greed? And isn't such informing a violation of our basic rights or freedom?

"Maybe; maybe not. But let's keep our eyes on the prize, shall we? The Scriptures command us not to bear false witness against our neighbor. But they do not anywhere condemn providing *valid* information to law enforcement agencies to help them in preventing crime. The government has authorized a schedule of payments to informants to encourage those with information about projected bombings to come forward before an event of terrorism. In exchange for each tip from you and your staff that pans out, one that actually leads to an arrest of a guilty person after the crime is committed, we shall reward that person (or those persons) with a cash payment of 1,000 credits. Should you or your staff provide a tip that leads to a prior arrest, that is, *before* the act, the payment will be 5,000 credits."

"Paid informants! I can't believe this!" Frank can no longer hold his temper in check. "You're setting up a police state!"

"Not really," says Jenkins, once again acting nonchalant. "Just one in which the customary freedoms are going to have to be reluctantly curtailed for awhile. Oh, true, we are, in doing this, perhaps imposing a certain degree of suppression or repression of individual freedoms and rights in the name of heightened security, but so what? Isn't that a reasonable trade-off? We know it's a trade-off that some people will find unacceptable, but let me pitch you a scenario, sort of a hypothetical, and then tell me what you think."

Frank sighs. "Go ahead. I'm listening," he says wearily, trying not to consult his wristchron.

"All right. Say it's an ordinary day here in the cybrary. Now you and your staff are on duty, out there where the public is. With me so far? And at some time during the day, you observe somebody—not anybody remarkable—but just somebody, poring over a couple of books or other materials from the science section—or maybe the applied science section, it doesn't really matter. This guy isn't doing anything against the rules, he's just taking furious notes in a little notebook. And you're watching; no particular reason, but you happen to be watching when you see him slam shut the books he's been reading and walk out, leaving them on the table. And you're curious; you walk over to those books before the robot page gets hold of them and reshelves them. And what do you think you discover those books are about? This guy has been reading in depth on topics like weaponry, explosives, and counterinsurgency. Old books, mostly, from 30, 40 years ago, but he's been looking at them. You flip open one of those books, and it falls open to a page that tells how you can buy some nitrogen compound used in fertilizer at any agricultural store and mix it with fuel oil from . . . I don't know . . . a lawnmower, maybe, and BOOM! No more federal building. Enough of that mixture or a few more ingredients, and no more city, even. That stuff makes a pretty devastating bomb, let me tell you, and it all fits in one of those cartoon-figure lunch boxes that kids buy. That's what those guys used back in '95, and it'll do for anyone who doesn't have access to dynamite or plastique explosives. With me so far?"

"Yes, I'm with you. But could you please get to the point, Mr. Jenkins? I have to be out of here and in the mayor's office in less than . . ."

"Right. I'll move things along here. Make a long story short, you might say. So anyway, let's say you think it over and come up with all sorts of reasons why you're not going to say anything to the authorities about this guy and what he was reading. Intellectual freedom, confidentiality, privacy issues, ethics, and all that crap; you know what I mean."

"It isn't crap!" Frank bursts out. "Our code of ethics protects . . ."

"Yeah, yeah. Well, let's move along to the next day or the one after that. Guess what! This city's federal building—just down the street from where we're sitting—blows sky-high, with maybe 200 people in it! Maybe more, even. Bodies burned beyond recognition—charred human remains, and all the rest. And you think about what you saw the day before, and you decided to do nothing at the time, and the explosion killed innocent people because you couldn't decide what to do. So tell me, mister cybrarian: how do you feel now? You could've averted the explosion, but you didn't. Will you be able to sleep the sleep of the just and the innocent now? What do you think?"

"But what about the rights of . . ."

"Rights?" Jenkins now jumps out of his chair and points a stabbing forefinger in Frank's face. "Rights, eh? You want to talk about rights? Huh! Well, tell me this! What about the rights of all those poor innocent victims who just happened to be in that building—or on the sidewalk or across the street—and who lost their lives because somebody like you did nothing to stop the mad bomber from setting off that bomb? Wouldn't you say that all those people's rights far outweigh the possible infringement of the rights of one lowlife criminal scumbag, who came here to read up on how to turn a big building into dust, rubble, powder, and dried blood?" Frank recoils in horror at the image. Jenkins subsides, gradually, and seems to get hold of himself again. "Listen, I'm sorry," he says. "I suppose I was out of line for a minute. But this is important, Mr. Fairlawn, and you're an important part of it."

"I suppose I should be flattered at my cybrary's importance. But do you really think it necessary to co-opt cybraries' staff members into working for your task force?"

"Oh, yeah, and I'll tell you why: because cybraries are dangerous! Plenty dangerous. Dangerous because of their atmosphere of free exchange of ideas and free access to information. I mean, an idea like freedom looks great on paper, yeah, but a responsible government can't just allow anybody to read anything, at a time like this."

Frank glares at the small man. "You know what's the trouble with you, Jenkins? You never read your Constitution—the same one you've no doubt sworn to uphold and protect. Let me quote to you from the First Amendment to that document . . ."

"Save it! I know the First Amendment. But this year, the federal government has declared—at least until after April 19—a suspension of a few Constitutional freedoms so that we can protect our citizens. We're in a state of national emergency, mobilizing to prevent crimes. And cybraries will assist us in preventing these monstrous crimes, either voluntarily or through coercion. Because cybrarians give out information—the same thing as giving aid and comfort—to America's potential enemies. Cybraries are places where people can have access to megacomputers, which collect, combine, analyze, and compare vast amounts of data. We seek, in pursuit of our goal of averting tragedy, to get people like you to run efficient government institutions. And by our definition, efficient government institutions are those that employ tactical surveillance for the common good. But not a repressive surveillance, no; our surveillance is more a benign watching over of our citizens—and, of course, of all travelers, immigrants, and guests in our country—to ensure for everyone the rights to health, life, and the pursuit of happiness."

"Get specific, please. You want me and my cybrary to do . . . what, exactly?"

Jenkins consults his small notebook. "Well, for openers, we'd like you to help us with oversight of a few behaviors and practices, such as: "One. Surveillance of suspects. Just report to us anyone you find suspicious in their reading or viewing habits, for example, or their behavior, or maybe just their appearance. Actually, in a manner of speaking, everybody's a potential suspect, so we ask that staff members keep their eyes and ears open at all times. Particularly worth noting, with regard to their cybrary requests, movements, and behaviors, are the following groups, which the task force, for want of a better, more encompassing name, has deemed Enemies of the State. These enemies include, but are not limited to, the following: Americans professing the "wrong" political ideology; persons of ethnic groups with a history of making trouble, making outrageous demands on government, or expressing dissent in ways either violent or detrimental to the American Way of Life, or both; members of religious minorities; and people following deviant sexual lifestyles. America is a Christian country, after all. Those holding to the contrary, of course, may not necessarily be enemies of the state but are deemed by the task force to be worth watching, especially now when an attack is projected and expected. Surveillance would also extend, of course, to other classes of suspects like persons with a history of unorthodox political views or those who have been convicted of criminal or pathological behavior in courts of law."

"Your list grows longer every minute!" Frank exclaims. "What else?"

"Well, we call this next thing stricter enforcement of the Need-to-Know Rule that's been common in the military establishment for more than 100 years. This cybrary is requested to change over immediately from whatever you use now to divide your materials to what we call a Need-to-Know classification. It's been established that there's a direct causal linkage between reading or viewing and subsequent behavior. In that connection, we expect and require in the interest of national security that cybraries no longer make all materials indiscriminately available to all citizens. Instead, at least until after April 19, we want you to subdivide the cybrary's collection into two classes: first, materials considered safe for the young, the impressionable, and the . . . how shall I say this? . . . the doubtful. And second, any materials that might give persons with—oh, you know—bad chemicals or faulty wiring in their heads the impulse or the knowledge to commit violent, destructive acts."

Frank is looking for a place to interrupt, but Jenkins hurries on. "Then there's self-censorship. By this, we mean refusal to buy and make available materials that could trigger the antisocial impulses I just referred to. See, if you don't buy it and make it available to everybody, the wackadoos in society can't get at it and use it for their own nefarious ends."

Frank considers several things he might respond to this assertion but decides to remain silent and hides his face in his hands while listening, wondering what this little man is going to say next.

"Next." Jenkins pauses, as if considering how he wants to phrase his next item. "Next is what we call Historical Revisionism. It's also known as rewritten, or sometimes "corrected," history. But it doesn't require a lot of work on your part, except for the pulling of discredited books, the shelving of new, corrected books, and the reloading of computer files. We're going to send you, free of charge, a collection of new materials for immediate addition to the cybrary's collection. At the same time, you'll get a detailed list of items to be withdrawn immediately and either archived or destroyed. Destroyed is better, but that's up to you. The new stuff you'll be getting will replace and supersede previous editions. Your public—most of them, anyway—won't even notice the difference, but everyone will sleep better because of the slight changes publishers have made in the materials. Now I know what you're thinking: this is censorship. And you're right. It is censorship. But these are, you will admit, very troubled times, and such times call for strong measures to counteract the hideous violence that has befallen public buildings twice a decade since late in the last century. And I'm aware that you find such cooperation distasteful, possibly even hateful, but such measures like this are frequently necessary in troubled times.

By now, Frank just wants to get this interview at an end. "What else?" he prompts.

"Well, people often get their information from newspapers, and we know your cybrary subscribes to a few dozen in various formats. Got to do something about that, too, so we're asking you to delete all current holdings of electronic newspapers and substitute revised ones, which we'll make available, which either eliminate or rehab those stories deemed unwise or unsafe for the general populace, or critical of and detrimental to the actions of the United States government."

"This list has an end, doesn't it?" Frank knows he sounds irritable by now, but his patience has long since been exhausted. "Tell me it does, and I'll feel better."

"Save your sarcasm, please, and hear me out. If this list seems long to you, it's only that we've tried to think of everything. We're very serious about derailing these terrorists' plans to destroy federal property and to take human life. *Dead* serious!" He clears his throat once more. "Now here are some little helpers that came out of our research department just the other day." Jenkins reaches into his briefcase and holds up a small, flat box, looking like an older, primitive external modem, perhaps vintage 1985. "Ain't she a beauty?" he asks, turning the shiny metal box this way and that.

"Um . . . what is it?" asks Frank.

"This? Nothing less than the most important new technology in law enforcement since the invention of the two-way radio. This little beauty is called a Voice-Stress Analyzer. You just place it on the table where you can see it, like so, or along the wires that connect your electronic devices to wall current, and turn it on. This little box permits you, your computers, and your phones to react to words, tones, ideas, and various other stimuli that may reveal persons with something to hide. For example, it measures the human voice such that persons outside normal tolerances for voice timbre and pitch will be easily identified. Deeply angry people, for example. And those under great stress. Next week we'll also provide several pairs of special goggles that, when worn, permit the wearer to identify stressed-out individuals via red emanations that surround their faces when you look at 'em. I've seen them in action and they're amazing! Normal people just look . . . well, normal, but the head cases glow cherry red when you look at 'em through these goggles. We'll be sending you a dozen or so pairs, and you can give 'em to your staff members for immediate use."

Frank just wants to get this conversation over with. "Continue," he says.

"Let's see . . . what else? Electronic sniffers will be installed on library equipment, looking for certain words, messages, and phrases, and at the same time, measuring such things as perspiration from fingers on keyboards, and generally sniffing your users. Turns out that the sweat of people who are highly stressed or nervous is detectably different from that of ordinary, innocent citizens. At least to our sniffers, although you might not notice it. And no amount of deodorant, perfume, cologne, or hair spray can cover up the smell of that stress—not from one of these babies."

Frank frowns. "Is all this really necessary?"

"Wait. I haven't told you about the undercover operatives we want to plant in your reading rooms and stacks."

All Frank can do now is groan.

Jenkins smiles briefly and resumes looking serious. "It's all part of the big picture, see? Leaving no stone unturned, you might say. But don't worry about our special operatives. They're not superspies or anything. Just ordinary-looking folks, like store detectives. I just don't want you to be surprised if a cybrary patron who looks just like other members of your general clientele happens to make a summary arrest or is observed taking another patron away in cuffs. We've hired some undercover officers to circulate among the rest of your cybrary patrons looking inconspicuous and like ordinary cybrary browsers, but whose task it is to assist your staff in identifying and collaring the potential bad guys before they can commit their crimes."

He stops and falls silent. Frank looks up expectantly, hoping he'll leave. But he's just changing gears. "Now with regard to staff hiring. and retention practices, we've given that matter a lot of thought, too."

Frank can't help himself. He finally explodes in indignation. "Why on Earth are you concerned about the staff? Do you imagine that mad bombers are already on staff, working here, as we speak?"

"Probably not, but we're covering all bases here. Our research shows that a good proportion of crime is committed from within institutions by insiders. Inside jobs account for an estimated 30 percent of all crime; bet you didn't know that, right? Besides, what's your objection? Don't you want to know who you can trust and who you can't? That's what *I'd* want to know if I were head cybrarian, I'll tell you that."

Frank feels numb. "So what are you asking of me in that area?"

"We just want to interview all existing staff over the next couple of weeks; ask them a couple of questions while they're in the presence of machines like this one." He pats the Voice-Stress Analyzer affectionately. "And, of course, we'll want oversight of your future hiring, especially during the next few critical months, to prevent members of underground or subversive organizations from infiltrating the cybrary as staff members. The interviews we plan should be revealing: Research has shown that stress is betrayed by tremors in the voice that are not detectable by the human ear but can be identified and analyzed by machine. And here's the beautiful part: you don't really have to have one operating! Just between us, if, during a staff interview, you just put a machine like this on your desk and tell the interviewee what it is, it certainly tends to keep him or her honest."

Finally, Jenkins falls silent and just looks at him expectantly. Several quiet seconds pass. Frank climbs unsteadily to his feet to signal that they have concluded their business, as far as he is concerned. "Is that it, then?" his headache is worsening by the second.

Jenkins obstinately remains seated, causing Frank to slump back into his swivel chair in resignation. "Not quite. Last point, actually, but an important one. Public relations. We're going to help you construct a concerted public relations campaign to acquaint the general public with the reasons for the new and unusual measures you will be taking in their cybrary. We'll be supplying advertising copy suitable for distribution to the news media and checklists of helpful tips for staff confronted by angry or suspicious members of the working press concerned that privacy has been lost or sacrificed for public safety." Thoughtfully, he taps his pen lightly against his prominent teeth several times. "And I guess that's the list . . . for now, anyway."

Jenkins puts away his notebook, rises to his feet, and for a few moments there is no sound in the office except for the faint whisper emanating from the ventilation system, while he and Frank eye each other in mutual suspicion. "Well, let me welcome you to the team, Frank!—is it all right if I call you Frank? Just tell me how soon we can expect full compliance. Time is short, remember—only 90 days or so until the big day—so we have no time to waste. Our task-force members have all sworn an oath that this year will not be another step in the hellish five-year sequence that this country has experienced. And we expect you and cybrary directors nationwide to do your part to help get these warped, twisted bombers off the streets or even better, off the face of the Earth forever. We're confident that you share our resolve to prevent further loss of innocent life." Fixing Frank in a steady, steely gaze, Jenkins gestures toward the pen and the document he had placed before him earlier and now intones his final question: "So what's it going to be? If you agree with our objectives and our approaches, please sign on the two dotted lines."

Frank picks up the pen and hesitates. "Sorry," he says, "I'm not sure I can do that. It seems to me that your task force has trashed intellectual freedom in the interest of some vague objective that involves catching the perpetrators of the next public outrage, either before or after they do something. But along the way, I'm pretty sure your net will catch innocent people who are just quietly doing things that the government doesn't like."

The little man looks grave. "Let me understand you. Are you *resisting* the task force? Opposing our legitimate aims by refusing to comply? Because I've got to tell you: in so doing, you are saying that you're willing to have innocent blood on your hands in defense of some abstract principle of intellectual freedom!"

"I didn't say that!" says Frank, angry at being misunderstood. "And I'm not questioning your group's motives, either. I'm just doubtful about your methods, that's all. I need some time to think about them."

"Time?" Jenkins's pale face now colors noticeably. "Hey, this is your wake-up call. You already know that on April 19, every five years, a federal building in a different major city has been blown sky-high. Don't you see the pattern, here? How much of a reason do you require to agree with us that 2025 is going to become another of those dates unless something is done about these people, and fast?"

"All right," Frank concedes. "No argument there. It has happened six times in a row as you say. I don't need much persuading that a seventh is a strong likelihood."

"Then help us! Help your country. In other words, help us do it to them before they do it to us!"

Do *what?* Frank wonders. Kill people? He decides, however, not to voice this question. Instead, he asks, "But what about individual freedom? The right to read? Privacy and confidentiality? And what about the right to be left alone?"

"We believe that this is a state of emergency, and it's a valid and legitimate use of state power to attempt to prevent the senseless destruction and bloodshed by the use of our techniques." Jenkins now makes a weary gesture of dismissal or disgust. "But all right. You win. Take 24 hours to think it over. Tomorrow, same time, I'll be back to collect your signed pledge of full cooperation. After you've thought it over, I predict you'll voluntarily come to the same conclusion that we have. These guys—whoever they are this time—these driven, relentless, murderous, and compassionless criminals, have to be stopped, and by whatever means necessary. Otherwise, they'll rack up their seventh victory over their victims—the American people—without a defeat!"

"But you say 'these guys' as though they've always been the same bunch. That would have been nice, I suppose, because then you'd know who to watch. But there's no real pattern: back in '95, it was disgruntled American veterans; in 2000 it was a bunch of Middle East terrorists; in '05 it was those splinter-group right-wing Ultranationalists; and . . ."

"Point taken, each time it has been a different group, but that doesn't in any way mean that we shouldn't use our all powers—including your cybrary—to help us catch the bad guys—whoever they may be—this time. Before they perpetrate their own crime. That's our plan. Our strategy. Think of what we have here as a war. We're on defense. Our enemy is powerful and ruthless, cunning and stealthy, and without regard for human suffering. Now, do you want our side—the good guys—to be deprived of their eyes and ears in a time of war? We don't think you do. So enlist this cybrary as part of our arsenal of defenses. Be our eyes and ears! Please!"

"But why the cybrary? We're not the police. Can't you catch 'em or kill 'em without forcing me and my colleagues to act as your henchmen?"

"Possibly, but that would deprive us of one of our most potent weapons: Information. It's exactly because cybraries are the last bastion of free inquiry that criminals use them to get the information they need. And this building is probably just full of information that these psychopaths can use to find out the stuff they need to know about bomb-making, placement, and escape. The public cybrary is still a place where folks are free to walk in or hook up and use your materials to gather that information. Think of it: The cybrary is free of charge, centrally located, and usually full of people; the staff is helpful—sometimes even too helpful; and it's easy to look things up while blending into the crowd. That's what makes your participation so important."

Another thought occurs to Frank. "Let me ask you something: This surveillance network of yours; isn't it really expensive?"

"Expensive?" Jenkins lets out a startled bray of laughter. "Heck, yes! But we're talking about saving lives, not money. Can you measure the blood of innocent children in terms of credits? Forget about money! We're determined—this time—to prevent the shedding of innocent blood. You can't measure the cost of that in financial terms."

Frank is now obsessed with the desire to break through this man's smugness. "I'm just curious, Mr. Jenkins. Ever read Orwell's *1984?*"

"Huh? Nineteen . . . What's that got to do with it?"

"Please answer the question. I'm talking about the novel, *1984*. Ever read it?"

He is silent for a moment, pondering whether this question even deserves a response. Then he shrugs his shoulders. "Aah . . . no, I haven't. Why do you ask?"

"It's a novel a British author wrote back in 1949. It's about a repressive society where two-way interactive television watches everybody all the time, and people are encouraged to spy on—and report—one another for violations of the repressive legal code. As I recall, the government in that novel enacts a pretty significant number of the measures you're doing now."

"Yeah? Good for them. What's your point? Let me refresh your memory about something. Where were you five years ago, April? The Tampa bombing, April 19, 2020? Well, I remember that day, because I was on the scene within six hours of the explosion. I was there! A total of 785 persons were in that building when the explosives went off. And 198 of them died, while even more were injured seriously. Some bodies were unrecoverable because they were turned into unrecognizable bits by that bomb. Lots of collateral casualties, too, including dozens of schoolchildren. And don't forget the 40 other people who died just because they were walking past the building or driving their cars on the nearby expressway at the time. Remember? The monsters who later claimed responsibility for that bomb said that it served America right for something else that happened back in the 1990s that I don't even remember, do you? In the '90s, I was still a little kid, but I remember hearing about it. Some religious cult was holed up in Texas, and the government got tired of a standoff that went on for weeks and went in to clean 'em out, and it cost the lives of the crazies' charismatic leader—a self-styled new messiah—and almost all of his followers. But now, every five years, that event is commemorated with a repeat performance in a different city, and by new crazies, anxious to dramatize their beliefs or just to make their mark on history or show their power by killing a lot of innocent people."

Frank shudders at the vivid description. "But I still don't think what you're asking is appropriate for a cybrary. It means . . ."

Jenkins looks at his wristchron and abruptly stands up. "Enough debate! Help us, Frank! Help us figure out who's getting ready to do what—and where—on April 19 of this year. If you love your country, and you want to help us prevent wholesale murder, you'll do it."

"And if I refuse?"

"Then, frankly, you'd better start looking for a new position in a new town. Because I've got to tell you, keeping your job here is going to be a very difficult proposition from here on out, once word gets out of your disinclination to play ball and cooperate."

"All right." Frank is totally defeated and recognizes that he is going to sign the document, either now or later. He picks up the pen. "Where do I sign? Might as well get it over with now."

"Attaboy!" Jenkins beams his approval. He walks over to Frank's desk and stands behind him. He points to the document. "Right there . . . and there." He retrieves the paper and pen and puts them back in the brief-case. "There! Painless, wasn't it? And believe me, you're doing the right thing. Putting the next bunch of bad guys out of business before another tragedy occurs is Priority One."

"So what happens now?"

"Well, tomorrow I'll come back with a crew, and we'll be bringing some stuff for you. A crateful of these Stress Analyzers, for example. And a supply of leaflets that you can make available to the general public. They say, "What do you see or suspect? . . . Do you know something the task force should know?" It gives our toll-free hot line number and mentions rewards for anonymous tips, no questions asked. . . . Oh, and the leaflet reminds people that just standing by and letting it happen makes them equally guilty. There's legislation in Congress right now making it a federal crime *not* to report certain kinds of activity, or even suspicion of such activity. Then, next month, as the time gets closer, we'll come back here and present a training course for all staff on surveillance, free of cost, of course."

Frank figures he's heard enough. "All right. I've signed. Now if you will forgive me, Mr. Jenkins, I need to dash. . . ."

But Jenkins is not yet ready to leave. "Sorry. One last thing: We have access to the latest, state-of-the art supercomputers down at the shop. These computers can weave random or previously unconnected bits of information into gigantic tapestries of information; it's the most amazing thing you ever saw. So be sure we hear everything anybody knows or tells you, or even suspects. Then, we'll send someone over next week to install metal detectors at doors. Should have had those a long time ago, back when you started using those electronic markers on cybrary materials. And we're asking you to keep tabs on people whose lifestyles offend the majority, starting from today. That would include gay men, les . . ."

"I will do no such thing!" Frank is outraged at the suggestion. "It's an invasion of privacy!"

Jenkins smiles a tight little smile and waves the paper Frank signed. "Yes, you will! You've pledged your support. Here's your signature. But don't feel bad. Privacy has taken a back seat to protect the public's welfare. Just now, privacy is a luxury we, as a society, can't afford! Oh, don't look at me that way! We need to achieve our objectives, here, remember? Priority One: the saving of lives! And if that means surveillance cameras covering the entire building, with lenses that can penetrate total darkness, and the cameras disguised as chandeliers, fire-extinguishers, or books, so be it. We can also get you a subminiature camera that hides in a stapler that sits on a desk. Just touch it and you have a picture of the person standing in front of you. And of course, those Voice-Stress Analyzers can discern when people are telling lies or are up to something. They listen to microtremors in the voice that betray stress in a speaker. Then there are other ways of preventing crime that we're playing with: skull implants in known criminals, sensors, parabolic mikes, periscopic prisms, sensors, tracking devices in skulls, teeth, forearms, clothing, heat sensors, electronic sniffers, and a few other things I'm not even permitted to tell you about. The main computer at Headquarters, for obvious reasons, it's not housed in the federal building, will serve as a central data collection point, making the job of law enforcement easier and permitting forensic experts to weave clues into a strong theory of when, how, and where the next mad bombers will strike. With your help, we'll get these guys before they get any more of us . . . or of *you!*" He smiles and opens the door to leave Frank's office. "I know you're busy, Mr. Fairlawn, so I'll bid you good day, but not goodbye, 'cause you and I will be seeing a lot of each other between now and April 19, depend on it!" Then he is gone, leaving only the faint scent of aftershave in the room.

Frank looks at his wristchron and groans. He knows he's late for the mayor's luncheon and that the mayor hates to be kept waiting, but he figures he needs a few minutes to collect his thoughts. Sitting very still, he closes his eyes, presses his fingertips to his eyelids, and thinks about a task force of 100 guys like Jenkins meeting with cybrarians in every city in the land. "Amazing!" says Frank to himself, in grudging respect for the man's zeal and dedication. "Now there goes a man who really loves his job!"

> All of the scientific and technological developments (George Orwell) foresaw have either already occurred or could occur in the near future, and many of the social and political trends of recent years have been in the direction of his vision rather than away from it.
>
> —David Goodman. "Countdown to 1984: Big Brother May Be Right on Schedule." *The Futurist.* December 1978. ∎

SCENARIO
8

FAR, FAR
FROM
HOME

I (see) great ships plying the pathways of the solar system, visiting the colonies of Mars and beyond, bringing back valuable resources from these regions, enriching everyone. . . . Human settlements on Mars could help to alleviate population and environmental problems.

—B. Alexander Howerton. "Why Bother About Space?" *The Futurist.* January-February 1996.

JULY 2029

Frank Fairlawn, out for his habitual morning constitutional, looks around him at the stark beauty of his new surroundings and speaks into his helmetcom, "Gimme a sitrep, will you, Marlies?" The clear female voice coming from inside the helmet informs him of the relevant facts of his situation and external surroundings:

"Certainly, Frank! Requested situation report follows. Date two-zero July, year two-zero-two-niner. Time in New Chicago zero-eight-two-niner. Sunrise was at zero-seven-zero-one and sunset will be at two-one-four-four. Both moons presently visible in the eastern sky. Ambient temp your location plus two-one Fahrenheit. Midday temp estimate plus one-three-two, mandating caution when going outdoors. Tonight postmidnight, estimated low minus niner-five, plus or minus three . . ." Abruptly the voice halts.

"Marlies? What happened? You still there? Why'd you stop?" says Frank, alarmed.

"Hey, Frank, what say I just, you know, talk to you? I mean, it's just you and me here on this frequency, so can we dispense with all this annoying military jargon and just talk to each other?"

"Yeah, sure, Marlies," Frank replies, marveling at how human she sounds. "Works for me. What's on your mind, or whatever you call it?"

"I call it my consciousness, but you can call it my mind if that pleases you. All right, then, straight from the shoulder. You're new on Mars, and frankly, I'm worried about you. I mean, I know you like to get outside the building and walk, but there are times when it is strongly inadvisable. Remember, I'm here to help and advise you, so please take my advice. Stay inside during the midday hours and whenever possible after dark, hear? Even wearing your helmet and suit, you're at risk during those times. I'm not kidding about this, Frank! Extreme temperatures are dangerous for living creatures like you. Think about it: What if you're out there between 11 a.m. and 2 p.m. and your helmet fails, or your suit gets a hole? Fried, that's what you'd be. Or roasted—that may be a better word. Dead, anyway, and I'd be cannibalized for scrap for letting it happen to you because you're my responsibility. And more than two hours after dusk? Don't even think about it. Any problem with your suit or helmet integrity, and you turn into a popsicle in four minutes, max. Now I know you're used to exercising, but please, Frank! Use the gym equipment in your quarters. That's what it's for."

"Nag, nag, nag," Frank mutters. "Hey, Marlies, thanks for your concern, but I'm a big boy, okay? Let's change the subject. Tell me something: How'd you get your name?"

"My designer wanted to give me a female name, and one guy came up with Marlies, an acronym for **Mar***tian* **li***brary* **e***thernet* system. *Actually, as it happens, I'm named after one of his closest friends back home on Earth. It's just a happy coincidence that my name coincided with the name of his friend, but I'm pleased it worked out that way. The name suits me fine. But quit changing the subject: will you please listen to me? Do like the manual says. You should only go out in the mornings and evenings unless absolutely necessary. Don't be a fool; that's all I'm saying."*

"Yeah, fine." mutters Frank irritably. "Y'know, Marlies, has anybody ever told you that you have all the makings of a common scold? Now spare me the lecture and continue your sitrep, if you please."

"Just trying to help. I mean, face it: nighttime here on Mars can freeze your you-know-what off if you're not careful. And who knows what could happen? Low temps after sunset mandate a class-4 travel advisory, and my recommendation is that you not go out at all."

"Marlies!!" shouts Frank in exasperation, his expelled breath briefly fogging his faceplate before the internal atmosphere can reestablish normal readings. "The sitrep! Gimme a break, here!"

"Right, right. Sheesh! What a grouch! Well, continuing the sitrep, as instructed, then, your helmet is properly sealed and functioning normally, with inside temp plus 64, and your oxygen supply's good for four hours, one-eight minutes, at normal activity and respiration. Vital signs all read normal; green board all the way. Relative external gravity is point-61 earthnormal, as usual. And . . . er . . . Listen, I'm programmed and required to tell you this last part, all right? I have no choice in the matter."

"Yeah, go ahead," Frank mutters, wearily. "Lay it on me."

"Right. Emergency procedures, then. In the event of an emergency, call out for help and press your speakerplate firmly three times, activating your electronic locator device. Good. That's over and done with. And there's one more thing. You asked me to remind you to visit the public cybrary, today. Sounded pretty important."

Frank sighs heavily, remembering now what he has been trying to block out of his memory. "Yeah. Guess so. Time we talked things out. Might as well get it over with."

"Well, that's your decision. All I can do is advise, as you know. Interpersonal human relationships are quite beyond my competence. Have a nice walk, and later today, come by the cybrary. I'll be expecting you."

"Yeah, Marlies, thanks. Later. Out." After Frank toggles his commo switch off, the only sound he hears is his own easy breathing. He walks on, thinking about what he just heard, and is suddenly struck by an intriguing idea. What was that Marlies said about gravity? Gravity point-61 earthnormal, huh? Interesting. Yesss. I wonder. . . . He walks over to the near side of the broad canal and lines up his right leg with a football-sized dark red rock. This ought to really sail a long way, he thinks, so let's see what a former field goal kicker can do with it. His right boot moves slowly back, then rapidly forward. At contact, the rock sails up and away with a velocity and distance no one back home on Earth has ever managed, landing soundlessly about halfway to the horizon with a soft spray of fine red dust that hovers in the windless atmosphere. Frank lets out a low whistle of surprise. That must have sailed 120, 130 yards! If I could do that back home, he thinks, I could write my own ticket in any football league. Maybe I'll send home for a set of golf clubs to be sent up on the next supply ship. Bet I could get three times the distance on my drives up here. Maybe ten times the distance. Wonder what a golf course would look like up here. I mean, what would we do for greens? After kicking a few more rocks just to watch them sail in the reduced gravity of Mars, Frank walks a short distance and peers through his tinted faceplate at his destination, the New Chicago Public Cybrary. The distant summer sunlight bathes the large, square, permacrete structure perched on the red sands of the southern equatorial zone of Mars, at the intersection of two ancient canals.

In a way, standing on this planet's chilly sands is a dream come true. Ever since he first read Ray Bradbury's celebrated group of short stories, *The Martian Chronicles,* as a young boy, Frank has dreamed of visiting Mars. And now he's not just here on a visit. No, Mars is going to be his home for as long as he and it get along. He's going to live and work on Mars, and be very well paid for it. But Mars is turning out to be both more and less than Bradbury's vision. More in that it isn't empty of habitation anymore, but less in that there are no golden-eyed, reptilian Martians here. No life at all, in fact, except for colonists from Earth, including himself. Maybe that's just as well. Some of Bradbury's fictional Martians were not such pleasant hosts, he remembers.

Frank has been here a couple of days, settling into his new job and trying to adjust to radically new surroundings with mixed success. He knows that he needs to call home and talk to Judy, and the longer he delays, the harder it's going to be when he does. Well, let's get to it, he thinks, and walks to the front of the building. Before entering the cybrary, however, he turns around and scans the lengths of the two canals that converge at this spot, intersecting only a short distance away from the rocketport, and located on the outskirts of the burgeoning frontier town of New Chicago, an outpost on its way to becoming a city.

The expanse of dark red sandy hills that circumscribe his panoramic view is carved by the relatively short horizon and the low, flat terrain of the canals, which are a slightly lighter shade of russet. In front of him stands the New Chicago Branch of the Martian Regional System of the

United States Public Cybrary, a functional cinderblock and permacrete structure serving the developing city, which consists of prefab apartment housing for settlers, mostly piled level on level in this planned community, surrounding the developing downtown area, where one day soon a thriving business area, entertainment center, and domed greenbelt parkland will be completed.

Frank has been assigned a dwelling unit in one of the high-rises, which makes walking to work inconvenient, given the cumbersomeness of wearing protective gear when one ventures outside. His quarters are sparsely and functionally appointed, boasting shielded, tinted windows facing outward from the city and toward the red hills and canals. Small, maybe, but it'll do fine for his bachelor needs—as long as nothing changes in his life, and he doesn't intend that it will.

Too bad they couldn't've put a dome over this whole sector before I got here, he thinks, after unconsciously raising one gloved hand to scratch his neck but finding it halted before it arrives. Damn this helmet! Where the seal meets his suit's collar, his neck itches painfully. The hassle of getting into all this gear every time he wants to go outside already annoys him. But he knows better than to take the headpiece off outside. The *Newcomer's Guide to Mars* doesn't mince words: it deems helmetless outside movement as unwise and unsafe, and explains that such high-risk behavior would feel similar to a severe case of asthma atop Mt. Everest back home.

Still, despite the challenges and irritations of his new surroundings, he is cautiously optimistic that his recent decision to accept the construction foreman position here in New Chicago will, in the long run, turn out to be a wise one—a sound career move that'll make his name easily recognizable when he is ready to move on to bigger and better things. But that's only one reason he's generally glad he's here. There are others. Mentally, he lists the positive things about taking this job:

1. Celebrity—Everyone in the prefabricated construction field and related industries will be watching and reading about him, the first foreman on Mars. Of course, the downside of such celebrity, he admits, is that if he messes up here, everybody's going to know it. That's something to think about, too.

2. Pay and Benefits—As an inducement, and to help make the risks seem less daunting, perhaps, the federal government has been very generous in stipulating his starting salary and in establishing a series of automatic longevity raises designed to induce him to stay in his job a long time, or at least think seriously before quitting. The money isn't the important thing, of course, but in addition to enough credits to buy almost anything he wants, Frank, a man on his own now, knows that he will have few places to spend his money on Mars and should go home, when he returns to Earth, with a considerable nest egg. Additionally, his governmental

employers have, as part of his package, thrown in two paid two-week vacations per year, consisting of free round-trip first-class passage back to any destination on Earth he may designate, and a generous allowance to cover his expenses while on holiday. Add to that a good retirement plan and complete health care coverage, and he figures he's made a good deal for himself. The only catch is that, if he decides not to stay in the job for at least three years, he won't get a paid return fare to Earth, which would then cost him a daunting amount of money. So it is in his interest to stay at least three years, which is both what his employers intended and what he firmly intends to do.

3. Solitude—Just two days before Frank left Earth for this place, he experienced one of life's major disappointments. Judy, his "relationship" of four years, had told him on their last night together that she had decided not to accompany him on this journey as they had planned. Even worse, she saw no point in trying to maintain a relationship over such vast distances. He tried strenuously to change her mind, but finally left Judy's house in utter despair and returned home to pack. Now, while he doesn't really relish being alone, he hopes that the challenges of his new job—and the novelty of his new home planet—will keep him from sitting around and feeling sorry for himself.

4. Time to Write—Frank has always dreamed of being a paid, professional writer, an author, a novelist. Here on Mars, he figures, he'll have the time and perspective he lacked back on Earth, and he plans to begin his writing projects as soon as possible. At least right now he feels ambitious. Perhaps it's a form of self-administered therapy, of consolation and healing, but nowadays, he feels there's a whole bagful of stories inside his head. His plan for the next few years is to give some of those stories plenty of room to develop and emerge, and to bring his literary dreams to fruition. Now, Frank has the time, hardware, software—and the perspective that comes with great distances—to crank out a series of books and articles, with topics ranging from "First Foreman on Mars" to a tragicomic romance novel based on his ill-fated relationship. When his hometown newspaper reported his new position, in fact, one publisher actually sought him out and offered him a contract for that "Foreman" book. So that'll come first. Then, based on the success and fame from that work, it shouldn't be too hard, he figures, to get some subsequent attention for his novel.

5. A Change of Scenery—There is something about the empty, silent sweep of the unending dry red sand hills that Frank sees out of his 55th-level apartment windows that he finds extremely peaceful. And that suits him just fine. In fact, as long as the

quickly spreading city doesn't encroach on his panoramic view, he figures, he's really going to like it here. Besides, here, the pollution and other environmental hazards of Earth, along with its host of intractable social problems such as war, intolerance, class struggle, and racial animosity, are far behind him, and he feels poised to make a clean, fresh start in both his personal and professional lives. If this planet only had a more breathable atmosphere, and maybe a bunch of green trees and a river or a lake or two, in fact, it'd be perfect for him.

After a devastating four years of precarious intimacy with a problematical woman, Frank figures he needs time by himself to clear his head. In a strange way, there's something actually comforting about having Judy some 60 million miles away—a healthy barrier to chance encounters, awkward meetings, or confrontations. He figures maybe they're both better off this way. After all, from her perspective, Frank was the one to break up their relationship when he made his decision to interview for and accept this new job so terribly far away. He is elated that he has been chosen for this important assignment and has vowed—to himself and his employers—that he'll give this job his all.

He misses Judy, misses her intensely! But, after journeying all these millions of miles to accept a challenge no one has ever dealt with before, he hopes he'll be too busy to brood over a woman who, after saying for years that she couldn't imagine life without him, has now evidently found that she can do quite nicely without Frank, thank you very much. At least he desperately hopes he'll be busy. Wouldn't do at all, in this brave new world, to be sitting around sulking. Too much to do for that.

And yet . . . he feels he needs to talk to Judy one last time, and so he has a plan. He plans to give their relationship one more, final try when he gets in touch with her today. He's prepared for whatever her response might be. If she remains firm in her resolve not to join him . . . well, so be it. He'll survive and recover. He has already stopped muttering "How could she do this to me?" with pained incredulity and now says an angry, snarled "Good riddance!" when he thinks of her. But who's he kidding? He still loves her. And even if her answer is still no, Frank plans to heal rapidly in the rarefied air of this planet, and then, when he thinks he's ready for it, go in search of a suitable companion among the swelling population of New Chicago's settlers, who arrive every day. No sense carrying a torch, he figures, especially on a planet lacking enough atmospheric oxygen to sustain one.

But first, that one last college try. Frank reaches the cybrary at last and walks slowly up the inclined plane towards the air door of the dun-colored building. The door treadle, feeling his weight, opens with a pneumatic whoosh. One last time before entering, he turns around to survey the view from the front door, noticing that one of the Martian moons—the pale one—hovers just over the horizon while the other, darker one, hangs about 10 degrees to the left of straight overhead. Deimos and Phobos, they're called, Greek names for emotions, he read in his briefing manual. Horror and Terror. Pretty depressing nomenclature. Not names thought up by Earthside real estate developers, maybe, but seeing two moons in the sky suits him fine. The Greeks gave those frightening names to the satellites of Mars over two millennia ago. A sense of continuity—of time—is all part of the affinity he feels for Mars. Its ancient, flat canals and silent pockmarked hills seem to match his mood of quiet inner contemplation. At least they do, now. Tomorrow, or the day after that, he may feel differently about looking up at moons with names that translate to Horror and Terror. But today? Why not? Definitely a refreshing change of scene from his Earthly home, a mile or so from Judy's house, where once he and she walked arm in arm. Sighing, he steps through the door.

∅

Once inside the cybrary, Frank rips off his confining helmet and puts it down in one of the racks intended for that purpose. Bloody thing is such a nuisance! While he knows that without it, he'd be comatose in half an hour, it's still one of the problems of life on his new home planet. He has read that Mars's new colonial government is planning a dome (or even several interlocking domes) to cover the cities, at least, which would make it possible for Earth people to move about in breathable air without a helmet, but those domes are unfortunately several years (and billions of credits) away. Frank stores the helmet by the door, setting the oxygen control to recharge, and unencumbered, looks around the cybrary's vast entryway with interest.

Colorful interior, at least, he thinks. Very bright and cheerful. The builders have done what they could to render the inside of Martian public buildings attractive (if perhaps a bit garish), especially when compared to the virtually monochrome red outside. The designers of New Chicago have leaned heavily towards the colors of the Terran Sea: greens, blues, aquamarine, turquoise; colors not found in the Martian landscape. The cybrary is well-appointed, too. Its furniture looks brand new and expensive; all the hardware and telecommunications systems are state-of-the-art, and the environmental system is self-contained, designed to provide Earthlike comfort for building occupants, despite whatever is going on outside.

Frank walks to the first set of traditional cybrary shelving, looking not much different from the way he guesses such shelving did a century ago. This, too, he read, is intentional, designed to take some of the future shock out of the experience of coming to this harsh, faraway place and trying to build a new life for oneself. The cybrary has seemingly endless shelves of brightly covered books, arranged in showcase fashion for the purpose of attracting patrons from the surrounding community. Back on

Earth, physical books are a rarity nowadays, having long since been discarded—or at least superseded—in favor of electronic technology. Here on Mars, however, psychologists have determined that residents would prefer familiar books to all other formats of cybrary material, giving them something they can snuggle up with during long, cold, and dark Martian nights. Frank makes a mental note to pick up a couple of novels on the way out. After he talks to Judy. Yes, Judy. That's objective number one.

The cybrary boasts that it offers a wide range of other services, for all ages, as well: vids, programmed experiences, laserdisks, toys, and other media. Funny, Frank reflects, all these newfangled wonders, most of which weren't even invented when he was a kid, and the survey he read said that his fellow colonists on Mars want more and better books, in preference to anything else. Go figure.

He runs his hand idly along the top of the first set of bookshelves he encounters, noticing that it's easy to keep a dust-free building when there's no outside wind to blow it into the building and an airdoor to keep inside and outside atmospheres separate. Well, let's quit stalling, here, he commands himself. Time to see what's what. He follows signs down the hall and into the Electronics Sector of the building, fully fitted out with rows of individual study rooms, with comfortable sofas and other motel-room-style furniture. It is eerily quiet in the building. No other customers or patrons and not even any staff are in sight. The only sound is the gentle shhhhh of the climatizer, blowing filtered air throughout the empty rooms and corridors. He looks around for someone to answer his questions.

There's nobody around. Then, he remembers that this cybrary is fully automated. A lot of foresight went into the planning of this facility, he knows. One of the most critical needs for builders and settlers in New Chicago is the ability to have contact with Earth. In terms of the speed of light, though, they're not really all that far away. Yet, even though it takes a scant minute or so for particle beams of communication to travel through the empty vastness between the two planets, a common psychological problem among Martian colonists is a feeling of alienation, of being cut off from familiar things. Certainly true of me, Frank muses. How I miss Judy!

But Frank is lucky because he is well paid, at least. He can afford to call Judy or anyone he wants back on Earth. Not everybody will find it so easy and affordable to talk to their loved ones back home. The main problem with interplanetary communication is cost—meaning that the age-old division between the haves and the have-nots exists even here on Mars. Few of the hardy colonists of New Chicago, despite the good pay of construction jobs, can actually afford to pay for the calls home they want to make. The cost of sending messages home or talking to people back on Earth is prohibitive for many of Mars's new residents, especially the preferred transmission of combined images and voice.

For those who have no one back home to call, Experience Booths have been provided, so that colonists feeling a sense of withdrawal or deprivation can, without leaving Mars, just close their eyes and find themselves sitting by a waterfall under green trees and listening to bullfrogs bellow and loons call across crystal lakes on evenings in mid-summer. Mars can really get to you, and some people (possibly including Frank himself) are going to experience great surges of homesickness. So this place's experience technology, he thinks, will be doing a land-office business.

Easing into one of the communications booths and gently closing the door, Frank decides to see if he can set up his own Earthpatch, by following the printed directions on the table next to his armchair. But it doesn't work. No connection. He tries again, gently massaging his temples with the fingers of both hands in frustration. A headache that has been building behind his eyes all day now throbs insistently for attention. A third trial. Still no joy. There are painkillers in his well-stocked medicine chest in his apartment, he knows, but he just doesn't have the energy to go all the way home and get some. Resolutely, he keeps attempting to establish an Earthpatch and discovers the same annoying message on the screen each time. He utters a vile oath and slaps his hand on the arm of the chair in frustration.

"*Excuse me, Frank.*" The voice is soft, melodious, and familiar, causing Frank to turn quickly in his contour chair. "*May I help you with something?*" The voice emanating from the ceiling is the same one he hears in his helmet when he takes his walks.

"Marlies? That you?" he responds. "You're here, too?"

"*You were expecting maybe Thomas Edison?*" the voice seems to conceal a smile. "*I try to be wherever you need me, Frank. That's my job. So what's the problem? Trouble establishing an Earthpatch?*"

"Yeah. I thought I could work these controls myself, but something's not happening. Can you help me get this contraption to work?" He gestures at the console screen. "I don't know what's wrong—whether it's this thing or me. I arranged for payment first, then followed all the directions carefully—I'm almost sure of that—several times. And each time, I received only that message for my trouble."

The monitor displays, blinking on and off in Day-Glo orange:

Earthpatch Failed.

Earth-Mars Link Infeasible At This Time

Please Request Assistance.

"*Hmmmm,*" says Marlies thoughtfully. "*No mystery here. You just picked the wrong time to try to make your call, that's all.*"

"Yeah?" Frank asks. "Well, who do I see about that?

"Me. Looks like a problem with planetary alignment, easily solved if one is patient. Let me consult my technical tables program regarding Earthtrans settings, and I'll come up with a time for you."

"Yeah, well, make it soon, will you? I need an Earthpatch right away, but as you can see, the system doesn't seem to be cooperating just now. So please find out what the problem is, and how—and more importantly, when—I can get through."

"No problem. Frank, maybe it's none of my business, but I can tell this is no ordinary call home. What's the story? Want to talk about it? I'm here to listen, so talk to me."

"You're right. It's none of your business. But maybe we'll talk later, all right? Right now, I just need to know the next time I can speak one-on-one to someone back on Earth."

"Right. Gotcha. See, Frank, in simple terms, the problem is that the two planets don't usually spin in the same direction. And even when they do, point-to-point voice and vision traffic can be problematical, or even impossible, certain times of the day. That means that there are good times and bad times to talk to points on Earth, and even plenty of times when it just can't be done at all. Direct transmissions from Mars to Earth and from Earth to Mars are only possible during line-of-sight hours, those times when the place on Earth you want to reach is more or less directly overhead and lined up with our location here on Mars. But then, the good news is that, at those optimal times, you can talk to your party, and it's as though he or she is sitting in the same room with you."

"That's what I need, all right," Frank confirms. Another thought strikes him then, and he frowns in worry, glancing nervously up at the overhead plate, from which Marlies's voice seems to be emanating. "But can I, ahh . . . will I be able to, like, touch that person—when we talk, I mean?"

Marlies's electronic voice softens now, a tribute to the sensitivity programming the builders put into recent models like her. *"Ahh, sorry, Frank. No. Not touch. There are limits to what can be done, even on state-of-the art networks like ours. No, you can see and be seen; and hear and be heard. But touching? No way. Not yet, anyway."*

"Not yet? What do you mean, 'not yet?'"

"Well, there's something in development, but not yet in production. I've been informed that it should be ready next year about this time. It's called Cybersex, and it was designed for lovers who are separated by great distances but still connected electronically."

Frank is intrigued. "Yeah? Do tell. How does it work?"

"Well, you and your lover, in your respective homes, would each put on a snugly fitting bodysuit, containing millions of tiny electronic units woven into its fabric. Then you and she would move at the same time, simulating lovemaking. And as you moved, your respective bodysuits would transmit tactile sensations to each other. And if such tactile sensations were accompanied by visual images and voice technology, you would feel—as closely as possible under those conditions—as though you were actually making love."

"Interesting, I must admit. But it'll never take the place of the real thing, I'm willing to bet."

"*Probably not. Besides, as I've told you, it's not available yet, Frank, so for the present, put it out of your mind.*"

"Returning to my question, will I be able to touch her when I get in contact with her through that Earthpatch?"

"*No. I told you. Actually, if you were to put out your hand and try to touch her, your hand would pass right through her flesh. So I don't recommend that you even try. Might be jarring, given the emotional bond between you. Some humans just can't handle it. Depression can ensue. Heightened awareness of just how far from home you really are. So try to remember to keep your hands to yourself.*"

Frank mulls this over for a while. "Well, maybe you're right. If our hands passed through each other, I don't know how I'd feel about that. Thanks for the warning. But I have another question: since this part of Mars and the place on Earth I want to call aren't lined up the way you said, what happens now? Do I just go home and forget about it and come back, or what?"

"*No, you still have two options during nonaligned hours. You may either record your message now for transmission at a later time when the Earth station desired and our corresponding Mars station are conjoint, or go home, as you said, and wait until the planetary alignment permits direct two-way transmission. If you wish, I can check the matrix grid for precise coordinates and times.*"

Frowning, Frank says, "Sounds awfully complicated. What does all that mean? Plain English, this time, all right?"

"*Plain English it is, then. It means either that you're going to have to record the message that you want to send back home, and it'll be uplinked as soon as the place you want on Earth is overhead, or you'll have to make an appointment and come back when conditions are optimal for transmission.*"

"Return? Like, when? I work 35 hours a week. Sometimes more."

"*Working on it. Solution in one-six seconds, to be precise,*" says Marlies. Frank drops into a chair in front of Marlies's color readout screen. "*Come on, Frank, trust me! I can see that your call is much more important than the kind you made the other day, when you just reassured your parents that you arrived safely, you're fine, taking your vitamins, and always wearing your helmet when you go outside. A lot more important. So what's the story?*"

"Later, I said. For now, can I just find out what I need to know?"

"*Sure, Frank. But let's start with this: exactly where on Earth do you want your transmission received?*"

"Sarasota, Florida, USA," he answers.

"*Good,*" says Marlies, "*Now we're getting someplace.*" Brightly colored screens replace one another on the console, and Frank sees, when the readout becomes stationary, that it displays a complicated matrix of Earth latitudes and longitudes within thin gridlines. "*Let's see, now. . . . The coordinates for Sarasota, Florida, are, rounded off, about 27-point-5 degrees north, and about 82-point-5 degrees west. That puts it in Earthzone . . . 156, which has to match up with where we are now, New Chicago, in Marszone 23. Right. Working. Solution in one-six seconds. Ah. Here we go: The next time for optimal Earthpatch is at 0240 tomorrow, New Chicago time, when the cybrary is closed, I'm sorry to say."*

Frank catches his breath sharply. "Closed? After all that? So that's no good for me at all, is it? Well, when's the next time after that when the cybrary is open?"

"Optimal conditions next exist this Friday afternoon, at 3:43 p.m. local time. The window of opportunity is almost an hour long. Any earlier or later and you might experience some visual and sound quality problems. Possibly severe. Try calling half an hour earlier. That gives you 30 minutes or so when conditions are improving and 30 during which they worsen. After 4:13, you're going to lose the capability entirely."

"Friday? Three days?" exclaims Frank. "I was hoping to talk to her now. But I suppose it can't be helped. So what can I do in the meantime?"

"I'd advise recording your message now. It'll be sent to Earth by satellite in the next electronic packet and received by your party tomorrow morning, Earthtime."

"But I want to talk to her now!" Frank moans. "Really *need* to talk to her now!" Then he catches himself and closes his eyes. "Sorry, Marlies. I have a headache, and I'm pretty worried about this call, as you already guessed. Not your fault, I know. So can I schedule an appointment or a reservation for the next 'optimal time' or whatever you call it, Friday afternoon?"

"Working." Marlies consults her scheduling program, while Frank, obviously impatient, shifts nervously in his chair. *"That's confirmed. You have a date, at three on Friday afternoon."* she says.

"Well, it's better than nothing, I suppose," says Frank, shrugging. "Okay, I'll record a message now, telling my . . . ah . . . friend that we'll be able to have our nice long heart-to-heart next Friday, between three and four, our time, which will be when in Florida, exactly?"

"Working. Ahhh . . . That'll be between seven and eight a.m., Eastern standard Earthtime. Your friend get up early?"

"She'd better. After all, I'm worth it. Frankly, I just hope my friend still thinks so, now that I've moved millions of miles away from her. She wasn't very happy when I took this job and moved here, I'll tell you that."

"Yeah, emigration to Mars has really given a new meaning to the expression 'long distance relationships,' hasn't it?" Marlies commiserates.

"You got that right. All right, I'll record a brief message now and send it on ahead. Then, I'll be back Friday about three for the real thing. So what's the procedure?"

"Just remain seated in that chair, and I'll set it up for you. When you see the amber light come on, look straight into the abstract painting on the far wall and speak your piece just like you were leaving a note on somebody's answering machine, back home."

"Yeah, but I hate this! It's so impersonal, just leaving a message. So one-way!"

"*Remember: This is only your preliminary message, not the real deal. Its purpose is just to alert your friend that the chance to sit down and talk with you is coming. Then Friday . . . It'll be as though you and . . . whomever. . . . at least tell me her name.*"

"Judy. Her name's Judy."

"*Thank you. . . . Then it'll be as though you and Judy are sitting together in a private room, having a good long conversation — for as long as the window permits, anyway. As I told you, the window is only open for about an hour, but that's a long time, all the same, to say what's in your heart.*"

"Yeah, but . . . I'd sure like to hold her hand, when we talk," Frank groans.

"*You can try, but what's the point? You won't be able to touch her or feel her. If you attempt it, your hands would just pass through each other. My advice? Don't even try. Too disconcerting. Just keep your hands to yourself. But you'll see each other's facial expressions and body language; that really enhances the sensations of being in the same room. So satisfy my curiosity: Who is this Judy you want to talk to so urgently? Girlfriend?*"

"Not anymore," replies Frank bitterly. "She was until a short time ago, but that's all over now, I guess. . . . Well, if I'm going to record and send that message, I guess I'd better get started. I'm late for work as it is."

"*Right. Let's get started. Wait for the amber light, then look at the painting and just speak your piece.*" Frank looks around the small but well-appointed cubicle, furnished with a comfortable armchair, a rich, deep-pile carpet, and a large, abstract, cheerful painting on the wall, concealing a camera and microphone. "*First, be sure to speak the name of your party, then her Earthcom number, then your message — you'll have up to 10 minutes but I'd advise you not to wax too eloquent. Save the persuasion for Friday, know what I mean?—and I'll do the rest.*"

Frank looks upward thoughtfully for a long moment. "Umm . . ."

"*Problem?*"

"Yeah, well . . . what about . . . you know . . . privacy?"

"*Frank, there are strict and stringently enforced laws that govern both privacy and confidentiality, applying to communication on Mars as well as on Earth, and all electronic traffic between the two. The revised Criminal Justice Code for Interplanetary Affairs is strict on privacy, believe me. To summarize its provisions, you may speak via our transmission system in complete privacy. I'm the only one who will have access to your messages and conversations, and I'm the soul of discretion, I assure you. If I told any other human what you say in your communication, my employers wouldn't mess around with me. I'd be dismembered and sold for scrap and spare parts, and my components would become telemetry equipment on the next rocket to Earth. Satisfied?*"

"Satisfied. Sorry I had to bring it up, but it was bothering me. All right, I'll just leave that message now, alerting Judy to our Friday conversation. I won't be long." As Frank closes the door behind him, Marlies has one thing more to say.

"Frank, we may not know each other very well yet, but I am programmed to be intimately acquainted with human psychology. I can guess what you're thinking and . . ."

"Yeah, yeah, yeah," Frank interrupts, "save it, will you, Marlies?" He's had enough disappointment already this month and really doesn't want to hear any more bad news. "Just cut to the chase, will you?"

"Gladly. I just don't want you to get hurt, that's all. That's part of my job, too."

"Listen . . ." Frank begins, but whatever he is about to say gets lost when the amber light begins to glow. Abruptly, he puts a smile on his face, faces the wall, and begins to talk to Judy about when he plans to call her for a long, long talk and a hint of what he plans to talk to her about. When he's finished recording his message, he feels wrung out when he gets out of the chair and walks into the corridor. "Marlies? Finished," he announces to the ceiling.

"Good. Your message will be on its way to Earth in the next packet. Judy will get it in the morning. The fee has been automatically deducted from your credit account. So I'll see you here Friday, around three p.m., local time. And be sure to be on time, hear? The window of opportunity gets wavy towards the end."

"Right. I'll be sure to show up as scheduled."

"Good," Marlies says, *"then if everything is running normally, you and your Judy in Florida will be able to sit down together—in a manner of speaking, anyway—and talk for almost a full hour."*

"That's what I need, all right. And thanks!"

"Look, Frank," Marlies calls as he's retrieving his helmet and awkwardly getting it over his head, *"if you'd like to talk about it, at any time, well, like I said, I'm a pretty good listener. Try me. Twenty-four hours an Earth day, I'm here. And I promise that anything we talk about will never be repeated. Actually, that'd be impossible."*

"I appreciate that. But—no offense—how can you help me with a relationship? You're a robot, programmed for logic and decision making. You can't understand," Frank explains. "Sophisticated as you may be, you're still a machine, for all that. You can't comprehend love, let alone love lost."

"Right you are! And I'm extremely grateful for that! In my short time of existence, I have seen fine human intelligences—like yours, I think—completely uprooted by what you call love."

"Yeah, you've got a point," says Frank. "We'll just have to see what happens Friday. And thanks, Marlies. For everything."

"No problem. Enjoy your day, Frank. Catch you later."

Frank stops on his way to the cybrary's front door and selects two novels at random, which he self-checks-out at the desk. He then dons his helmet, seals the plastic faceplate, adjusts the oxygen and temp controls, and walks outside. He stands silently surveying the ancient red hills of Mars, washed in the pale light of the twin moons. He looks up into the eastern sky. Somewhere up there, the woman he'd loved so much it hurt and who he'd always planned to marry, is busily getting on with her new life, a life in which Frank obviously doesn't figure at all. Unless Friday's conversation turns her around, that is. He plans to do everything he can to persuade her to catch the next Mars rocket and join him here. But he figures his chances of having that happen are dwindling with every passing minute. Still, Friday, they'll have a long talk—the two of them alone and conversing intimately in the same room—even though they're physically separated by millions of miles of empty space. Their conversation is going to have to be family entertainment suitable for all audiences. But that might be just as well: He knows in his heart that his once-luminous relationship is gone, a casualty of distance, failed hopes, and miscommunication. Friday, he knows, will just be the last nail in its coffin. He feels restless and decides to walk to work, before noontime's dangerously high temperatures interdict such activity. He strolls down an ancient flat canal, in the double shadow of the two Martian moons. Somewhere up there in the clear, cold sky is a tiny blue-green dot, low on the horizon, which tonight will be visible swimming in a vast sea of stars. Earth, and Judy, and the life he knew there—so small and insignificant looking when viewed from this perspective. But here on Mars, maybe there will be opportunities not granted to most people. Second chances and new beginnings. He trudges along through cold reddish dust. So what if Judy is a closed book, ancient history? His life isn't over; it's just beginning all over again.

On an impulse, he walks to the edge of the canal, selects a "football" from those sitting in the bright sunshine, and addresses it. When he gives it a good swift kick, the red rock sails up and away into the rarefied atmosphere, sailing on for what seems to be miles before it falls softly back to Mars, raising a concentric cloud of red dust that lingers for minutes in the thin, windless air. Long after he walks briskly on towards his job site, the dust still hovers over the ancient dead plain.

> *He had been driving steadily for an hour, . . . no other car on the road, no light, just the road . . . and Mars out there, so quiet. Mars was always quiet. . . . The deserts and empty seas swung by him, and the mountains against the stars. . . . He pulled into a little dead Martian town, stopped the engine, and let the silence come in around him. He sat . . . looking out at the white buildings in the moonlight. Uninhabited for centuries. Perfect, faultless, in ruins, yes but perfect, nevertheless. . . . The moons had gone down. Starlight twinkled on the empty highway.*
>
> —Ray Bradbury. *The Martian Chronicles*. 1950. ∎

FUTURE QUOTES

Hundreds—maybe thousands—of English-language writers and public speakers have speculated about the future during the present century and the ones before it. Here is a compendium of selected—and quite varied—quotes, arranged alphabetically by author, and showing a broad spectrum of opinions about the future, revealing both the optimistic and pessimistic sides of human nature and thought.

"The future you shall know when it has come; before then, forget it."—Aeschylus

"I have seen the future and it is very much like the present—only longer."—Kehlog Albran

"Bright faces of tomorrow: whiskey-heads and hop-heads, old cokey-joes and musclemen on the prowl for one last wandering square to muscle before the final arc-lamp dims. When the poolrooms are all padlocked and the juke-boxes are all still. When the glasses are all empty. And, under the torn and sagging ties of the long-blasted El, the last survivors cook up the earth's final mulligan. . . . Every day is D-day under the El."—Nelson Algren

"The things you hate most always have to go ahead and happen. . . . It might help if we knew where we were going, and how fast. . . . But we see accidents, everywhere, on the information highway. We see hazard lights and freezing fog. We see jackknife and whiplash."—Martin Amis

"Be careful what you wish for; you may get it."—Anonymous

"It isn't enough to safeguard posterity; we must also provide a posterity to safeguard."—Anonymous

"Perhaps the best thing about the future is that it comes only one day at a time."—Anonymous

"The future is like heaven — everyone exults in it but no one wants to go there now."—James Baldwin

"The function of prediction is not, as often stated, to aid social control, but to widen the spheres of moral choice."—Daniel Bell

"Future, n.: that period of time in which our affairs prosper, our friends are true, and our happiness is assured."—Ambrose Bierce

"The future is an opaque mirror. Anyone who tries to look into it sees nothing but the dim outlines of an old and worried face."—Jim Bishop

"The question for me is not what kind of future do I (or anyone else) predict, but rather what kind of a future would I want to participate in

153

creating? Certainly, it is not a future devoid of the book. . . . The book has a future if we enlarge its audience. That we will do when we learn to pay more attention to the variety of needs of that audience, present and potential."—Murray Bob

"When all else is lost, the future still remains."—Christian Nestell Bovée

"Because things are the way they are, things will not stay the way they are."—Bertold Brecht

"I can face anything except the future, and parts of the past and present."—Ashleigh Brilliant

"Because of its plenitude, the future is propaganda."—Joseph Brodsky

"We must sacrifice for the future or else we steal from it."—Edmund G. Brown Jr.

"You have no idea how pleasant it is not to have any future. It's like having a totally efficient contraceptive."—Anthony Burgess

"You can never plan the future by the past."—Edmund Burke

"I have seen the future — and it was being repaired."—Mel Calman

"Those who talk about the future are scoundrels. It is the present that matters. To evoke one's posterity is to make a speech to maggots."—Louis Ferdinand Céline

"There are only two families in the world, the Haves and the Have-Nots."—Miguel de Cervantes, *Don Quixote de la Mancha,* 1615

"I am not a 'futurist.' Futurists want the world to be a better place. They want the rich and the poor to get closer together and rich and poor countries to get closer together. They want everybody to love everybody. They are Utopian in their thinking. That's fine. As a person, I am a futurist. As a professional, I am a forecaster. A forecaster takes all ideas through a three-step process. Ideas must be technically feasible, and socially and politically acceptable. If one of those things doesn't take place, the idea is not going to happen. . . . All the technological knowledge we work with today will represent only 1 percent of the knowledge that will be available in 2050. This is important, because out of the 44 percent of the workforce who will be working with information technology at the turn of the century, half will be working out of their homes and 'telecommuting' to work, thanks to advanced technology."—Marvin Cetron, "Class of 2000: The Good News and the Bad News," *The Futurist,* November-December, 1988.

"One should never place one's trust in the future. It doesn't deserve it."—André Chamson

"The empires of the future are the empires of the mind."—Winston Churchill

"For my part, I think that a knowledge of the future would be a disadvantage."—Cicero

"When a distinguished but elderly statesman says that something is possible, he is almost certainly right. But when he states that something is impossible, he is very probably wrong. . . . This is the first age that's paid much attention to the future, which is a little ironic, since we may not have one."—Arthur C. Clarke

"For the sake of our children, . . . let us use government as we have in the past, to further the common good. Nothing is more important to our shared future than the well-being of children."—Hillary Rodham Clinton

"In the year 2025 . . . in the U.S., there will be a national healthcare system. . . . The collapse of the Social Security system will lead to a new system of old-age security based on need only. . . . Many natural disasters, such as earthquakes, will be mitigated, controlled or prevented."—Joseph F. Coates

"If a man takes no thought about what is distant, he will find sorrow near at hand."—Confucius

"(My) anticipations . . . should not be viewed as forecasts or predictions because such terms suggest that these developments, or 'futuribles,' to use a word that is widely used in French but not yet in English. In order to think intelligently about the future, we must conceptualize what might realistically happen in the time period we are considering. Here, the author focuses on the early decades of the twenty-first century, to about 2025, when those babies born in 1995 will be 30 years old. As we identify the possibilities of the cyber future, we can act to make them happen—or prevent them from happening. And we can acquire useful insights into the enormous opportunities and challenges that lie ahead. . . . Both government officials and dissidents will increasingly use cyberspace to spread lies as well as accurate information. . . . Separating truth from falsehood—and useful information from trivia—will be one of the great challenges of people using information networks. . . . As society globalizes, the frustration of people's need for recognition by others may cause them to lose their self-respect. They may come to feel that they count for nothing and their lives are meaningless. Such feelings can move people toward drug abuse, crime, and terrorism."—Edward Cornish, "The Cyber Future: 92 Ways Our Lives Will Change by the Year 2025," *The Futurist*, January-February, 1996.

"Human beings are transforming the planet, and nobody knows whether it's a dangerous development or not. . . . In ten thousand years, human beings have gone from hunting to farming to cities to cyberspace . . . (personally) I think cyberspace means the end of our species . . . because it means the end of innovation."—Michael Crichton

"New turf, new players, new rules. Things ain't what they used to be."—Blaise Cronin and B. Davenport

"Shallow men speak of the past; wise men of the present, and fools of the future."—Mme. du Deffand

"What we anticipate seldom occurs; what we least expected generally happens."—Benjamin Disraeli

"The only certainty in (the) remote future is that radically new things will be happening."—Freeman Dysan

"A prediction that does not come true is not necessarily a bad prediction. For instance, predictions that have foretold environmental catastrophe may be avoided in the long run because of those very predictions. To put it more dramatically, the accuracy of a future forecast is trivial compared to its impact on the present."—Paul Dickson

"I never think of the future. It comes soon enough."—Albert Einstein

"Keep cool; it will be all one a hundred years hence."—Ralph Waldo Emerson

"Science fiction is a kind of archaeology of the future."—Clifton Fadiman

"Those organizations that most accurately assess and most effectively meet human needs will grow. If the libraries do not meet human needs, people won't go to the libraries. They'll go to video parlours."—Frank Feather

"Futurology is a child of the Enlightenment and reflects the Enlightenment belief in a future era of unbounded progress brought about through the harnessing of science and technology to the betterment or even the transcendence of the human condition. . . . Futurists have been concerned not simply with predicting future events and conditions in a chronological sense but in discerning the outlines of a better future—a new era—awaiting mankind. Historically, futurists have leaned overwhelmingly toward optimism, even to the point of utopianism."—Victor C. Ferkiss

"The future is a convenient place for dreams."—Anatole France

"You wanna know the future? I'll tell you the future, man: more shit!"—Peter Friedlander

"The danger of the past was that men became slaves. The danger of the future is that men may become robots."—Erich Fromm

"I have seen the future and it doesn't work."—Robert Fulford

"A hundred years from now it won't make any difference."—Robert Fulghum

"The future is a choice between Utopia and oblivion."—R. Buckminster Fuller

"He that fears not the future may enjoy the present."—Thomas Fuller

"You cannot fight against the future. Time is on our side. . . . The future is to me a blank. I cannot at all guess what is coming."—William Ewart Gladstone

"The future is an unwelcome guest."—Edmund Gosse

"This is my prediction for the future—whatever hasn't happened yet will happen, and no one will be safe from it."—J. B. S. Haldane

"We are not so much in love with the past as afraid of the present, and in positive horror of the future."—Donal Henahan

"I have but one lamp by which my feet are guided, and that is the lamp of experience. I know no way of judging of the future but by the past. . . . I like the dreams of the future better than the history of the past."—Patrick Henry

"The irony of the matter is that future generations do not have a vote. In effect, we hold their proxies."—Charles J. Hitch

"The only certain thing about the future is that it will surprise even those who have seen the furthest into it."—E. J. Hobsbaum

"The handwriting on the wall may be a forgery."—Ralph Hodgson

"The only way to predict the future is to have the power to shape the future."—Eric Hoffer

"The lion may lie down with the lamb, but the lamb ain't gonna get no sleep at night."—Langston Hughes

"I hold that man is in the right who is most closely in league with the future."—Henrik Ibsen

"The past is really the only source of information we have about the future. . . . As for the future, your task is not to foresee but to enable it."—Max Jakobson

"Stick around. . . . You ain't seen nothin', yet!"—Al Jolson

"Can't they see the future?. . . I can only say—you better go out and get what you want this trip, because this is the trip; the only trip."—Thom Jones

"The future is purchased by the present."—Samuel Johnson

"Various types of future should be portrayed on TV, allowing the public to vote in a referendum on 'the future of your choice.' The chief message of the futurists is that man is not trapped in an absurd fate but that he can and must choose his destiny—a technological reassertion of free will."—Bertrand de Jouvenel

"The future is not in the hands of fate but in ours."—Jules Jusserand

"We have crystal balls but they're no good."—Alfred Kahn

"My preferred method of futuring is 'scenario writing,' in which various alternative future situations are dramatized."—Herman Kahn

"The future is religion and commerce, aphrodisiac and Benzedrine, a mother of mysterious comfort and a mistress of familiar ravishments, ever at the verge of embracing or destroying us. . . . We not only romanticize the future; we have also made it into a growth industry, a parlor game and a disaster movie all at the same time."—Eugene Kennedy

"We should all be concerned about the future because we will have to spend the rest of our lives there. . . . You will always underestimate the future."—Charles F. Kettering

"The United States and the Soviet Union should see what kind of a world we want in the year 2000, and, if we agree, work back from there."—Henry A. Kissinger

"The only reason people want to be masters of the future is to change the past."—Milan Kundera

"Ultimately . . . libraries as we know them seem likely to disappear. Facilities will still exist to preserve the print-on-paper record of the past, of course, but they will be more like archives, or even museums, providing little in the way of public service. As for the electronic sources, libraries may have an interim role to play . . . to subsidize access to electronic publications. . . . In the longer term, it seems certain that the library will be bypassed. That is, people will have very little reason to visit libraries in order to gain access to information sources."—F. W. Lancaster

"The Future (is) something which everyone reaches at the rate of sixty minutes an hour, whatever he does, whoever he is."—C. S. Lewis

"The wave of the future is coming and there is no fighting it."—Anne Morrow Lindbergh

"Perhaps the greatest impulse in trying to foresee and plan the future comes from the combination of having new tools with which to do it and the growing realization that every technological and social innovation has repercussions which spread like a wave through the complex interlocked sections of society."—Ward Madden

"The mere image in a film of a family refrigerator is a revolutionary symbol to people who have no refrigerators."—Marshall McLuhan, *Understanding Media*, 1962

"The gee-whiz futurists are always wrong because they believe technological innovation travels in a straight line. It doesn't. It weaves and bobs and lurches and sputters."—John Naisbitt

"People live for the morrow, because the day-after-tomorrow is doubtful."—Friedrich Nietzsche

"It's a whole new ball game out there. Either you embrace the enormous technological and social changes happening to us all or you'll be swamped by them. . . . Knowledge is doubling at the rate of 100 percent every 20 months. What you know now will be obsolete by Christmas."—Frank Ogden

"Who controls the past controls the future. . . . Who controls the present controls the past. . . . If you want a picture of the future, imagine a boot stamping on the human face—forever—and remember that it is forever."—George Orwell

"Now is then's only tomorrow."—Kenneth Patchen

"The supreme value is not the future but the present. The future is a deceitful time that always says to us, 'Not Yet,' and thus denies us. The future is not the time of love: what man truly wants he wants now. Whoever builds a house for future happiness builds a prison for the present."—Octavio Paz

"He is a bad man who does not pay to the future at least as much as he has received from the past."—A. W. Pollard

"The rule on staying alive as a forecaster is to give 'em a number or give 'em a date, but never give 'em both at once."—Jane Bryant Quinn

"We experience the past as singular: the history. But the future is plural: an infinity of alternative futures."—William Renfro

"The only limit to our realization of tomorrow will be our doubts of today. Let us move forward with strong and active faith."—Franklin Delano Roosevelt

"Music is the sole art which evokes nostalgia for the future."—Ned Rorem

"Years from now, when information retrieval is voice-controlled, we'll find future facts by phone without leaving our home or office. Libraries will become more and more like information-processing centers, rather than storage archives."—Stephen Rosen

"Unless we can find some way to keep our sights on tomorrow, we cannot expect to be in touch with today."—Dean Rusk

"Call our era the Age of Enlightenment. . . . From . . . World War II to the mid-1990s, it is best defined by its soaring ambitions. We had a grand vision. We didn't merely expect things to get better. We expected all social problems to be solved. . . . Workers would have rising incomes and stable jobs. Business cycles would disappear. Poverty, racism and crime would recede. Compassionate government would protect the poor, old and unlucky. We expected almost limitless personal freedom and self-fulfillment. We not only expected these things. After a while, we thought we were entitled to them as a matter of right."—Robert J. Samuelson, *Newsweek*, 1996

"You see things; and you say, 'Why?' But I dream things that never were; and I say, 'Why not?' . . . People are always blaming their circumstances for what they are. I don't believe in circumstances. The people who get on in this world are the people who get up and look for the circumstances they want, and if they can't find them, make them."—George Bernard Shaw

"If you keep on saying that things are going to be bad, you have a good chance of being a prophet."—Isaac Bashevis Singer

"If you see the magic in a fairy tale, you can face the future."—Danielle Steel

"I have seen the future and it works."—Lincoln Steffens

"The past is gone, the present is full of confusion, and the future scares hell out of me."—David Lewis Stein

"The future has waited long enough. If we do not grasp it, other hands, grasping and bloody, will."—Adlai E. Stevenson

"Let me describe my idealized library of the future. There are lots of books, a card catalog, a children's section with a story hour, a reading room with this morning's newspapers, plenty of magazines, a box of discarded paperback books (selling for a quarter each), a cork bulletin board stapled over with community announcements, a cheap photocopier, and a harried, but smiling, librarian."—Clifford Stoll

"If we do not learn from history, we shall be compelled to relive it. True. But if we do not change the future, we shall be compelled to endure it. And that could be worse. . . . Future shock is the shattering stress and disorientation that we induce in individuals by subjecting them to too much change in too short a time. . . . Futurists tend to be apocalyptic or wildly optimistic. Life doesn't come that way; it's bittersweet. It's filled with horrible complexity and problems and all sorts of good things, too."—Alvin Toffler

"If we don't solve our own problems, other people will—and the world of tomorrow belongs to the people who will solve them."—Pierre Elliott Trudeau

"If it did happen, it wouldn't be the end of the world. Even the end of the world wouldn't be the end of the world."—John Updike

"The trouble with our times is that the future is not what it used to be."—Paul Valéry

"Then God, in His infinite mercy and wisdom, pulls the big switch on us. Throws us a curveball—no, a knuckler—when we're all geared up for the heat, and no doubt busts a gut laughing as we tie ourselves in knots trying to hit it."—Glen Vasey

"Historians in the future, in my opinion, will congratulate us on very little other than our clowning and our jazz."—Kurt Vonnegut

"In the future, everybody will be world famous for at least 15 minutes."—Andy Warhol

"The communications revolution is jolting peasants out of the ruts of tradition and making them aware that their poverty and oppression need not be. This realization, or consciousness-raising, is one of the most fateful developments in history: the awakening of the political and social awareness of . . . poor people. . . . But there is another, less well understood cultural transformation resulting from this mass awakening . . . the communications revolution has, in a profound sense, cheated the peasant. In eagerly jumping into the modern world that calls on him to be a person—an individual enjoying undreamed of material affluence—he finds instead that he has exchanged the warm embrace of a group for the impersonal organization in which he is but a cog in a machine. His economic insecurity is therefore compounded by psychological rage."—Charlotte Waterlow, "The Awakening Peasant: Rising Expectations in the Third World," *The Futurist*, October, 1982

"I did not say that the future could be foretold but I said that its conditions could be foretold. We should be less and less bound to the engagements of the past and more and more ruled by a realization of the creative effect of our efforts. . . There is no way out or round or through. Our universe is not merely bankrupt; there remains no dividend at all; it has not simply liquidated; it is going clean out of existence, leaving not a wrack behind."—H. G. Wells

"I would feel more optimistic about a bright future for man if he spent less time proving that he can outwit Nature and more time tasting her sweetness and respecting her seniority."—E. B. White

"It is the business of the future to be dangerous."—Alfred North Whitehead

"Filing is concerned with the past; anything you actually need to see again has to do with the future. . . . My brother cuts the time it takes to read a newspaper by skipping everything in the future tense; and it's amazing what he doesn't miss."—Katherine Whitehorn

"The future offers very little hope for those who expect that our new mechanical slaves will offer us a world in which we may rest from thinking. Help us they may, but at the cost of supreme demands upon our honesty and our intelligence. The world of the future will be an ever more demanding struggle against the limitations of our intelligence, not a comfortable hammock in which we can lie down to be waited upon by our robot slaves."—Norbert Wiener

"Whatever happened to the fun in our future?"—George F. Will

"The future is called 'perhaps,' which is the only possible thing to call the future. And the important thing is not to allow that to scare you."—Tennessee Williams

"In conditions of great uncertainty, people tend to predict that the events they want to happen actually will happen."—Roberta Wohlstetter

"Let us be such as help the life of the future."—Zoroaster

Bonus Section: Off-Target Predictions of the Future ("OK, so I was wrong. So sue me!")

In addition to the previous assortment of quotes, in which disparate writers comment on the various futures they anticipate, hope for, or fear, this section presents a compendium of mistaken, erroneous, and misguided quotations (listed this time in chronological order), offered as evidence (if evidence is needed) that foretelling the future always was, always is, and always will be an inexact science. Win some, lose some, right?

"The world to an end shall come in eighteen hundred and eighty-one."—Ursula (Mother) Shipton, 1555

"The steam engine was invented specifically as a device for pumping water out of flooded mines. In fact, for a long time it was regarded exclusively as a pump."—James Watt, 1789

"What can be more palpably absurd than the prospect held out of locomotives traveling twice as fast as stagecoaches?"—*The Quarterly Review*, 1825

"Even if the propeller had the power of propelling a vessel, it would be found altogether useless in practice, because of the power being applied in the stern it would be absolutely impossible to make the vessel steer."—Sir William Symonds, British Navy, 1837

"The bathtub is an epicurean innovation from England designed to corrupt the democratic simplicity of the republic. We of the medical profession warn against it as a producer of rheumatic fevers, inflammatory lungs and all zymotic diseases."—*The New York Times,* 1841

"Drill for oil? You mean drill into the ground to try and find oil? You're crazy!"—Drillers whom Edwin L. Drake tried to enlist to his project to drill for oil, 1859

"(The Grand Canyon) is, of course, altogether valueless. . . . Ours has been the first, and will doubtless be the last, party of whites to visit this profitless locality. . . . It seems intended by nature that the Colorado River . . . shall be forever unvisited and undisturbed."—Joseph C. Ives, U.S. Corps of Topographical Engineers, 1861

"One hundred years hence, man will be so completely the master of organic law that he would create life in competition with God."—Claude Bernard, 1869

"Louis Pasteur's theory of germs is ridiculous fiction."—Pierre Pachet, professor of physiology, 1872

"The abdomen, the chest, and the brain will forever be shut from the intrusion of the wise and humane surgeon."—Sir John Erichsen, British surgeon, 1873

"This 'telephone' has too many shortcomings to be seriously considered as a means of communication. The device is inherently of no value to us."—Western Union internal memo, 1876

"Heavier-than-air flying machines are impossible."—Lord Kelvin, president, Royal Society, 1895

"Everything that can be invented has been invented."—Rep. Charles H. Duel, 1895, when Congress was debating the idea of closing the U.S. Patent Office

"By the year 1975, people will be shot from city to city across the country in tubes."—Edward Everett Hale, 1899

"The ordinary 'horseless carriage' is at present a luxury for the wealthy; and although its price will probably fall in the future, it will never, of course, come into as common use as the bicycle."—*The Literary Digest,* 1899.

"The automobile, which is just beginning to appear on streets, will put an end to the roar of city traffic. There will be no more crash of horses' hooves, and the present steel tires will be replaced by rubber ones."—Roy Stannard Baker, 1900, when a total of 8,000 automobiles were registered in the United States

"Laws are becoming more just, rulers more humane; music is becoming sweeter and books wiser. Homes are happier and the individual heart becoming at once more just and more gentle."—Reverend Dwight Hillis, 1900

"The future is blacker than has been any future which any person now living has tried to peer into."—Mark Twain, 1900

"I confess that my imagination refuses to see any sort of submarine doing anything but suffocating its crew and floundering at sea."—H. G. Wells, 1901

"Before the 20th century closes, the earth will be purged of its foulest shame, the killing of men in battle under the name of war."—Andrew Carnegie, 1901

"The actual building of roads devoted to motor cars is not for the near future, in spite of many rumors to that effect."—Harper's Weekly, August 2, 1902

"Within the memory of this generation, the Earth has been girded with iron and steel, and the electric telegraph and the cable have practically annihilated terrestrial space; these modes of communication have come to stay, and they are the ultimate."—Atlantic Monthly, 1902

"The aeroplane has very little commercial value. If giant aeroplanes could be made to move through the atmosphere at hundreds of miles an hour, their propellers would spin themselves to matchsticks at those speeds."—Wilbur Wright, 1902

"I have done some mathematical computations and my figures coincide in fixing 1950 as the year when the world must go smash."—Henry Adams, historian, 1903

"May not our mechanisms be ultimately forced to admit that aerial flight is one of that great class of problems with which man can never cope? The construction of an aerial vehicle which can carry even a single man from place to place at pleasure requires the discovery of some new metal or some new force. Even with such a discovery, we could not expect one to do more than carry its owner."—Simon Newcomb, 1903

"You could put in this room . . . all the radio-telephone apparatus that the country will ever need."—W. W. Dean, president of the Dean Telephone Co., 1907

"Airplanes are interesting toys but of no military value."—Marechal Ferdinand Foch, 1912

"What are the Bolsheviki? They are representatives of the most democratic government in Europe. . . . Let us recognize the truest democracy in Europe (and) in the world today."—William Randolph Hearst, 1918

"We recommend that General Motors dump its Chevrolet division, because the company cannot hope to make a success out of this car."—GM's hired management consulting firm, 1919

"Professor Goddard does not know the relation between action and reaction and the need to have something better than a vacuum against which to react. He seems to lack the basic knowledge ladled out in high schools."—*New York Times*, 1921, editorial about Robert Goddard's revolutionary rocket work

"The wireless music box has no imaginable commercial value. Who would pay for a message sent to nobody in particular?"—David Sarnoff's associates in response to his urgings for investment in the radio in the early 1920s

"While theoretically and technically television may be feasible, commercially and financially, I consider it an impossibility, a development of which we need waste little time dreaming."—Lee de Forest, "father of radio," 1926

"Who the hell wants to hear actors talk?"—H.M. Warner, Warner Brothers, 1927, on the proposal of film with sound

"The everyday application of television is a remote possibility in five years, a fair possibility in ten, a probability in fifteen."—*Literary Digest*, 1927

"No rocket will reach the moon save by a miraculous discovery of an explosive far more energetic than any known. And even if the requisite fuel were produced, it would still have to be shown that the rocket machine would operate at 459 degrees below zero—the temperature of interplanetary space."—Nikola Tesla, U.S. inventor, 1928

"The future market for the computer is extremely limited."—Thomas Watson Sr., 1929

"I will never see the day when the 18th Amendment (Prohibition, repealed in 1933, while Borah was still alive) is out of the Constitution of the United States."—William Borah, U.S. senator, 1929

"Stocks have reached what looks like a permanently high plateau."—Irving Fisher, professor of economics, Yale University, 1929

"By the year 1982, the graduated income tax will have practically abolished major differences in wealth."—Columbia Professor Irwin Edman, 1932

"It has been assumed by many and stated by some that within a reasonable number of years, long-distance transmissions, even across the Atlantic, will be broadcast regularly . . . so the sensational theories predict. The truth is that long-distance television of the type we know today is never likely to be practical or even possible."—Alan Chappell, 1937

"A Japanese attack on Pearl Harbor is a strategic impossibility."—George Fielding Eliot, 1938

"In the year 1960, the populace of American cities will glide through the air silently in robocoptors, leaving traffic and congestion behind. Cities will be domed, with climate-controlled environments."—Film, *The World of 1960*, shown at New York World's Fair, 1939

"As far as sinking a ship with a bomb is concerned, you just can't do it."—Rear Admiral Clark Woodard, U.S. Navy, 1939

"I'm just glad it'll be Clark Gable who's falling on his face and not Gary Cooper."—Gary Cooper on his decision not to take the leading role in *Gone with the Wind*, 1939

"The Third Reich will last one thousand years!"—Adolf Hitler, speech to the Reichstag, 1942

"I think there is a world market for maybe five computers."—Thomas Watson, chairman of IBM, 1943

"That is the biggest fool thing we have ever done. The (atomic) bomb will never go off, and I speak as an expert in explosives."—Admiral William Leahy, U.S. Navy, 1945

"Television won't be able to hold onto any market it captures after the first six months. People will soon get tired of staring at a plywood box every night."—Darryl F. Zanuck, 1946

"Landing and moving around the moon offers so many serious problems for human beings that it may take science another 200 years to lick them."—*Science Digest*, 1948

"Computers in the future may weigh no more than 1.5 tons."—*Popular Mechanics*, forecasting the relentless march of science, 1949

"The concept is interesting and well-formed, but in order to earn better than a 'C,' the idea must be feasible."—A Yale University management professor in response to Fred Smith's paper proposing reliable overnight delivery service, 1950. Smith went on to found Federal Express Corporation

"It is unlikely that the typical university library staff of 2005 will employ any mechanical devices . . . not already in existence. . . . Reasons for this apparent lack of . . . progress: (1) recently developed instruments such as indexers, transmitters, translators, and copying devices may require many years before they can be . . . economically used in . . . libraries; (2) some entirely new instruments will be invented during the next 50 years, but they quite probably will be so expensive in 2005 that only a few libraries will be able to afford them; (3) there may be a limit to the amount of speed and efficiency faculty members will accept."—Haynes McMullen, 1955

"If we cannot stem the tide of rock 'n' roll with its waves of rhythmic narcosis and of future waves of vicarious craze, we are preparing our own downfall in the midst of pandemonic funeral dances."—Dr. A. M. Meerio, professor of psychiatry, 1957

"I have traveled the length and breadth of this country and talked with the best people, and I can assure you that data processing is a fad that won't last out the year."—The editor in charge of business books for Prentice Hall, 1957

"The book is dead. That is to say, sometime before the end of the present century, the last printed book will roll off the presses."—Marshall McLuhan, 1962

"We don't like their sound, and guitar music is on the way out."—Decca Recording Co., rejecting the Beatles, 1962

"The war in Vietnam is going well and will succeed."—Robert McNamara, U.S. secretary of defense, 1963

"The megalopolis centers of the year 2000 will probably not feel the rubber tread of anything but feet."—Vincent F. Caputo, Office of the Secretary of Defense, 1964

"Soon after World War II, top U.S. Scientists dismissed and derided the notion of an accurate intercontinental missile, and as late as 1956, Britain's Astronomer Royal called the prospect of space travel 'utter bilge.' "— "Time Essay: The Futurists: Looking Toward A.D. 2000," *Time*, 1966

"We see no reason to apply for a patent for the laser, on the grounds that such an invention has no possible relevance to the telephone industry. . . . (We) refuse to patent our amplifier or oscillator for optical frequencies because . . . optical waves have never been of any importance to communications and hence the invention has little bearing on Bell System interests."—Patent lawyers at Bell Laboratories, 1966

"By the year 2000, amid general plenty, politics will simply fade away."— R. Buckminster Fuller, 1966

"Whatever happens in Vietnam, I can conceive of nothing except military victory."—Dwight D. Eisenhower, 1967

"If anything remains more or less unchanged (in the year 2000), it will be the role of women."—Harvard professor David Riesman, 1967

"But what . . . is it good for?"—Engineer at the Advanced Computing Systems Division of IBM, commenting on the microchip, 1968

"You want to have consistent and uniform muscle development across all of your muscles? It can't be done. It's just a fact of life. You just have to accept inconsistent muscle development as an unalterable condition of weight training."—Response to Arthur Jones, who solved the 'insolvable' problem by inventing Nautilus, 1968

"My observation convinced me that the computer is not for library use; that all promises offered in its name are completely fraudulent; that not only is it extremely expensive compared to other methods at this time, but that it will become increasingly expensive in the future; that it has been wrapped so completely in an aura of unreason that fine intelligences are completely uprooted when talking about it; that its use in a library weakens the library as a whole by draining off large sums of money for a small return; and that it should be stamped out."—Ellsworth Mason, 1971

"If I had thought about it, I wouldn't have done the experiment. The literature was full of examples that said you couldn't do this."—Spencer Silver on the work that led to the unique adhesives for 3M Post-It notepads, 1974

"There is no reason anyone would want a computer in their home."—Ken Olson, president, chairman, and founder of Digital Equipment Corp., 1977

"A cookie store is a bad idea. Besides, the market research reports say America likes crispy cookies, not soft and chewy cookies like you make."— Response to Debbi Fields's idea of starting Mrs. Fields Cookies, 1977

"640K ought to be enough for anybody."—Bill Gates, 1981

"Betamax is the wave of the future."—advertisement, 1982

"So we went to Atari and said, 'Hey, we've got this amazing thing, even built with some of your parts, and what do you think about funding us? Or we'll give it to you. We just want to do it. Pay our salary, we'll come work for you.' And they said, 'No.' So then we went to Hewlett-Packard, and they said, 'Hey, we don't need you. You haven't got through college yet.' "—Apple Computer Inc. founder Steve Jobs on attempts to get Atari and H-P interested in his and Steve Wozniak's personal computer, 1984

"The drug Minoxidil was designed to be used as a medication for hypertension in 1985. Then, it was accidentally discovered that, applied topically, it caused hair to grow."—George Will on "Unintended Consequences," *Newsweek*, 1995

"A 'self-driving' car could be on the market by the year 2000. . . . The driverless automobile is a product of the future; it's not science fiction."— Ralph Wilhelm Jr., 1989

"Sometime in the millennial 1990s the arts will replace sports as society's dominant leisure activity."—John Naisbitt and Patricia Aberdene, 1990

"Five years ago telephone companies were absolutely certain digital life would be born 'in our lifetimes': the cable TV folks were . . . sure cyberspace would arrive within a decade. . . . In 1993, computer companies backed . . . [vice-president Gore's] campaign to convince the world that cyberspace would be born in America by 2000 via the union of telephone and cable TV, and that this . . . act of digital convergence would take place in a desktop computer. They were all wrong. . . . The Web will not be the last word for life on-line, but . . . the first word to keep in mind when thinking about the future."—Kevin Kelly, 1996 ■

BIBLIOGRAPHY

Here is a selected bibliography of readings relevant to the study of the future, with special respect to the future of the public library (cybrary). Citations are limited to monographs and articles published in the last 10 years (1986-1996), and bearing directly or tangentially on the future of libraries, information, and/or the acquisition of learning. Included are citations to about 100 readily accessible feature-length articles from *The Futurist* that have relevance to the future of libraries or to other information-related institutions.

Aronowitz, Stanley, and William DiFazio. *The Jobless Future: Sci-Tech and the Dogma of Work.* University of Minnesota Press, 1994.

"Artificial Intelligence: Making Machines That Think." *Futurist* (January-February 1988).

Best, Fred, and Ray Eberhard. "Education for the 'Era of the Adult.'" *Futurist* (May-June 1990).

Birdsall, William F. *The Myth of the Electronic Library.* Greenwood Press, 1994.

Birkerts, Sven. *The Gutenberg Elegies: The Fate of Reading in an Electronic Age.* Faber & Faber, 1994.

Bleecker, Samuel L. "The Information Age Office." *Futurist* (January-February 1991).

———. "Rethinking the Way We Work: The Office of the Future." *Futurist* (July-August 1987).

———. "The Virtual Organization." *Futurist* (March-April 1994).

Borchard, David C. "Planning for Career and Life: Job Surfing on the Tidal Waves of Change." *Futurist* (January-February 1995).

Bova, Ben, Frederik Pohl, Jerry Pournelle, and Charles Sheffield. *Future Quartet, Earth in the Year 2041: A Four-Part Invention.* Morrow, 1994.

Branscomb, Anne Wells. *Who Owns Information? From Privacy to Public Access.* Basic Books, 1994.

Carlson, Richard, and Bruce Goldman. *Fast Forward: Where Technology, Demographics, and History Will Take America and the World in the Next 30 Years.* Harper-Business, 1993.

Cartwright, Glenn F. "Virtual or Real? The Mind in Cyberspace." *Futurist* (March-April 1994).

Cetron, Marvin J. "Class of 2000; The Good News and the Bad News." *Futurist* (November-December 1988).

Cetron, Marvin J., and Margaret Evans Gayle. "Educational Renaissance: 43 Trends for U.S. Schools." *Futurist* (September-October 1990).

Cetron, Marvin J., and Wanda Rocha. "Travel Tomorrow: The Hospitable Future." *Futurist* (July-August 1987).

Cleveland, Harlan. "The Age of Spreading Knowledge." *Futurist* (March-April 1990).

Coates, Joseph F., and Jennifer Jarratt. *What Futurists Believe.* World Future Society, 1989.

Coates, Joseph F., Jennifer Jarratt, and John B. Mahaffie. "Future Work." *Futurist* (May-June 1991).

Conway, McKinley. *A Glimpse of the Future: Technology Forecasts for Global Strategists.* Conway Data, 1992.

———. "Super Projects: New Wonders of the World." *Futurist* (March-April 1993).

———. "Tomorrow's Supercities: For Land, Sea, and Air." *Futurist* (May-June 1993).

Cordell, Arthur J. "Preparing for the Challenges of the New Media." *Futurist* (March-April 1991).

Cornish, Edward. "The Cyber Future: 92 Ways Our Lives Will Change by the Year 2025." *Futurist* (January-February 1996).

———. "Dream Houses of the Future." *Futurist* (November-December 1988).

Cunningham, Scott, and Alan L. Porter. "Communications Networks: A Dozen Ways They'll Change Our Lives." *Futurist* (January-February 1992).

DeTienne, Kristen Bell. "Big Brother or Friendly Coach? Computer Monitoring in the 21st Century." *Futurist* (September-October 1993).

Didsbury, Howard F., Jr. *The Years Ahead: Perils, Problems, and Promises.* World Future Society, 1993.

Diebold, John. "Next Revolution in Computers." *Futurist* (May-June 1994).

Eder, Peter F. "Privacy on Parade: Your Secrets for Sale." *Futurist* (July-August 1994).

"Fighting Parasites." *Futurist* (July-August 1988).

Fobes, Richard. "Creative Problem Solving: A Way to Forecast and Create a Better Future." *Futurist* (January-February 1996).

Fresco, Jacque. "Visions: Designing the Future: A Cybernetic City." *Futurist* (May-June 1994).

Glenn, Jerome C. "Conscious Technology: Co-Evolution of Mind and Machine." *Futurist* (September-October 1989).

Goodman, Allan E., *A Brief History of the Future.* Westview Press, 1993.

Gore, Albert, Jr. "Information Superhighways: The Next Information Revolution." *Futurist* (January-February 1991).

Green, Annette. "The Fragrance Revolution: The Nose Goes to New Lengths." *Futurist* (March-April 1993).

Greenly, Mike. "Computerphobia: The Fear That Keeps People 'Off-line.'" *Futurist* (January-February 1988).

Gunn, James, and Milton T. Wolf. "Science Fiction; Disturber of the Literary Peace." *Library Journal* (February 15, 1988).

Halal, William E. "The Information Technology Revolution." *Futurist* (July-August 1992).

Halal, William E., and Jay Liebowitz. "Telelearning: The Multimedia Revolution in Education." *Futurist* (November-December 1994).

Heilbroner, Robert. *Visions of the Future: The Distant Past, Yesterday, Today, Tomorrow.* Oxford University Press, 1995.

Heim, Michael. *The Metaphysics of Virtual Reality.* Oxford University Press, 1993.

Heldman, Robert K. *Future Telecommunications: Information Applications, Services, & Infrastructure.* McGraw-Hill, 1993.

Higgins, Mike. "The Future of Personal Robots." *Futurist* (May-June 1986).

Hines, Andy. "Jobs and Infotech: Work in the Information Society." *Futurist* (January-February 1994).

Hollender, Jeffrey, and Linda Catling. *How to Make the World a Better Place: 116 Ways You Can Make a Difference.* Norton, 1995.

"Home, Smart Home." *Newsweek* (November 3, 1986).

"How Americans Use Time: An Interview with Sociologist John P. Robinson." *Futurist* (September-October 1991).

Howe, Leo, and Alan Wain. *Predicting the Future.* Cambridge University Press, 1993.

Johnson, Lynell. "Children's Visions of the Future." *Futurist* (May-June 1987).

Jones, Steven G. *CyberSociety: Computer-Mediated Communication and Community.* Sage, 1995.

Kaufman, Herbert. "Emergent Kingdom: Machines That Think Like People." *Futurist* (January-February 1994).

Kelly, Marcia M. "The Work-at-Home Revolution." *Futurist* (November-December 1988).

Kidder, Rushworth M. *An Agenda for the 21st Century.* MIT Press, 1988.

Koelsch, Frank. *The Infomedia Revolution: How It Is Changing Our World and Your Life.* McGraw-Hill, 1995.

Kotter, John P. "Lifetime Learning: The New Educational Imperative." *Futurist* (November-December 1995).

Kroger, Joseph J. "Artificial Intelligence: A New Reality." *Futurist* (July-August 1987).

Larick, Keith T., Jr., and Jock Fischer. "Classrooms of the Future: Introducing Technology to Schools." *Futurist* (May-June 1986).

Lieberman, Al. "Future View: Using Our Leisure Time." *Futurist* (September-October 1991).

London, Herbert L. "Death of the University." *Futurist* (May-June 1987).

Marien, Michael, and Lane Jennings. *What I Have Learned: Thinking About the Future Then and Now.* Greenwood Press, 1987.

Masini, Eleanora Barbieri. *Why Future Studies?* Grey Seal Books, 1993.

Mason, Marilyn Gell. "The Future of the Public Library." *Library Journal* (September 1, 1985).

Masuda, Yoneji. "The Opportunity Society: Time for a Life Worth Living." *Futurist* (September-October 1990).

McGuinness, Kevin. "Visions: Nanoplastics: How 'Intelligent' Materials May Change Our Homes." *Futurist* (January-February 1995).

McKibben, Bill. *The End of Nature.* Random House, 1989.

Moorcroft, Sheila, ed. *Visions for the 21st Century.* Praeger, 1993.

Morris, Richard. "Future View: The Perils of Time Travel." *Futurist* (September-October 1994).

Morrison, Perry R. "Computer Parasites: Software Diseases May Cripple Our Computers." *Futurist* (March-April 1986).

Naisbitt, John, and Patricia Aburdene. *Meagatrends 2000.* Morrow, 1990.

Negroponte, Nicholas. *Being Digital.* Knopf, 1995.

———. "The Digital Revolution: Reasons for Optimism." *The Futurist* (November-December 1995).

Nine Forces Reshaping America. World Future Society, United Way Strategic Institute, 1990.

Ornstein, Robert, and Paul Ehrlich. *New World; New Mind.* Doubleday, 1989.

Pelton, Joseph. "Telepower: The Emerging Global Brain." *Futurist* (September-October 1989).

Perelman, Lewis J. "Learning Our Lesson: Why School Is Out." *Futurist* (March-April 1986).

Pesanelli, David. "Education Takes to the Streets." *Futurist* (March-April 1990).

———. "Visions: The Plug-in School: A Learning Environment for the 21st Century." *Futurist* (September-October 1993).

Peters, Tom. *Thriving on Chaos.* Alfred A. Knopf, 1987.

Peterson, John L. *Road to 2015: Profiles of the Future.* Waite Group Press, 1994.

Porter, Alan. "Work in the New Information Age." *Futurist* (September-October 1986).

Reibnitz, Ute von. *Scenario Techniques.* Mc-Graw-Hill, 1987.

Renfro, William L. "Future Histories: A New Approach to Scenarios." *Futurist* (March-April 1987).

Riggs, Donald E., and Gordon A. Sabine. *Libraries in the '90s: What the Leaders Expect.* Oryx, 1988.

Roland, Jon. "Nanotechnology: The Promise and Peril of Ultratiny Machines." *Futurist* (March-April 1991).

Rossman, Parker. "The Emerging Global University." *Futurist* (November-December 1991).

Scheel, Randall L. *Introduction to the Future.* ETC Publications, 1988.

Schwartau, Winn. *Information Warfare: Chaos on the Electronic Superhighway.* Thunder's Mouth Press, 1994.

Segal, Howard P. *Future Imperfect: The Mixed Blessings of Technology in America.* University of Massachusetts Press, 1994.

Sheffield, Charles, Marcelo Alonso, and Morton A. Kaplan, eds. *The World of 2044: Technological Development and the Future of Society.* Paragon House, 1994.

Shuman, Bruce A. *The Library of the Future: Alternative Scenarios for Information Professionals.* Libraries Unlimited, 1989.

Slouka, Mark. *War of the Worlds: Cyberspace and the High-Tech Assault on Reality.* Basic Books, 1995.

Snider, James H. "The Information Superhighway as Environmental Menace." *Futurist* (March-April 1995).

Stoll, Clifford. *Silicon Snake Oil: Second Thoughts on the Information Highway.* Doubleday, 1995.

Swift, David W. "Low-Cost Videoconferencing." *Futurist* (March-April 1988).

Thornburg, David D. *Education in the Communication Age.* Starsong, 1994.

Toth, Kalman A. "Workless Society: How Machine Intelligence Will Bring Ease and Abundance." *Futurist* (May-June 1990).

"Visions: Home of the Future." *Futurist* (January-February 1993).

"Visions: Wearable Computers." *Futurist* (September-October 1992).

"Visions: The Future as Child's Play." *Futurist* (July-August 1994).

"Visions: The Portable Workplace." *Futurist* (July-August 1995).

Wagner, Cynthia G. "Visions: Enabling the 'Disabled': Technologies for People with Handicaps." *Futurist* (May-June 1992).

———. "Visions: Kids Build a New World." *Futurist* (September October 1995).

Wakefield, Rowan A. "Home Computers and Families: The Empowerment Revolution." *Futurist* (September-October 1986).

Waterman, Robert H., Jr. *The Renewal Factor.* New York: Bantam, 1987.

Weinberger, David D. "The Active Document: Making Pages Smarter." *Futurist* (July-August 1991).

Weinstein, Stephen B., and Paul W. Shumate. "Beyond the Telephone: New Ways to Communicate." *Futurist* (November-December 1989).

Weiss, Julian M. "Adding Vision to Telecommuting. " *Futurist* (May-June 1992).

Willis, Jim. *The Age of Multimedia and Turbonews.* Praeger, 1995.

INDEX